Linking Macroeconomic and Agricultural Policies for Adjustment with Growth

The Colombian Experience

A World Bank Publication

Linking Macroeconomic and Agricultural Policies for Adjustment with Growth

The Colombian Experience

Vinod Thomas

with contributions from

Sebastian Edwards
John Nash
Jorge García-García
José B. Sokol
Ai Chin Wee
Mateen Thobani

Published for The World Bank
THE JOHNS HOPKINS UNIVERSITY PRESS
Baltimore and London

The Johns Hopkins University Press
Baltimore, Maryland 21211, U.S.A.

First printing November 1985

Library of Congress Cataloging-in-Publication Data
Thomas, Vinod, 1949–
   Linking macroeconomic and agricultural policies for adjustment with growth.

   "A World Bank publication."
   Includes index.
   1. Colombia—Economic policy—Addresses, essays,
lectures.   2. Agriculture and state—Colombia—
Addresses, essays, lectures.   3. Colombia—Commercial
policy—Addresses, essays, lectures.   4. Price
policy—Colombia—Addresses, essays, lectures.
5.   Coffee trade—Colombia—Addresses, essays, lectures.
I. Title.
HC197.T38   1985   338.9861   85-45105
ISBN 0-8018-3121-0

Foreword

DURING THE 1980s many developing countries have faced increasingly complex issues of adjustment and growth. The difficulties can be attributed to both external and internal factors. One set of problems relates to the varying fortunes of exports and imports of the developing countries in world markets; uncertainties concerning the availability of external capital have produced additional difficulties. Meanwhile, domestic policies have not always been adequate to stimulate growth in the economy and to provide stability in the balance of payments and fiscal accounts.

This book deals with economic policies for growth and adjustment during periods of rapidly changing circumstances and links them to developments at the sectoral level. It is based on the experience of Colombia, which, after a long period of successful performance, has been experiencing a downturn in economic growth and increased deficits in the external and fiscal balances. The study analyzes factors that have contributed to the country's long-term development. Turning to the more recent events, it addresses policy measures that are needed to adjust the economy, bring about a resumption of growth, and generate more employment.

In the exploration of growth prospects, the focus of the investigation is on options for revitalizing the agricultural sector, which in the past has been a major source of long-term growth. A variety of policy alternatives in the areas of coffee diversification, price supports, price stabilization, input subsidies, and investment strategy are evaluated. In addition, trade-related issues of adjustment which go beyond the typical concerns of any single sector are emphasized. Such a macroeconomic framework has been necessitated by the close links in Colombia among agriculture, trade, and growth. The performance of coffee exports, in particular, has strongly influenced the course of macroeconomic events. In turn, macroeconomic policies—the exchange rate, import controls, fiscal and monetary measures—have substantially affected progress in agriculture, both directly and indirectly.

The broader focus that is brought to bear on sectoral analysis is a noteworthy aspect of this work, which could be useful in the study of sectoral strategies in other countries with similarly complex economic problems. It highlights the importance of coffee and agriculture in driving economic developments and the behavior of sectoral dynamics in an economywide context. A second feature of this volume, one that is of particular concern to policymakers, is the review of long-term sector-specific options for growth in the context of pressing economic choices: in the present case, economic stabilization measures such as exchange rate adjustments and fiscal restraint are evaluated jointly with pricing and investment decisions at the sectoral level. Finally, a variety of technical analyses are employed that could be applied in other studies of a similar nature. In the area of macroeconomic policy, analyses are provided of the effects of a major commodity—and a leading sector—on the rest of the economy, and the effects of key policy variables such as the exchange rate. Price policy analysis includes measurement of the benefits and costs of various price intervention options. Finally, the volume provides some of the data used in the estimations.

During the final work on this study in 1984 and subsequently, the government has taken a variety of policy measures—some of which are recorded here—with the goal of achieving adjustment while protecting economic growth and employment generation. The reforms have by no means been easy to adopt, and they reflect the vision of the policymakers in making politically difficult decisions in order to sustain the country's medium-term performance and prospects. The World Bank has provided its support for this economic program, both through policy analysis and through a major policy loan designed to strengthen the country's external trade. There is evidence of a restoration of stability in the economy so far and of the maintenance of the international financial community's confidence and involvement in the country during this difficult period. The equally important task of sustaining the policy improvements and restoring rapid development through the medium term remains.

The World Bank has maintained a fruitful relationship with Colombia for more than thirty years. The first World Bank economic mission to a developing country visited Colombia in 1949. The first World Bank Economic Report in 1952 and the first publication of a country report in book form in 1972 also concerned Colombia. The present volume is the result of the World Bank's more recent economic and sector work in the country. It has grown out of a 1983 study in Colombia, led by Vinod Thomas, and the author's subsequent findings. Its publication reflects the continuing involvement of this institution in the analysis of the country's economic policies, and it represents a timely contribution to discussions of its developmental achievements and prospects.

A. DAVID KNOX
Regional Vice President
Latin America and Caribbean Office
The World Bank

June 1985

Contents

Preface

COLOMBIA HAS EXPERIENCED a rapid and sustained economic development during the past three decades. In the early 1980s, however, the country's economic performance slowed. During 1983–84, when this study was completed, Colombia's external accounts were facing significant difficulties. Faced with growing balance of payments problems, the government has initiated an adjustment program that emphasizes export development and fiscal and monetary restraint. With a substantial depreciation of the real exchange rate, a selective opening up of imports is envisaged.

Some of the problems of the external sector during the first half of the 1980s could be attributed to a slowdown in the expansion of noncoffee production and exports combined with a downswing in coffee prospects. Equally important, however, were the unfavorable trends in the capital markets, which were responding to the economic and debt woes of Latin America. Thus, even while Colombia was achieving a significant adjustment in its current account of the balance of payments, the pressure on the capital account continued to hurt the external sector balances. Given continuation of policies for adjustment with growth and attention to generation of employment, a strengthening in the balance of payments and a revitalization of development are to be expected.

While international factors are crucial to an understanding of the evolving situation, this study is focused on domestic measures managed by policymakers. Even though the near-term issues of stabilization are of great importance, the book also establishes some of the requirements of medium-term performance. Emphasizing the need for sectoral revitalization, the work reviews growth options in agriculture. These issues, however, cannot be divorced from the trade-related macroeconomic concerns, not only because of the pressing nature of the latter but also because of their close relationship with agriculture.

The book is in four parts. Part one is a discussion of trade-related macroeconomic policies, with special attention given to their connection with agriculture. Chapter 1 begins with an overview of issues and the effects of macroeconomic policy on the agricultural sector. The next chapter is a review of export policy focused on management of export incentives, while in chapter 3 import policy alternatives are considered. Part two is an assessment of price policies in agriculture, including price support and import restrictions (chapter 4); price stabilization issues (chapter 5); and policies regarding coffee production and pricing, and issues related to agricultural diversification (chapter 6). In part 3 nonpricing issues that influence the production environment in agriculture are examined, including public and private sector investment in agriculture (chapter 7) and direct policies aimed at increasing agricultural productivity (chapter 8). A final chapter draws out the main conclusions of the work. The appendixes contain technical analyses to support some of the conclusions.

This work has gained from the contribution of several people to whom I am most grateful. Enrique Lerdau, Miguel Schloss, and Guy Pfeffermann gave critical guidance at a very early and formative stage of this work. Roberto Junguito Bonnet, minister of agriculture and subsequently minister of finance of Colombia, provided an orientation to the study that has proved to be extremely valuable. The study has drawn on the contributions of Alberto Ararat, Deepak Bhattasali, Ana Rita Cárdenas, Laurens Hoppenbrouwer, Kei Kawabata, and German Rioseco.

This project benefited from the support of several government and private officials in Colombia, particularly Edgar Gutiérrez-Castro, former minister of finance; Gustavo Castro Guerrero, minister of agriculture and later minister of development; Jorge Ospina Sardi, director of planning; Hugo Palacios Mejía, general manager of the Central Bank and later minister of finance, Jorge Cárdenas Gutiérrez and Hernán Uribe Arango, general manager and deputy manager, respectively, of the Coffee Federation; and Carlos Ossa Escobar, president of the Sociedad de Agricultores de Colombia. I am grateful for the advice and suggestions given by Nicholas Carter, Melvin Goldman, Juan Carlos Jaramillo, Fernando Montes, Diego Pizano, German Valenzuela, and Hugo Valdez. I would like to acknowledge the comments of Takamasa Akiyama, David Argyle, Mauricio Cabrera, Ricardo Candelo, Ramon Lopez, Jayati Datta Mitra, Enrique Ospina, Gabriel Montes, José Olivares, Jairo Ramírez, Franz Schorosch, Alvaro Silva, Naveen Verghese, and the reviewers who commented on the manuscript for the World Bank, Raymond R. Frost and J. Peter Neary. David Howell Jones carefully edited the book. Myrna Hanson provided valuable assistance throughout the preparation of the study.

In the absence of the proverbial understanding wife and children, I would like to thank my parents and sister for their recognition of the contribution made by my prolonged bachelorhood to the completion of this work.

VINOD THOMAS

Abbreviations and Acronyms

ABOCOL	Abonos Colombianos S.A. (a Colombian private sector fertilizer company)
ACOSEMILLA	Asociación Colombiana de Productores de Semillas (Colombian Association of Seed Producers)
AGD	Almacenes Generales de Depósito (General Storage Facility)
ALADI	Asociación Latino Americana de Desarrollo y Integración (Latin American Association for Development and Integration)
Almagrario	Almacen Agrario (Agricultural Storage)
Almapopular	Almacen Popular (Popular Storage)
ASOCAÑA	Asociación de Cultivadores de Caña de Azúcar de Colombia (Sugar Mills Association of Colombia)
ASOCOLFLORES	Asociación Colombiana de Productores de Flores (Colombian Association of Flower Producers)
Banco Ganadero	Livestock Bank
Bolsa	Bolsa Nacional Agropecuaria, S.A. (National Stock Exchange for Agriculture)
BOR	Banco de la Republica (Central Bank)
BP	Bono de Prenda (subsidized storage credit)
Caja, or Caja Agraria	Caja de Crédito Agrario, Industrial, y Minero (Agricultural, Industrial and Mining Credit Bank)
CAT	Certificado de Abono Tributario (tax credit certificate)
CD	Certificado de Depósito (term certificate of deposit)
CECORA	Central de Cooperativas de la Reforma Agraria, Ltda. (Union of Agrarian Reform Cooperatives, Ltd.)
CERT	Certificado de Reembolso Tributario (tax reimbursement certificate)
COFIAGRO	Corporación Financiera de Fomento Agropecuario y de Exportaciónes (Financial Corporation for Agricultural and Export Development)
COLPUERTOS	Puertos de Colombia (Colombian Port Authority)

CONPES   Consejo Nacional de Política Económica y Social (National Economic and Social Policy Council)

CORABASTOS   Corporación de Abastos de Bogotá (Central Wholesale Market of Bogotá)

CVC   Corporación Autónoma Regional del Valle del Rio Cauca (Autonomous Regional Corporation of Rio Cauca Valley)

DANE   Departamento Administrativo Nacional de Estadística (National Department of Statistics)

DNP   Departamento Nacional de Planeación (National Planning Department)

DRI (IRDP)   Programa de Desarrollo Rural Integrado (Integrated Rural Development Program)

EEC   European Economic Community

EMCOPER   Empresa Comercializadora de Productos Perecederos (Enterprise for Marketing of Perishable Products)

ERP   Effective Rate of Protection

FAO   Food and Agriculture Organization

FEDEARROZ   Federación Nacional de Arroceros (National Rice Producers' Federation)

FEDEGAN   Federación Colombiana de Ganaderos (Colombian Cattle Owners' Federation)

FEDEPALMA   Federación Nacional de Cultivadores de Palma Africana (National Federation of African Palm Growers)

FEDEPAPA   Federación Colombiana de Productores de Papa (Colombian Producers of Potato)

FEDERACAFE   Federación Nacional de Cafeteros de Colombia (National Federation of Colombian Coffee Growers)

FEDERALGODON   Federación Nacional de Algodoneros (National Cotton Producers' Federation)

FEDESARROLLO   Fundación para la Educación Superior y el Desarrollo (Foundation for Higher Education and Development)

FENALCO   Federación Nacional de Cooperativas (National Federation of Cooperatives)

FFAP   Fondo Financiero Agropecuario (Agricultural Financial Fund)

GATT   General Agreement on Tariffs and Trade

HIMAT   Instituto de Hidrología, Meteorología, y Adecuaciónes de Tierras (Institute for Hydrology, Meteorology and Land Improvement)

ICA   Instituto Colombiano Agropecuario (Colombian Agricultural Institute)

ICA   International Coffee Agreement

ICO   International Coffee Organization

IDB   Inter-American Development Bank

IDEMA	Instituto de Mercadeo Agropecuario (Agricultural Marketing Institute)
IFS	International Financial Statistics
IICA	Instituto Interamericano de Ciencias Agrícolas (Inter-American Institute for Agricultural Sciences)
INCOMEX	Instituto de Comercio Exterior (Foreign Trade Institute)
INCORA	Instituto Colombiano de la Reforma Agraria (Colombian Institute for Agrarian Reform)
INDERENA	Instituto Nacional de los Recursos Naturales Renovables y del Ambiente (National Institute for Renewable Natural Resources and the Environment)
LP	Licencia Previa (prior licensing)
MUV	Manufactured unit value index
NCF	National Coffee Fund
NER	Nominal exchange rate
n.f.s.	Nonfactor services
OECD	Organisation for Economic Co-operation and Development
OPSA	Oficina de Planeación del Sector Agropecuario (Agricultural Sector Planning Office)
PAN	Plan Nacional de Alimentación y Nutrición (National Food and Nutrition Plan)
PLANIA	Plan Nacional de Investigación Agropecuario (National Agricultural Research Plan)
PLANIF	Plan Nacional de Investigación Forestal (National Forestry Research Plan)
Plan Vallejo	Import duty drawback for exporters
PPP	Purchasing power parity
PROCAÑA	Productores de Caña (Cane Producers)
PRODESARROLLO	Programa de Diversificación y Desarrollo de Zonas Cafeteras (Program of Development and Diversification of Coffee Areas)
PROEXPO	Fondo de Promoción de Exportaciones (Export Promotion Fund; also denotes Export Promotion Agency)
REER	Real effective exchange rate
RER	Real exchange rate
SAC	Sociedad de Agricultores de Colombia (Colombian Farmers' Association)
SEA	Special Exchange Account
SENA	Servicio Nacional de Aprendizaje (National Apprenticeship Service)
Situado Fiscal	Revenue earmarking
USDA	United States Department of Agriculture

Currency Equivalents

Currency unit—Colombian peso (Col$)

Exchange rate as of January 1, 1985:
  US$1 = Col$113.890
  Col$1 = US$0.00878

Dollar amounts given are in U.S. dollars unless specified otherwise.

Average exchange rate

1981	*1982*	*1983*	*1984*
US$1 = Col$54.491	US$1 = Col$64.102	US$1 = Col$78.861	US$1 = Col$100.992
Col$1 = US$0.0184	Col$1 = US$0.0156	Col$1 = US$0.0127	Col$1 = US$0.0099

Part One

Macroeconomic Policy and Agriculture

1

An Overview of Trade and Agricultural Policies

THIS BOOK addresses issues in economic policymaking in Colombia, a country confronting rapidly changing external circumstances. A central issue is the slowdown in the performance of the Colombian economy during the first half of the 1980s, after a long period of rapid expansion. The economic record has been closely associated with success in the agricultural sector. Agricultural and other exports have been the mainstay of favorable outcomes in the external accounts in the past and a significant source of economic growth. At the same time, a proximate cause of the recent difficulties has been the setback in the external sector, particularly that related to the performance of exports. For these reasons, a primary objective of this work is to consider ways and means of stabilizing the external sector of the country and revitalizing growth, in particular by enlarging the net contribution of agriculture to foreign exchange.

Since the latter half of the 1960s Colombia has managed the economy with a well-integrated package of exchange-rate, fiscal, and export-incentive policies that have succeeded in promoting the development and growth of its exports. Through the 1970s the performance of industry was more striking than that of agriculture, partly because the former started from a smaller base. Nevertheless, agriculture maintained an average growth rate of about 4 percent, and the development of agricultural exports other than coffee was impressive. The economy steadily diversified into one that was more urban and more resilient to external shocks.

The policy package, however, began to unravel during the latter half of the 1970s, even as the country was enjoying a coffee boom. The expansion in total noncoffee exports began to slow down, although it was hidden by the coffee boom during 1976–80. By the early 1980s, however, this was accompanied by a downturn in real coffee earnings, contributing to increasing deficits in the current account of the balance of payments. During 1982–83 this deficit amounted to more than 7 percent of gross domestic product (GDP). As in the mid 1960s, problems began to appear in the external sector, although at this time the situation was aggravated by growing capital-market constraints. The underlying domestic economic situation, however, remained far stronger than it had been twenty years earlier. Noncoffee exports from agriculture and the rest of the economy had established a high plateau of performance, and the real price of coffee was higher.

A way to correct the problems in the external sector would be to reestablish the previous basis for export development and growth. Restoration of agricultural incentives would be essential to the revitalization of this important sector. At the macroeconomic level, however, new constraints need to be addressed. The government budget has grown rapidly during the 1980s; the surplus that existed during most of the 1970s has changed to deficit, and considerable efforts have been required to achieve a better balance. Wage-rate and interest-rate expectations have also been related to exchange-rate policy, making improvements in the real exchange rate more complex. Nevertheless, recent experience has shown positive results in reversing these trends through careful macroeconomic management. More remains to be done.

In this Colombian context, macroeconomic policies and sectoral initiatives in agriculture for achieving the needed overall adjustment while sustaining growth will be examined. In recent work the connection between macroeconomic and agricultural developments has been noted.[1] The present study extends the analysis through an explicit focus on this interrelationship in Colombia and also provides a framework suitable for other country studies. Macroeconomic developments in Colombia have been strongly influenced by the fortunes of agriculture, particularly by its external performance. In turn, the record in agriculture has been substantially affected by macroeconomic policies. In view of these links, a part of this work is devoted to an analysis of trade-related macroeconomic policy, which has a significant bearing on agricultural performance. After this broader perspective has been established, the focus will be narrowed to a study of sectoral policies that affect agriculture directly; then even more specific financial issues will be addressed. The sectoral initiatives that will be investigated include price interventions, particularly price support and import controls for import-competing commodities, storage and price-stabilization measures for cereals, tax policies in the case of coffee, and credit subsidies that affect most products.

Taken together, the various pieces of analysis will seek to shed light on possible ways of achieving stability and accelerated growth in the external sector, particularly as they involve incentives to produce and export agricultural commodities. The domestic prices of traded commodities in relation to prices of other commodities are determined not only by international price trends but also by domestic policies toward the exchange rate, production costs, and, more generally, the rate of inflation within a country. Inducements to produce and to export are also derived from various export-promotion and import policies. In addition, a variety of policies that are confined to agriculture can alter output and input prices and in turn affect farm incentives. Finally, considerations of microeconomic production that involve yields and farm budgets influence the production environment and affect actual performance.

Long-Term Performance and Its Sources

The Colombian economy has shown rapid and sustained growth in output and employment since the mid 1950s. Even from the mid 1970s to the early 1980s, while most other countries in the region suffered significant declines in growth, Colombia's GDP rose at a trend rate of 4–5 percent a year. Juxtaposed with an annual population growth rate of about 2 percent, this produced a respectable long-term growth in per capita output. For much of the 1970s, the country enjoyed a substantial balance of payments surplus, and prudent management of the external sector contributed significantly to the confidence in Colombia's creditworthiness shown by international financial markets. On the domestic front, the country realized an extraordinary boom in employment and improvements in real wages during most of the 1970s, which accompanied the rapid expansion of labor-intensive production and exports. Although fortuitous external circumstances have been helpful, it is also true that a favorable policy environment that has prevailed over the long term has been instrumental in producing these results.[2]

The contribution of agriculture to growth has been sizable. Agriculture accounts for between a fifth and a quarter of GDP, some two-thirds of export earnings, and a third of total employment in the economy. The sector continues to influence major macroeconomic trends, not only through its contribution to foreign-exchange revenues and import capacity, but also directly through its effect on employment and incomes in both agricultural and nonagricultural activities. An important segment of the sector that deals primarily with food production is predominantly traditional in its production processes.

Vigorous economic growth in Colombia has been positively related to the development of exports. The country's success in increasing exports during the period 1967–75 was based on an outward-looking policy that was in part the result of significant domestic inducements to export promotion. Activism in exporting diminished significantly after the mid 1970s, partly on account of the increase in foreign-exchange earnings that accompanied the commodity price boom of 1976–79. Rapid increases in external demand for Colombian agricultural products were the most significant development of this period, with the demand for coffee and illegal drugs leading the rest of exports.

The rate of economic growth fell between 1981 and 1983. Colombia's external sector has been in difficulty in part because of the economic problems of its neighbors and the debt problems of Latin America. Although an important source of long-term growth, agriculture suffered a sharp downswing, attributable to weak export demand and low international prices and to domestic developments.

Growth in noncoffee exports, agricultural and others, decelerated during 1975–83, first as the relative producer prices in the domestic markets for these commodities declined and later as international export conditions became less and less favorable.[3]

Sectoral Contributions to Growth

From the late 1960s through much of the 1970s growth in GDP averaged a sizable 6 percent, although it decelerated during the second half of the decade. An even sharper turning point came at the beginning of the 1980s, when the growth rate in GDP began to dip (see table 1-1). During the long term agriculture has grown at a rate about 1.5 percentage points less than the average for the whole economy. Although long-term growth rates in manufacturing and services have been higher, the contribution of agriculture to growth has been just as great in view of the larger share of agriculture in GDP, and the sector has been the mainstay of economic performance since the mid 1970s. During 1960–82 agriculture contributed, on the average, about a fifth of the increase in GDP.

Manufacturing grew at an unaccustomed rate during 1967–75; the contribution of the manufacturing sector to the increment in GDP during that period was more than 23 percent, whereas its contribution was much smaller during the following period. The vitality of the sector has weakened significantly since the mid 1970s for a number of reasons: an appreciated (lower) real exchange rate for exports in the

Table 1-1. *Total and Sectoral Growth Rates, 1960–82*
(percent)

Period	Agriculture[a]	Manufacturing	Selected services[b]	Total GDP
1960–67	2.9	5.4	5.6	4.6
1967–75	4.5	7.8	7.7	6.4
1975–80	4.5	5.2	6.5	5.5
1975–82	3.8	3.4	4.8	4.6
1960–82	4.1	6.0	6.4	5.5
Contribution to growth[c]	21.1	22.8	19.5	100.0

Note: In making these calculations we relied on data from the Central Bank, which are a longer series than those of the Departamento de Administrativo Nacional de Estadistica (DANE, the National Department of Statistics), which has been revising the national accounts; the revised data from DANE are presented in appendix tables SA-1–4. The direction and orders of magnitude are the same in both sets of data. Growth rates are those of GDP at factor cost, calculated by the least-squares method.

a. Includes fishing, hunting, and forestry.

b. Commerce, banking, finance, and insurance.

c. Sectoral contributions to growth are measured as sectoral growth rates weighted by the corresponding shares of the sector in GDP. These do not add to 100 because some sectors are excluded.

Source: Author's calculations based on Central Bank data.

face of the coffee bonanza; the slowdown in domestic economic activity; lagging technological progress in the highly protected domestic industrial sector; and, more recently, the downturn in the world economy. During 1980–82 manufacturing declined in real terms, accounting for a good part of the domestic recession. Services that support the productive sectors sustained a fairly steady and high rate of growth, accompanying high growth rates either in manufacturing or in agriculture. Through the long term, this sector's contribution to the increment in GDP has been about the same as that of agriculture or manufacturing. Following the late 1970s, however, as both agriculture and manufacturing suffered setbacks, the growth in services also dipped.[4]

Components of Total Demand

The significant contribution of increases in exports to aggregate demand, particularly in industries, has been noted in earlier work.[5] Outward-looking strategies have contributed positively to the record of agriculture. The period 1970–75 saw a growth rate of about 5 percent a year in noncoffee agriculture, while it was less than 4 percent in the years following 1975. There was a distinct switch in emphasis from external demand-driven growth to domestic demand-based expansion between one period and another, as shown in table 1-2. The contribution of exports to total demand fell sharply, while that from import substitution turned negative between the two periods. The slowdown in domestic activity during the early 1980s was in part attributable to the downswing in world economic expansion. Additionally, the inward-looking nature of development in agriculture during the latter half of the 1970s compared to that in the previous half has also been associated with a slowdown in noncoffee growth.

Although Colombia is only moderately open by international standards—according to a criterion of the share of trade in total output—a finer disaggregation of economic activity makes it immediately apparent that for most of the period under consideration trade has indeed been an important source of growth in the economy. In addition to fortuitous external circumstances, the establishment of an outward-looking policy environment during the period 1967–75 was instrumental in creating the basis for a dynamic response to external market conditions. As a result, values of total exports and imports have increased significantly in real terms since the mid 1960s, producing a modest increase in their shares of GDP in the long term.[6]

Trade in Agriculture

As a whole, agriculture has had a strong orientation toward trade, in large measure because of the importance of coffee in international trade. During 1982–83 agricultural exports represented some 65 percent of total exports, which roughly corresponds to the behavior of a country with the per capita income of Colombia.[7]

Table 1-2. *Shares in Growth of Components of Agricultural Aggregate Demand, 1970–75 and 1976–81*
(percent)

	Domestic demand					External demand			Total agriculture
Period	Intermediate consumption	Final consumption	Fixed capital formation	Changes in stocks	Sub-total	Exports	Intermediate consumption for exports	Sub-total	Import substitution	
1970–75	43.0	24.5	2.3	−1.2	68.6	7.4	16.8	24.2	7.2	100.0
1976–81	43.0	32.6	0.8	10.6	87.0	3.4	15.9	19.3	−6.3	100.0

Note: The method used to estimate the average contributions of the components of total demand during a given period is explained by Gabriel Montes and Ricardo Candelo in "El crecimiento industrial y la generación de empleo en Colombia," *Revista de planeación y desarrollo*, vol. 12, nos. 1 and 2 (January–June 1981), p. 87.
Source: Calculations of the Departamento Nacional de Planeamento (DNP, the National Planning Department), using DANE data.

Exports have been a far more significant component of GDP in agriculture, with or without coffee, than imports, and the net foreign-exchange position of agriculture has been strongly positive in the long run.[8] During 1970–83, the share of agricultural commodity exports averaged roughly a third of agricultural GDP. Excluding coffee, this proportion—that is, noncoffee agricultural exports over noncoffee agricultural GDP—falls to about 9 percent, which is about 1 percentage point higher than the share for nonagriculture (see tables SA-5–7). During the same period agricultural imports constituted only 3 percent of sectoral GDP but about 18 percent in the rest of the economy.

An alternative approach to measuring the trade orientation of agriculture is demonstrated in a recent review in which an attempt is made to estimate the share in agriculture of tradables—that is, exportables and importables—defined as the total value added in domestic production of categories that are or have been exported and imported.[9] The purpose of this estimate is to show the full size of value added of a category—in addition to the share actually traded—that would be affected by an export or import intervention. Including coffee, total exportable and importable agricultural commodities are estimated to constitute 70 percent of sectoral output—60 percent exportables and 10 percent importables, primarily food items. The remaining 30 percent is made up principally of food items for domestic consumption. Excluding coffee, agricultural tradables are estimated to constitute 40–45 percent of noncoffee agricultural output.

In contrast, the rest of the economy is characterized by a larger proportion of nontradables: a proportionately larger part of nonagricultural production is derived from generally nontradable sectors such as transport, communication, commerce, banking, and public services. The conclusion is that on the average agriculture contains a larger tradable component than the rest of the economy, and in that sense trade policies can influence agriculture more on the average than they can affect the rest of the economy. Furthermore, because of the greater share of exports than imports in agricultural GDP, incentives to agricultural exports—given a satisfactory demand environment—would have a more significant effect on the balance of payments than a comparable protection given for import substitution in agriculture.

During 1970–83 as a whole, agricultural exports grew at an estimated (by least squares) rate of nearly 5 percent a year in constant prices, coffee growing at a rate slightly above this average and other exports slightly below. During this period, flowers, bananas, fresh meat, hides and skins, and tobacco have grown at impressive rates, albeit from small bases. It is noteworthy, however, that after a growth rate of 5 percent a year in constant prices during 1970–75, noncoffee agro-based exports grew at a rate of only 1.7 percent during the period 1975–83, and even with its own recent decline in growth, coffee has been the mainstay of export growth. Agricultural imports have grown steadily, although at a rate below the average for the rest of the economy: in 1970–83 agricultural imports grew at 5.5 percent, while the rate outside the sector was more than 6 percent. The larger part of the increases in agricultural imports have come from increased domestic consumption of imported foods, which have not been quantitatively very significant in the balance of payments. The decline in the growth of noncoffee agricultural exports in recent years has been a more serious source of concern, although improvements were estimated for 1984 and early 1985.

The position of agriculture as a net exporter is true regardless of whether coffee is included or not. Including coffee, the trade surplus during 1970–83 was nearly 30 percent of sectoral GDP. For noncoffee commodities, exports and imports have represented fairly small proportions of domestic production, and during 1970–83 the trade surplus of the noncoffee portion was nearly 5 percent of value added of the same category. The country has remained a net exporter of food products also, steadily registering a small trade surplus. With this trade surplus, food production has been slightly above net domestic supply in all years since 1975. The net supply of food is estimated to have grown by roughly 4 percent a year in constant pesos. The gross value of food output is about 65 percent of the agricultural total, and it is a highly diversified output, the growth of which can contribute enormously to the domestic food supply. Fears of undue reliance on international markets for food and expectations of benefits from heavy protection of domestic food production or from export controls are somewhat misplaced, in view of the trade surplus and the small share of agricultural imports in GDP and in total imports.

Recent Developments and Some Explanations

In addition to the international recession—and particularly that in Latin America—internal developments have also contributed to emergence of the recent problems mentioned at the outset of this study. To understand this process better, it is helpful to disaggregate agriculture into two categories—coffee and the rest. This makes it possible to see that the country has exhibited the symptoms of the booming-sector syndrome observed elsewhere in the world, where the rapid growth of a few primary exports and the resultant inflow of foreign exchange have been coupled with a real appreciation of the exchange rate, defined as Colombian pesos per unit of foreign currency, causing significant changes in the deployment of labor and the use of resources that have hurt other productive sectors by drawing resources into the booming sectors.[10] In Colombia, the coffee and drug export windfalls of the second half of the 1970s produced these adverse effects on noncoffee agriculture and the rest of the exportables and importables, and the effect persisted even after the end of the commodity boom period.[11]

External Factors

Exports to Mexico, Argentina, Brazil, Ecuador, Costa Rica, and Chile, which had expanded significantly during 1970–1982, declined after 1982. Speculation against the Colombian peso following the 1983 and 1984 Venezuelan devaluations and the ensuing tight import restrictions in Venezuela exacerbated Colombia's problems. During the first quarter of 1984, the Colombian peso remained appreciated in relation to the currencies of a number of Latin American countries, particularly to the Venezuelan bolivar. Venezuela used to account for about 25 percent of Colombian exports of goods and services and for much of the transfers received from abroad. In 1984 foreign-exchange receipts from these sources were expected to be less than a fifth of what they were in 1982. The external debt problems of other Latin American countries have been a proximate cause of the pressure on the capital account also. The availability of external financing from commercial banks has shrunk, and the terms and conditions of the loans have hardened.

In general, domestic performance has been positively associated with growth in world production and trade. During the period 1965–73 worldwide export volumes grew at an estimated 8.7 percent; they grew at only 4.9 percent during 1973–80. The downturn in the world economy during 1980–82, when growth in industrial countries averaged barely 1 percent a year, by dampening international demand for Colombian exports, undoubtedly hurt Colombia's performance. In general the country's terms of trade have been positively related to domestic performance. After the mid 1960s Colombia's terms of trade began gradually to improve. Having fallen between 1974 and 1975, they improved after 1975 because of sharply rising coffee prices, which compensated for the decline in real prices of noncoffee exports during 1977–79. After 1979 noncoffee export prices began to recover in real terms, partly offsetting the decline in coffee prices. The overall terms of trade in 1983 were above the level of 1975 (see table 1-3). Excluding coffee, in fact, the terms of trade showed an improvement over those of 1975. For noncoffee agriculture alone, however, they had not regained the 1974–75 level (see chapter 4).

Coffee exports are determined in part by special arrangements under the International Coffee Agreement (ICA), while domestic incentives for coffee production and exports are provided in a manner quite distinct from those for other commodities (see chapter 6). The value of coffee exports rose during 1978–80 and fell during 1980–82, following the ups (1976–78) and downs (after 1979) in world coffee prices. Although domestic prices of coffee were considerably stabilized, the higher producer prices in 1976–78 induced a dramatic increase in production. The higher prices were the main reason for increased export values in 1976–77. The record export sales in 1978–80, on the other hand, were the result both of higher prices and of greater volumes. During 1981–83, export volumes declined from the 1978–80 levels and stabilized at levels that were nevertheless higher than the 1970–75 average. The decline in export values during 1981–83 were also on account of the decline in prices.

Noncoffee exports in real terms—that is, total value adjusted by a price index—did not do well during 1979–83, after a modest increase in the second half of the 1970s, although they were estimated to have improved in 1984 and early 1985. The fall in an index of international real prices of these commodities between 1977

Table 1-3. *Real Prices of Exports, Imports, and the Terms of Trade, 1970–83*
(1975 = 100)

Year	Coffee[a]	Noncoffee exports[b]	All exports[b]	Terms of trade[c]
1970	124.8	77.1	101.3	99.0
1971	102.6	80.9	91.6	92.5
1972	107.2	80.3	94.0	97.3
1973	120.2	84.2	102.2	103.6
1974	105.8	121.1	112.4	108.1
1975	100.0	100.0	100.0	100.0
1976	190.3	102.6	144.4	140.3
1977	263.8	129.4	193.2	194.6
1978	176.7	104.0	140.1	145.3
1979	154.1	89.1	122.0	129.8
1980	137.4	108.5	124.0	132.0
1981	97.8	123.0	110.4	111.3
1982	109.9	115.9	112.9	107.8
1983	104.8	124.2	114.5	110.4

Note: For additional details of agricultural prices, both external and domestic, see chapter 4. These export prices have been deflated by a July 1985 World Bank estimate of a unit-value, U.S.-dollar price index of manufactured exports from developed to developing countries.

a. New York price of Colombian coffee, from IFS yearbook, line 76e.

b. Based on indexes of export unit values from IFS; the noncoffee export index was calculated from price indexes of coffee and all other exports, weighted by their respective shares.

c. Export price index divided by import price index for Colombia, as in IFS.

Sources: International Financial Statistics (IFS) (Washington, D.C.: International Monetary Fund, annual publication); World Bank estimates.

and 1979, particularly in relation to coffee, may have contributed to the poor export performance. Quantities of these noncoffee commodities exported may have slackened in the 1980s in response to previously depressed international prices. External prices, however, cannot fully explain the declining export trend following an improvement in world prices and Colombia's overall terms of trade. Within agriculture alone, a fall in external prices has been a more serious impediment than in the rest of the economy. In general, however, domestic price developments and nonprice factors must also be accounted for in explaining recent trends.

Evolution of Internal Relative Prices

Prices of exports and imports in relation to those of nontraded commodities in the domestic market reflect the degree of competitiveness of the traded goods. Between 1975 and 1977, when the relative price of coffee was rising, the internal relative prices of both noncoffee exports and imports with respect to nontradables declined, and this reduction continued in 1978 (see table 1-4). Between 1979 and

Table 1-4. *Internal Relative Prices of Exports and Imports, 1970–83*

Year	All exports	Coffee exports[a]	Noncoffee exports	Imports
1970	88.9	111.6	68.3	82.6
1971	79.3	92.9	67.8	80.1
1972	86.3	104.6	73.3	78.7
1973	98.8	121.4	83.8	80.9
1974	104.7	102.9	106.0	97.3
1975	100.0	100.0	100.0	100.0
1976	120.6	165.1	90.6	91.9
1977	135.4	235.6	83.6	82.2
1978	111.2	151.7	78.9	77.0
1979	97.0	110.9	83.1	78.5
1980	102.4	111.9	93.6	80.2
1981	85.0	80.2	89.2	77.5
1982	80.8	83.6	79.0	71.5
1983	79.8	80.1	79.6	70.1

Note: Relative prices, as shown in this table, are the ratio of the implicit prices of exports and imports to implicit GDP deflators.

a. The export price of coffee divided by the GDP deflator. This is not the real internal price of coffee shown in table 6-6.

Source: Computed from DANE data by Jorge García-García, "Aspects of Agricultural Development in Colombia" (Bogotá, April 1983, processed).

 1980 this tendency was reversed, with the relative price of coffee dropping and the relative price of noncoffee exports and imports increasing. During 1981–83, the relative prices of coffee and noncoffee traded goods fell. These price developments would be expected to erode the incentives to produce noncoffee exportables and import-competing commodities, which is what has happened in recent years.

By raising disposable incomes and spending, the increase in the world coffee price increased the prices of nontraded products not only in relation to the price of coffee, but also in relation to the prices of products in other traded categories.[12] In view of the large component of traded products in agriculture, the effect of declining relative prices was felt particularly in this sector (see table 1-5). The relatively high rate of domestic inflation, coupled with a low rate of depreciation of the peso during the period 1976–82, further reduced the degree of competitiveness among traded goods other than coffee. The higher world price of coffee in 1976–79 generated a dramatic increase in international reserves, higher rates of growth of high-powered money, and a tendency toward a higher rate of inflation. The government responded by implementing a stabilization policy and sterilizing—that is, neutralizing—a part of the additional reserves and thus controlling other sources of inflation. Toward the end of 1979, most import restrictions were eased significantly (see chapter 3). Meanwhile, for stabilization, the rate of depreciation of the crawling

Table 1-5. *Internal Relative Prices of Agricultural Exports and Imports, 1970–82*

Year	Agricultural exports[a]	Agricultural exports[b]	Agricultural imports[c]
1970	134.1	183.5	74.0
1971	117.1	120.5	77.9
1972	130.9	135.4	78.9
1973	127.8	139.8	109.6
1974	107.6	105.4	121.3
1975	100.0	100.0	100.0
1976	94.3	147.4	87.8
1977	99.3	212.6	93.4
1978	90.2	148.4	58.3
1979	93.4	113.7	81.5
1980	81.4	107.0	89.2
1981	85.4	84.5	83.7
1982	96.6	89.2	79.7

a. In relation to nonagricultural exports; agriculture includes unprocessed coffee, other crops, and livestock.

b. In relation to nonbroad agricultural exports; "broad agriculture" includes—in addition to unprocessed coffee, other crops, and livestock—the sectors in which coffee and sugar are processed.

c. In relation to nonbroad agricultural imports; this column refers to imported agricultural commodities within the broad agriculture sector.

Source: Same as for table 1-4.

peg was reduced,[13] and the real exchange rate (pesos per unit of foreign currency) was allowed to decline—that is, appreciate—significantly, contributing to a reduction in the competitiveness of categories of traded products other than coffee.

The decline in producer prices in agriculture in relation to prices in the rest of the economy since the mid 1970s has hurt noncoffee agriculture. In addition, price interventions and other sectoral developments have contributed to the performance of the sector, as will be elaborated upon later. The government has intervened in the sector in an effort to provide special inducements to agricultural production, principally through import controls, domestic price supports for selected commodities, and credit subsidies. Import policies affect only a small proportion of these importables and have thus been largely ineffective and often inefficient. Furthermore, additional import controls constitute an indirect tax on exports, further eroding incentives in the part of agriculture in which exportable commodities are produced. The period of falling agricultural incentives, 1975–83, also coincided with declining government efforts in agricultural investment (see chapter 7). The private sector has taken the lead in investment, although a declining government contribution in such critical areas as research, extension, and development of infrastructure has been detrimental to sectoral development. Meanwhile, agricultural production costs have mounted, and yields of only certain products have increased significantly. Investments in a number of areas—research, extension, irrigation, input supply—together with improvements in the provision of credit and in marketing can make a significant contribution to increasing yields and reducing production costs (see chapter 8). The macroeconomic adjustment can help improve agricultural incentives, as evidence for 1984 and 1985 shows (see chapter 9).

Macroeconomic Policy and Inflation

Macroeconomic policy interacts with agriculture in good measure through its effects on inflation, the real exchange rate, and incentives to export and import. Particular macroeconomic policies may originate within the agricultural sector itself. Coffee is one source of such a linkage in Colombia.

Coffee Prices and Inflation

The increase in the price of coffee produced higher disposable incomes and an increase in the demand for both tradables and nontradables. Since the price of tradables other than coffee is, to a significant extent, determined by the world price and the exchange rate, this income effect caused the relative price of nontradables to rise (see appendix A). More important, the increase in the price of coffee tended to generate a balance of payments surplus and an accumulation of international reserves. Since the increase in international reserves was not fully neutralized, the monetary base also increased. Additional spending induced by the higher coffee earnings increased the demand for credit and probably increased velocity, and in the short run inflation tended to accelerate. A fairly close statistical relation between inflation and monetary growth has been documented.[14] Another avenue through which the higher coffee price affected the real exchange rate was discussed earlier. The monetary authority, worried about a higher rate of inflation, reacted to a higher price of coffee by trying to use exchange rate policy for stabilization and reducing the rate of nominal depreciation of the crawling peg.

As confirmed by the statistical analysis in appendix A, the higher coffee price was associated with an increase in the monetary base, which was related positively to a rise in the rate of domestic inflation and a fall—that is, an appreciation—in the real exchange rate. Additionally, the fiscal deficit of the central government rose from 1.2 percent of GDP in 1979 to about 4 percent in 1982 and 1983; a containment was estimated for 1984–85. (Colombia's fiscal year is identical with the calendar year.) These inflationary developments, combined with the inadequate exchange rate adjustment, meant a reduction in the relative prices of noncoffee tradable goods and a consequent loss in their competitiveness.

Fiscal Deficit and Inflation

With the decline in real prices of coffee in the 1980s, the trends in the international reserve position and the size of the monetary base were reversed. These tendencies should be expected to bring down the rate of inflation and, other things being equal, depreciate the real exchange rate. During the early 1980s, however, the growing fiscal deficit became a source of the upward pressure on domestic prices. Through most of the 1970s, the central government's cash balances were positive or modestly negative. A significant turnaround occurred during 1980–82, when current expenditures rose steadily as a result of real wage increases, earmarked revenues, and automatic transfers to decentralized public agencies, while current revenues hardly improved in real terms; in 1980–82 there were also rapid increases in investment. By 1982 the overall cash deficit of the central administration reached Col\$110 billion—that is, thousand million—or more than 4 percent of GDP (see table 1-6). The corresponding deficit in the consolidated public sector accounts was twice as high, although accurate data for this aspect are not available. Fiscal policy needs to curb expenditures in line with the generation of revenue, while protecting high-priority investments.

The government has been increasing—albeit from relatively low levels—expenditures that need to be financed by borrowing from private savings and from the creation of money. A part of the government deficit is financed by the creation of money and not met by a concomitant increase in aggregate supply.[15] Since 1980 there has been a sharp decline in the contribution of the growth of international reserves to the money base, while deficit financing has assumed increasing importance and has contributed to inflation. The rising deficit has also meant a diversion of part of investable funds from private savings toward current government expenditures, thus reducing the availability of such funds for the rest of the economy. Finally, the fiscal deficit has also reduced the degree of freedom of the government with respect to management of deficits in the balance of payments, given the need

Table 1-6. *Cash Deficit of the Central Government, 1978–84*
(billion pesos)

Item	1978	1979	1980	1981	1982	1983	1984[a]
Current revenue[b]	80.1	94.6	131.1	155.0	197.3	236.2	297.3
Current expenditure	57.2	83.0	121.8	154.2	211.5	277.6	358.9
Current account	22.9	11.6	9.3	0.8	−14.2	−41.4	−61.6
Investment	21.0	26.0	42.0	61.2	96.1	81.8	101.8
Overall deficit	−1.9	14.4	32.6	60.4	110.3	123.2	163.4
Net financing	−1.9	14.4	32.6	60.4	110.3	123.2	163.4
Net external financing	−2.2	5.4	16.8	19.1	14.9	2.5	19.6
Net domestic financing	0.3	9.0	15.8	41.3	95.4	120.7	143.8
Monetary financing	1.7	7.5	22.6	47.4	103.8	107.3	149.3
Domestic credit and other	−2.0	1.5	−6.8	−6.1	−8.4	13.4	−5.5

Note: In this study the word *billion* is used to mean one thousand million.

a. Estimated.

b. Excludes nontax proceeds from the special-exchange account and receipts from certificates.

Source: Calculated by Laurens M. Hoppenbrouwer on the basis of data from the Colombian treasury.

to finance a part of the budget deficit from external financing by reducing foreign reserves.

Appendix A shows the positive empirical relation between the government deficit and the rate of inflation. Such a positive association, however, may be difficult to discern by merely considering particular years without separating out the simultaneous effects of other important variables. It is possible in a given year for the deficit to increase while the rate of inflation declines. A recession can diminish tax revenues, thus increasing the deficit, while simultaneously putting a lid on the rate of inflation. In 1983, the reserves dropped drastically, holding the expansion in the rate of growth of the money supply and inflation in check without any decrease in the fiscal deficit. These observations, however, do not negate the partial positive effect of deficits on inflation.

Another implication of the foregoing is that under recessionary circumstances, an increase in the deficit may not increase inflation in the very short term. As the economy recovers, however, the inflationary effect becomes evident, other things remaining the same. The results depend on monetary policy as well. The inflationary effect of higher deficits can be offset by a tight monetary policy, but such a policy could lead to higher interest rates, which might arrest economic growth. During 1983–84 the real monetary base was reduced, mainly on account of falling reserves, which in the face of a rising budget deficit exercised an upward pressure on the interest rate. The determination of interest rate is also heavily influenced by the expected depreciation of the peso (see chapter 2).

Real Exchange Rate and Competitiveness

The data in table 1-7 support the more formal empirical analysis in appendix A, which establishes the statistical link between the price of coffee, the rate of growth of high-powered money, and inflation in Colombia. Together, the findings confirm some of the characteristics of the Dutch-disease type model: other things being equal, a higher price of coffee has led to a higher rate of inflation and an appreciation of the real exchange rate.[16] A growing fiscal deficit has aggravated the inflationary tendency, further lowering the real exchange rate.

According to table 1-7, during most of 1970–78 and 1981–83, the real price of coffee and the real exchange rate showed the above-mentioned relation. During 1978–81, however, the opposite seems to have been the case. It should be emphasized, nevertheless, that during the second half of the 1970s, real coffee prices remained at very high levels—even during years in which they declined—contributing to the appreciation of the real rate of exchange. Three factors seem to be noteworthy. First, the exchange-rate effect of coffee prices involves some lags—that is, the real rate continued to appreciate even after the price of coffee began in 1978 to fall from its extraordinarily high levels. Second, coffee revenues, not just prices, are relevant; revenues continued to rise through 1980, contributing to appreciation of the peso. Finally, during 1981–82, the real price of coffee hardly changed, but the

Table 1-7. *Selected Macroeconomic Variables, 1970–84*

Year	Real price of coffee[a] (1975 = 100)	Terms of trade[a] (1975 = 100)	Rate of growth of money base[b] (percent)	Central government cash deficit as percentage of GDP[c]	Rate of inflation[d] (percent)	Average rate of devaluation[e] (percent)	Real exchange rate[f] (1975 = 100)
1970	124.8	99.0	19.8	n.a.	6.7	6.5	81.1
1971	102.6	92.5	8.8	n.a.	11.6	8.1	83.1
1972	107.2	97.3	25.4	n.a.	13.8	9.7	86.4
1973	120.2	103.6	31.1	1.2	22.0	8.1	89.3
1974	105.8	108.1	18.8	1.5	25.2	10.3	94.7
1975	100.0	100.0	31.7	0.5	23.6	18.7	100.0
1976	190.3	140.3	41.6	− 0.6	19.9	12.2	97.3
1977	263.8	194.6	40.1	− 0.5	34.7	6.0	83.4
1978	176.2	145.3	35.2	− 0.2	16.7	6.3	83.5
1979	154.1	129.8	30.4	1.2	24.9	8.8	81.8
1980	137.4	132.0	28.8	2.1	27.2	11.1	82.0
1981	97.4	111.3	21.8	3.1	28.1	15.3	78.1
1982	109.9	107.8	17.7	4.4	24.6	17.6	73.4
1983	104.8	110.4	13.5	4.1	19.8	23.0	75.2
1984[g]	111.5	115.0	18.3	4.5	16.4	27.9	81.8

n.a. Not available.

a. From table 1-3.

b. Currency in the hands of the public plus reserves held by commercial banks in nominal terms.

c. Before amortization.

d. Percentage change in period averages of the consumer price index. Blue collar workers.

e. Period averages are from IFS.

f. Measured against a trade-weighted basket, as explained in table 2-3.

g. Preliminary estimate.

Sources: Banco de la Republica, IFS, International Monetary Fund, DANE, and World Bank data.

peso continued to appreciate. This was to a significant extent the result of a growing fiscal deficit.

The net result was to hurt the performance of noncoffee tradables. On the other hand, there has not been any significant output response from the relative prices of nontradables, which improved. The coffee boom hid the negative effect on the noncoffee-tradable economy. With a fall in noncoffee prices in the 1980s, a lower rate of inflation and an increase—that is, a depreciation—in the real exchange rate ought to be expected. The decline in the rate of inflation was slow until 1982, however; the continuing increase in the fiscal deficit combined with increases in real wages kept increases in aggregate demand higher than increases in aggregate supply.

Real Exchange Rate and Import Policy

While export development was depressed, imports showed a healthy growth during 1980–82. The share of imports—goods and nonfactor services—in GDP during 1980–82 was higher than its level during the early 1970s. The balance of payments effect was becoming steadily more negative, as evidenced by the growing resource gap during this period. The appreciated exchange rate has hurt the competitiveness of import-competing industries and has contributed to balance of payments difficulties.

As will be seen in chapter 3, imports are to a degree a policy variable, because the government influences the level of imports through licensing, tariffs, and some prohibitions. With the problems in the external sector, the controls increased during 1983–84, partly to offset the overvaluation (appreciation) of the exchange rate and partly to protect foreign exchange reserves directly. By the same token, when import restrictions have been effective, they have been observed to contribute to inflation in Colombia and to constrain domestic production.[17] As the balance of payments stabilizes and adjustments in the exchange rate are improved, therefore, gradual liberalization of the import regime will be desirable.

The Medium-Term Outlook

During 1980–83 GDP grew at an average of less than 1.5 percent a year.[18] Noncoffee exports fell in constant prices from 1980 through 1983.[19] Combined with the fall in coffee revenues, this meant a sizable decline in commodity exports in constant prices during 1980–83 (see table 1-7). Commodity imports, in the meantime, increased in constant prices in 1981 and 1982; this increase, combined with the slump in exports, produced deficits in the trade and resource balances during 1981–83—the first in seven years.

The economy remained modestly active during 1983–84. A significant outcome was the drop in inflation to 19.8 percent in 1983 and an estimated 16.4 percent in 1984, although this drop was partly the result of declines in reserves and in the growth of the monetary base. In four major cities, the average unemployment rate in 1983 was estimated to be 11.8 percent; it had been 9.2 percent in 1982, and it is estimated to have increased further, to 13.5 percent, in 1984. GDP in real terms is estimated to have increased by less than 1 percent in 1983 and about 3 percent in 1984. Exports and imports fell in 1983, as can be seen from table 1-8. A large deficit in the current account—only marginally lower than the deficit in the previous year—was estimated for 1983. Net capital inflow declined significantly in 1983, causing a drop of 37 percent in international reserves.

On the basis of preliminary data the current account deficit was estimated to have been reduced significantly in 1984–85. In the absence of a significant turnaround in capital inflows, however, the balance of payments position remained difficult in

Table 1-8. *The Balance of Payments Situation, 1970, 1975, and 1978–84*
(million U.S. dollars)

	1970	1975	1978	1980	1981	1982	1983	1984[a]
Exports[b]	1,000	2,165	4,039	5,747	4,678	4,785	4,050	4,542
Imports[b]	1,149	2,030	4,131	5,494	6,078	6,738	5,814	5,113
Current account balance	−339	−98	357	104	−1,722	−2,886	−2,826	−1,870
Percentage of GDP	−4.8	−0.7	1.5	0.3	−4.7	−7.4	−7.3	−5.1
Net year-end reserves	152	547	2,482	5,416	5,630	4,891	3,079	1,796
Equivalent months of imports[b]	1.6	3.2	7.2	11.8	11.1	8.7	6.5	4.2

a. Preliminary estimate.
b. Goods and nonfactor services.
c. Estimates made by the Banco de la Republica, Bogotá, and the World Bank.
Sources: Banco de la Republica and World Bank estimates.

1984. Any substantial improvement in world coffee prices would obviously produce an improvement in the external accounts. An increase in net capital inflows remains essential in order to stabilize the reserve position. According to a base-case or moderate projection, assuming world economic recovery and good domestic policies—some of which are discussed in this study—it is envisaged that, with faster depreciation of the real exchange rate combined with a vigorous export drive backed by efforts to strengthen aggregate supply, rapid economic growth could be resumed in the mid 1980s.[20] The balance of payments is expected to stabilize and improve significantly during the latter half of the 1980s, particularly as substantial exports of oil and coal come on stream.

Macroeconomic adjustments were initiated in 1984–85, and early indications show that the central government cash deficit as a proportion of GDP is being reduced. With a significant increase in the rate of the crawling peg and reduction in the domestic inflation rate, the real exchange rate is estimated to have depreciated substantially. These adjustment measures are to be deepened and complemented by some additional capital inflows, with borrowing policies kept within prudent limits. Once the near-term difficulties have been overcome through these developments, the medium-term outlook is expected to remain favorable for growth, employment, and the balance of payments.

A Policy Overview

Macroeconomic management in Colombia over the long term has successfully responded to emerging realities within the confines of a democratic process of policymaking. Policy decisions, however, have been found to be especially difficult when coffee prices fluctuate sharply. This arises from the uncertainty attached to assessments of the duration of price increases and, consequently, the degree of adjustment in macroeconomic variables that is required. During the coffee price boom, alternative means of stabilization were pursued to varying degrees and with varying effectiveness. To some extent, the increases in reserves were neutralized by the monetary policies adopted, some increase in imports, and appreciation of the real exchange rate.

A smaller appreciation of the peso might have been workable if it had been supported by a larger inflow of imports to absorb the increase in domestic demand and if borrowing had not increased sharply, as it did during 1978–82. It should be noted, however, that a major liberalization in the face of an already appreciated peso could exacerbate adjustment problems of import-competing domestic industries. Temporary protection for noncoffee exports in the form of special export incentives might be necessary for a short period and was, in fact, actually extended to a limited degree. Once the price boom has been diagnosed as transitory, however, a reversal of appreciation of the peso—even if the exchange rate might have been at an adequate level during the boom—would normally be the right approach to take. In this respect, the adjustment of the Colombian economy—in reducing inflation, improving the real exchange rate, and shifting resources into production of products other than coffee—could perhaps have been more timely.

The difference between domestic and external inflation during 1975–84 was large; domestic prices, measured at the official exchange rate, rose by some 100 percent, while the increase in one index of external prices was about 50 percent. Partly as a result, the producer prices of noncoffee tradables—which, as mentioned earlier, are strongly influenced by international prices—have fallen in relation to the price of domestic goods and services in this period. Since the share of tradables in agricultural output is greater than in the rest of the economy, this decline in relative producer prices has been especially adverse for the sector. Unfortunately, the shift of incentives in favor of nontradables has not produced any significant output response from this domestic sector as a whole, so there has been little offset to the losses in production and employment, which are the result of slower growth in the tradable goods sector.

Colombia now faces real coffee prices that are roughly comparable to those that existed during the mid 1970s but lower than the average real price during the first half of the 1970s. Colombian terms of trade today correspond roughly to the level of those of the mid 1970s. The direction of macroeconomic policy at present consists, among other things, of a depreciation of the peso to reach an equilibrium level as soon as possible. At the same time, a reduction of domestic inflation—which could otherwise increase as a result of accelerated depreciation of the peso—is sought through fiscal and other measures, such as a gradual opening up of imports as exports respond to greater incentives. A target of current policy is to bring the fiscal deficit of the central government down from the level of over 4 percent of GDP in 1982 and 1983 to less than 2 percent in 1985 and to reduce it thereafter. Corresponding decreases in the deficit of the consolidated public sector are also expected. These steps aimed at reducing inflation and improving the real exchange rate would in general be favorable to agriculture, reducing the pressure to provide special price incentives directly to the sector.

The government would also have to execute a more forceful strategy of return to export promotion to absorb any significant shift in the domestic supply of agricultural products. It should include an adequate general incentive system for noncoffee exports to regain competitiveness, a gradual reduction in the level and dispersion of protection across sectors, and an assurance to exporters of rapid access to foreign exchange and the imports needed to produce exports. A balance of payments projection consistent with a recovery of growth through the 1980s indicates also the need for some increased net capital inflows and investment in the near term. Accordingly, the country needs to continue to speed disbursements of existing loans and put together a program for some additional external financing.

This study suggests that both the world economic recession and an adverse shift in relative producer prices in domestic markets have been significant in explaining the performance of noncoffee exports, both agricultural products and others.[21] What is also needed is a product-by-product and country-by-country examination of external demand and of institutional and other arrangements required to break into new markets, supported by efforts to improve yield, quality, processing and marketing. An important aspect of agricultural adjustment revolves around the problem of reducing excess stocks of coffee—unless there is a dramatic increase in the demand facing Colombia—and the need to restrain the internal real price of coffee and to induce a shift of resources into noncoffee activities. A good part of diversification is likely to be in the output of additional food, domestic expenditure on which contributes nearly 40 percent of the consumer budget. The demand for noncoffee agricultural products—food and nonfood combined—is projected to grow sufficiently to absorb a significantly higher output level—by about 3 percent (domestic and external combined) during the 1980s under one set of "moderate" assumptions of a world recovery and improvements in Colombia's competitiveness.[22] Efforts to reduce production costs and increase yields (see chapters 7 and 8) will permit a better alignment of additional supplies with future demand.

Notes

1. Vinod Thomas and others, "Colombian Agriculture: Selected Issues and Some Directions for Strategy," Report no. 4275-CO (Washington, D.C.: World Bank, Latin America and the Caribbean Country Programs, Colombia Division, 1983).

2. In addition to the coffee boom, there was also rapid growth in drug trade during the 1970s, although assessment of it remains difficult. In Roberto Junguito and Carlos Caballero, "La otra economía," *Coyuntura económica*, vol. 8 (December 1978), pp. 103–39, drug exports were estimated to have grown from about $300 million to $850 million between 1974 and 1977 (dollar amounts are in

U.S. dollars unless another currency is specified). This growth would be equivalent to an additional 0.4 percent average annual growth in GDP, or an increase of nearly 10 percent in the growth rate, during that period.

3. The recession in Venezuela and increasing import restriction in that and other neighboring countries during the early 1980s seriously hurt Colombian exports.

4. A more detailed discussion of the economy is given in World Bank, *Colombia: Economic Development and Policy under Changing Conditions* (Washington, D.C., 1984). It should be noted that some of the calculations involving national accounts data obtained from the Central Bank in that study and the present one differ somewhat from the newly published data of the Departamento Administrativo Nacional de Estadistica (DANE, the National Department of Statistics). Greater use of the data base of DANE could be made in future work.

5. See Gabriel Montes and Ricardo Candelo, "El crecimiento industrial y la generación de empleo en Colombia: Entre la substitución de importaciónes y la promoción de exportaciónes," *Revista de planeación y desarrollo*, vol. 12, nos. 1 and 2, (January–June 1981), p. 87; and Francisco Thoumi, "International Trade Strategies, Employment and Income Distribution in Colombia," in *Trade and Employment in Developing Countries*, ed. by Anne O. Krueger and others, vol. 3 (Chicago: University of Chicago Press, 1981).

6. Details of this and other trade-related observations can be found in tables SA-1–10.

7. See Roberto Junguito and Diego Pizano, "Primary Products in Latin America," in *Latin America and the New International Order*, ed. R. Ffrench-Davis and Ernest Tironi (London: Macmillan, 1982).

8. The main agricultural export commodities, other than coffee, are cotton, sugar, bananas, flowers, leaf tobacco, livestock products, fish, and rice. Agricultural imports are defined here as outputs of agricultural origin, and they exclude processed foods and beverages as well as agricultural inputs such as fertilizer.

9. See Jorge García-García, "Aspects of Agricultural Development in Colombia" (Bogotá, April 1983, processed). Exportables are defined as coffee, rice, sugarcane, leaf tobacco, beans, bananas, sesame, cotton fiber, flowers, cattle, and sugar. Importables consist of cereals other than rice, green peas, other vegetables, other fruits, soybeans, cocoa, and milk products. Domestic commodities are brown sugar, tubers, tomatoes and other vegetables, plantains, oilseeds, noncotton fibers, hogs, sheep, horses, poultry, and eggs.

10. A decline in the number of Colombian pesos paid per unit of foreign currency is defined as a nominal appreciation of the peso. After adjustments have been made for differential movements in price levels in Colombia and externally, however, a measure of real movements in the exchange rate is obtained.

11. Although there are parallels, the monetization of export receipts and the fiscal effects of illegal exports of drugs would be quite different from those of coffee. Of course, the domestic social and sociological aspects of coffee and drug exports are worlds apart.

12. The measures of relative prices of exports and imports would by and large be representative of the trends for exportables and importables, respectively, as well. Therefore, often a finding concerning the competitiveness of traded goods is generalized for tradables in this book.

13. See "Evaluación de la estrategia de exportaciónes nuevas, 1979–1982" (Bogotá: Fondo de Promoción de Exportaciónes [PROEXPO, the export promotion agency], 1982).

14. James Hanson, "Inflation and Imported Input-Prices in Some Inflationary Latin American Economies" (Washington, D.C.: World Bank, Industry Department, 1982, processed); Laughlin Currie, "La demanda de dinero y la velocidad ingreso de la moneda en Colombia, 1960–80," *Desarrollo y Sociedad*, no. 6 (July 1981).

15. Juan Carlos Jaramillo and Armando Montenegro, "Cuenta especial de cambios: Descripción y analisis de su evolución reciente," *Ensayos sobre política económica*, no.2 (September 1982), pp. 109-86; and José Antonio Ocampo and Guillermo Perry, "La reforma fiscal, 1982–83," *Coyuntura económica*, vol. 13, no. 1 (March 1983), pp. 215–64.

16. A Dutch-disease type of model is formally explained in appendix A. See W. Max Corden and

J. Peter Neary, "Booming Sector and De-Industrialization in a Small Open Economy," *Economic Journal*, vol. 92 (December 1982), pp. 825–48; Arnold C. Harberger, "Dutch Disease: How Much Sickness, How Much Boon?" *Resources and Energy*, vol. 5 (March 1983), pp. 1–20; and Sebastian Edwards and Masanao Aoki, "Oil Export Boom and Dutch-Disease: A Dynamic Analysis," *Resources and Energy*, vol. 8 (September 1985).

17. See Hanson, "Inflation and Imported Input-Prices."

18. See, for a discussion, Edgar Gutierrez Castro, "Presentacion ante el Congreso Nacional sobre la Emergencia Económica" (Bogotá, 1983, processed); see also table SA-9.

19. See table SA-7. If dollar receipts are deflated by the declining international price index for manufactured goods in 1981 and 1982, however, in constant dollar terms no significant change is indicated.

20. Underlying the base case are, among other things, assumptions of good OECD growth and a set of good domestic policies concerning the exchange rate, monetary, fiscal, and financial matters, and management of external debt.

21. Even with faster world recovery, the success of Colombia's efforts to increase exports might be predicated on its ability to take into account the exchange-rate adjustments of its competitors (see chapter 2).

22. Thomas and others, "Colombian Agriculture."

2

Trade Policy and Export Promotion

TRADE POLICIES that have a significant influence on export performance are the subject of this chapter. The superior performance of outward-oriented economies has been related both to competitive exchange rates and to other incentives, such as access to duty-free imported inputs for exporting firms. Successful outward-looking economies have been known for their policies to ensure similar incentives to production for export and home markets. Equally important have been quality control, prompt delivery, and flexibility in composition of products in response to variations in foreign demand. Furthermore, where import protection is not heavy, domestic production has had to compete with imports either for domestic sales or eventually for exports.[1]

Export incentives in Colombia usually involve exchange rate management, export loans, subsidies, and special facilities, as well as import policy. Import considerations having been set aside for chapter 3, a close examination will be provided of the way these incentives have varied with the passage of time. An important element of this analysis is the exchange rate, which since 1967 has been based on a crawling peg. In this chapter the way the exchange rate has varied in order to stimulate exports (1967–75), the way it has been used for stabilization purposes (1976–80), and the possibilities there are in the 1980s for restoring its function of export promotion will be reviewed.

Factors That Affect Policy Choice

In evaluating exchange rate policy, it is essential to distinguish between short-term fluctuations around long-term equilibrium levels and persistent disequilibrium levels. While short-term variations can be problematic, persistent deviation from a long-term or fundamental equilibrium is of greater concern. Purchasing power parity (PPP) suggests that changes in the nominal exchange rate should be in accordance with differences between domestic and external inflation, but it does not account for equilibrium departures from PPP when the price of an important commodity, such as coffee, changes significantly in more than a transitory way. PPP also does not indicate the base exchange rate level for comparison. Measures of changing competitiveness as guides for the appropriate exchange rate are also arbitrary, because they require choosing base years when the country's costs and prices are considered to be in reasonable balance and when a basic equilibrium may be considered to have existed. One alternative is to examine normal years, when the real exchange rates permitted the matching of balances in the current account with trends in capital flows.[2] The rate would have to provide sufficient incentives to productive sectors to allow a reasonable rate of growth in a framework of balance of payments viability *given* external conditions and domestic fiscal and monetary conditions.

Wide fluctuations in the country's external terms of trade have made it difficult to determine and maintain a long-term equilibrium exchange rate in Colombia. Most of these changes have been the result of variations in world prices of coffee—coffee representing some 56 percent of goods exported during the period 1970–82—which in turn have affected the level of the exchange rate the authorities consider sustainable for noncoffee commodities. During the 1950s and through the mid 1960s multiple exchange rates were used, with rates for noncoffee exports—sometimes separate rates for imports and for petroleum and other products—at times floating and often pegged at a level different from that for coffee. Instability and unpredictability of world coffee prices have also discouraged policymakers in the past from seeking long-term equilibrium rates, using import controls instead and export subsidies for commodities other than coffee. Since 1967 multiple rates have been abandoned, and the approach to an equilibrium rate has been more successful, although not always without difficulties.

With the trade reforms initiated in 1967, the peso depreciated significantly, reaching an equilibrium by the mid 1970s. The balance of payments was in reasonable equilibrium from 1973 to 1975. Commodity prices, especially those of coffee, were not abnormal in that period, and Colombia was still self-sufficient in petroleum, so there was no significant oil price effect. In fact, the terms of trade were about the same during 1973–75 as in 1983 (see table 2-1). These considerations support the use of the mid 1970s as a base for measuring the real exchange rate, although this will clearly need to be a flexible policy, to be revised upon the appearance of new evidence.

Past Policies and Exports

During the 1950s and through the mid 1960s, the peso was chronically overvalued from the point of view of competitiveness of noncoffee exports, effectively constraining export diversification.[3] Although isolated attempts at stimulating exports had been made before, it was not until 1967 that a coherent set of measures

Table 2-1. *Indicators of Performance in the External Sector, 1970–84*

Year	Terms of trade[a] (1975 = 100)	Current account balance[b] Million U.S. dollars	Current account balance[b] Percent of GDP	Net capital inflow[bc] (million U.S. dollars)	Change in reserves[bd]
1970	99.0	– 339	– 4.8	337	– 2
1971	92.5	– 484	– 6.4	409	– 75
1972	97.3	– 214	– 2.5	406	192
1973	103.6	– 80	– 0.8	305	225
1974	108.1	– 384	– 3.0	20	– 364
1975	100.0	– 98	– 0.7	237	139
1976	140.3	210	1.4	352	562
1977	194.6	449	2.3	403	852
1978	145.3	357	1.5	253	610
1979	129.8	562	2.0	675	1,237
1980	132.0	104	0.3	1,206	1,310
1981	111.3	– 1,722	– 4.7	1,936	214
1982	107.8	– 2,885	– 7.4	2,146	– 739
1983	110.4	– 2,826	– 7.3	1,014	– 1,812
1984[c]	115.0	– 1,870	– 5.1	587	– 1,283

a. Unit export price divided by unit import price, from IFS data.
b. From table SA-8.
c. The difference between the current account balance and the change in reserves, which means that errors and omissions are included.
d. A minus sign signifies a drop in reserves.
e. Preliminary estimate.
Sources: Banco de la Republica, IMF, and World Bank data.

was undertaken to promote nontraditional exports—that is, exports other than coffee and petroleum.

The 1967 Trade Reforms

The most important element of the new policies was the introduction of a crawling peg exchange rate system.[4] A package of export incentives was also introduced, including fiscal incentives—Certificados de Abono Tributario (CATS); concessionary credits for export-related activities from the Export Promotion Fund (PROEXPO credit); and an expanded and more effective import-export regime (Plan Vallejo). The new policies represented an attempt to compensate for the distortions in relative prices generated by the import-substitution effort. Together with the favorable development of world trade, this shift in policy emphasis brought about impressive results.

Between 1968 and 1974 manufactured exports, in current prices, increased from $58 million to more than $390 million, and their share in total exports rose from 8 percent to 28 percent.[5] Industrial value added increased 7 percent a year in real terms, and the growth in manufacturing employment of 8.5 percent a year reached unprecedented levels, largely as a result of the labor-intensive nature of the leading export subsectors—textiles, apparel, footwear, and leather products. This growth of manufactured goods and other minor exports also succeeded in easing the foreign exchange problems that had plagued the economy in earlier years.

About a third of Colombia's export growth during 1967–75 was attributed principally to the sharp expansion in world trade of manufactured goods, and the remaining two-thirds to the increased competitiveness of Colombian industry in international markets. This has in turn been linked to adjustments in the real exchange rate to reflect the effective value of the CAT export incentive, the effective value of subsidized PROEXPO credits, and the conditions of the import duty drawback scheme (Plan Vallejo). A variety of products took advantage of these incentives, and several new commodities entered the export market. A number of impressive results can be cited: Colombia's textile exports grew faster than those of Taiwan, Hong Kong, and Singapore during 1970–75; exports of cut flowers, beginning from negligible levels in the mid 1960s, climbed dramatically to reach $19 million in 1975 and $112 million in 1982; by 1978 Colombia had become the world's leading exporter of children's books, exporting $58 million worth, up from $2 million in 1970.

Several developments through the 1970s might not have been predicted at the beginning of that decade: cheese, bananas, frozen shrimp, footwear, refrigerators and stoves, work gloves, and false teeth are some of the products exports of which had reached impressive levels by 1980. These examples suggest that a favorable export climate can produce remarkable results, not all of which can be anticipated. Exports to the Andean Group have been roughly 15–16 percent in recent years, and this share has not changed significantly since the mid 1970s. Protection of agricultural imports in other countries is a potentially limiting factor for Colombian exports of certain commodities to certain countries or groups of countries. In the aggregate, however, there appears to be head room to increase Colombian exports; the issue of export markets, however, needs to be examined further.

Nonprimary exports benefited more from the exchange regime established during 1966–70 than did products based on natural resources, but both were encouraged to take advantage of a rapidly growing world market. This approach was continued in the 1970–74 development plan. The resultant growth reflected the use of excess capacity created during the period of substantial investment, 1962–66, and a judicious use of expansionary exchange-rate and aggregate-demand policies. Growth also reflected an improvement in allocation of resources, however. For example, no new and expensive import-competing projects were initiated. Growth in agriculture, particularly of export-oriented commodities, accelerated while output of less efficiently produced crops—such as wheat—fell sharply. These production effects, particularly the improvement in agricultural performance, also contributed to reduction of inflation.

Developments during the 1970s

Most of the thrust of the 1967 reforms was maintained in subsequent years, but their effectiveness has varied with changes in world conditions and occasional delays in policy responses. In the second half of the 1970s, an externally generated increase in the money supply gave rise to higher rates of inflation: world coffee prices soared and unrecorded exports and net capital inflows grew rapidly, while recorded imports as a percentage of GDP did not expand and aggregate real purchasing power rose significantly. In January 1977 the administration initiated a stabilization package, which consisted of sharp rises in reserve requirements, including those for foreign borrowing, the reimposition of prior deposits for imports to reduce the money base, the use of exchange certificates to delay the monetization of export receipts, a further tightening of fiscal policy, and a reduction in the rate of depreciation of the peso; efforts to contain inflation thus met with qualified success. A more rapid increase in selected imports than actually occurred could have, in addition to absorbing the rising liquidity, allowed the country to grow faster and enjoy efficiency benefits of liberalization, although the timing of such a policy during a coffee boom is not without problems. Smuggled imports, by all accounts, did increase.

Recent Developments and Outlook

While international coffee prices began to decline from their post–World War II peaks of 1977, the government's budget deficit began to climb steadily in the second half of the 1970s, contributing to inflation. Public investment and expenditures had been reduced by the stabilization efforts of the 1974–78 administration, and the new administration (1978–82) sought to reverse this trend. Both current and capital expenditures grew in 1979 and 1980, but these contributed to an increase in the fiscal deficit, in the absence of a matching tax effort. A large part of this deficit was financed by the use of the Special Exchange Account, a part of it representing the creation of money. The Central Bank's deficit-financing operations were estimated to account for more than 90 percent of the expansion in the money base during 1981, a sharp change from the preceding five years, when public sector borrowing had been negligible. Once the accumulation of reserves had been reversed in the 1980s, the rising fiscal deficit became a reason for a high rate of inflation. A growing government deficit squeezes the private sector out of the domestic credit market, with particularly serious effects given the present difficult circumstances of the international financial markets.

The recession hurt worldwide exports, which grew 1.5 percent in 1980, stagnated in 1981, and declined some 2 percent in 1982. Only a few developing countries managed to increase exports, mainly of manufactured goods, during this period by improving productivity and quality.[6] Colombia's exports also declined in constant prices during 1980–82. Agricultural exports other than coffee fell from $643 million in 1980 to $590 million in 1981, $507 million in 1982, and an estimated $420 million in 1983 (see table SA-8). A recovery of the world economy and a depreciation of the exchange rate and export promotion efforts would be vital to Colombia's export performance, as estimates of better performance in 1984 and early 1985 already suggest.

Competitiveness and the Real Exchange Rate

Alternative measures of competitiveness can be used in an attempt to capture changes in a country's production costs—evaluated at a suitable nominal exchange rate (NER)—in comparison to international changes. In this section estimates of the way domestic and international inflation have differed in the course of time will be presented; that the measures presented would capture changes in production costs only in a broad sense has been recognized. In addition, estimates of the real exchange rate (RER) are also presented. The RER captures the effect of changes in the nominal exchange rate in offsetting the difference between domestic and external inflation.

Colombia's crawling peg is defined by the rate of exchange between the Colombian peso and the U.S. dollar. Traditionally, in calculations of the RER comparisons of the peso and the dollar have been used, adjusting the nominal rate by the difference between domestic and U.S. inflation. Such comparisons, however, would still have to be modified to the extent that the peso, like some of the other principal currencies, floats in relation to the dollar. Depending on the relation between the dollar and these currencies, a particular change in the RER, as indicated by the rate of exchange between the peso and the dollar, may or may not be reflected by a similar change of the peso in relation to these other currencies. In particular, when the dollar has appreciated against other currencies—as in 1984—the peso has also, other things being equal, tended to appreciate in real terms against these currencies. A government policy to depreciate the peso-dollar rate in this case may not depreciate the peso in relation to a basket of the relevant currencies. The exchange rate movements in real terms against these currencies can be accomplished by constructing an index of the RER with respect to a basket of currencies of the trading partners, taking into account their rates of inflation (see table 2-3).

Estimates of the Real Exchange Rate

Between 1970 and 1975, the rise of Colombian prices in U.S. dollars was significantly slower than the rise of external prices. The opposite has been true since 1975, as shown in table 2-2. The RER indexes in table 2-3 use estimated 1975–84 noncoffee trade weights—that is, export and import—for fifteen most important

Table 2-2. *A Comparison of Colombian Inflation with International Price Movements, 1970–84*
(1975 = 100)

Year	Colombian price index in Colombian pesos[a]	Official rate of exchange[b]	Colombian price index in U.S. dollars[c]	International price index[d]
1970	44.2	59.5	74.3	55.6
1971	47.8	64.4	74.2	58.5
1972	54.2	70.8	76.6	63.7
1973	65.4	76.4	85.6	73.9
1974	81.4	84.5	96.3	90.0
1975	100.0	100.0	100.0	100.0
1976	120.2	112.3	107.0	101.4
1977	160.0	119.1	134.3	111.4
1978	188.4	126.5	148.9	128.3
1979	235.0	137.9	170.4	145.3
1980	297.4	153.1	194.3	159.3
1981	379.1	176.4	214.9	160.2
1982	472.1	207.4	227.6	155.5
1983	565.6	255.3	221.5	153.6
1984[e]	656.7	326.2	201.3	150.8

a. Consumer price index, average for the period.
b. Peso price of a dollar, average for the period.
c. Column 1 divided by column 2.
d. Manufactured unit value index (MUV) estimate, July 1985.
e. Preliminary estimate.
Sources: IFS and World Bank data.

partners.[7] Two of the more traditional measures of the RER are also presented. Both measure the peso-dollar exchange rate, one using the U.S. inflation wholesale price index, the other using the U.S. consumer price index. The 1975–82 appreciation—that is, a decline in the RER—is less serious if it is based on the latter dollar-peso measure of RER, as shown in the third and fourth columns of table 2-3. The measure against the basket—the second column in table 2-3—however, shows a more serious level of appreciation, on account of the appreciation of the dollar against other major currencies.

Effect of Special Incentives

The provision of special incentives for exports—CAT and, more recently, Certificado de Reembolso Tributario (CERT, tax reimbursement certificate) and PROEXPO credit—was increased following 1975 in order to offset a part of the appreciation of the RER for exports. During 1975–81 the RER against the U.S. dollar—including

Table 2-3. *Indexes of the Real Exchange Rate of the Peso, 1970–84*
(1975 = 100)

| | | Against the U.S. dollar | |
| | | | |
Year	Against a basket[a]	Wholesale price indexes	Consumer price indexes
1970	81.1	108.3	98.2
1971	83.1	108.5	101.5
1972	86.4	105.1	101.4
1973	89.3	100.4	96.4
1974	94.7	96.7	94.9
1975	100.0	100.0	100.0
1976	97.3	95.5	98.7
1977	83.4	84.8	83.7
1978	83.5	82.6	81.3
1979	81.8	79.2	79.0
1980	82.0	80.8	78.7
1981	78.1	81.9	78.5
1982	73.4	78.2	78.7
1983	75.2	80.1	83.5
1984[b]	81.8	88.6	95.8

a. Estimated 1975–84 noncoffee trade weights for Colombia's fifteen most important trading partners were used. A foreign-country index of WPIS was used to reflect external inflation, and the Colombian CPI was used to reflect domestic inflation. For 1983 and 1984, estimated weighted averages of official and parallel exchange rates and inflation rates for Venezuela were used.

b. Preliminary estimate, based on incomplete data.

Source: Computed from IFS data.

changes in CAT—is estimated to have declined (depreciated) by 19.8 percent, while the RER (excluding CAT) against the U.S. dollar fell 22 percent. In 1983 and 1984 CAT rates and the new CERT rates were significantly increased, as shown in table 2-4. Details of the rates for 1978, 1981, and 1983 before the August increase are given in table SA-12; the August 1983 reform raised the CAT rate to 20 percent for 265 products, while in 1984 many of these rates were increased further through CERT. With the CAT increases applicable from 1978 to mid 1983 on average, about 7 percentage points of the appreciation may have been corrected from the point of view of the exporters.[8] Such calculations, however, do not account for changes in export incentives in other countries. Other limitations of considering additional special incentives will be noted below.

Exchange Rate Depreciation and Special Incentives

A policy of faster depreciation of the exchange rate differs from one of higher export subsidies in several respects. First, a nominal depreciation of the peso that succeeds in generating a real depreciation raises the prices of all tradables as a

Table 2-4. *Aggregate Weighted Average of Tax Reimbursement Certificate (CAT) and Tax Reimbursement Certificate (CERT) Rates, 1978, 1981, and 1983–84*
(percent)

Year	Weighted average rate	
	Total	Agriculture[a]
1978	3.7	n.a.
1981	3.5	n.a.
1983[b]	11.3	9.8
1984[c]	12.3[d]	10.6[d]
1984[e]	15.0[d]	n.a.

n.a. Not available.

a. Percentage of export value, excluding coffee.

b. Before the August 1983 increase.

c. After the August 1983 increase, effective in 1984; a rough estimate based on the projected total additional fiscal expenditure on CAT and the 1982 value of exports other than coffee.

d. Preliminary estimate.

e. An estimate of the average rate of CERT, which in 1984, by Ley 48, replaced CAT.

Source: Table SA-12.

group—exportables and importables—in relation to the prices of nontradables. An increase in the export incentives alone excludes the import-competing industries. To avoid the latter effect, import tariffs can be increased, but only at some welfare cost, as will be seen in chapter 3. Differential rates of export subsidies and import tariffs can produce substantial inefficiencies and welfare losses. Second, export incentives promote only trade in merchandise, while an increase in the real exchange rate affects invisibles as well. Third, commercial policies—export subsidies and import tariffs—do not directly affect the peso value of foreign assets, whereas a depreciation of the peso would increase it. Finally, an expected faster rate of the crawl, which is the government policy, will tend to raise the nominal interest rate.[9] Commercial policies do not produce such effects on the interest rate.

In practical terms, further increases in export subsidies may not be feasible in view of various trade agreements. These incentives also have significant negative consequences for public finance. Where the diagnosis points to an overvaluation of the exchange rate, the primary policy tool would need to be the exchange rate, and the aim of accompanying policies should be to offset potential side effects, such as those on external debt repayments and the interest rate. Once the real exchange rate has attained an equilibrium level, therefore, special incentives might gradually be replaced by a further depreciation of the peso.

Stimulating Noncoffee Exports

While noncoffee exports expanded 5 percent a year in constant pesos during 1970–75, they increased only 2 percent during 1975–82. In agriculture, the share of noncoffee exports gradually increased from 18 percent in 1970 to 24 percent in 1982. In dollar terms, the most important agricultural export items are bananas, flowers, cotton, sugar, and livestock products, which constitute about 25 percent, 21 percent, 17 percent, 14 percent, and 10 percent, respectively, of the value of noncoffee agricultural exports; less important exports are tobacco, rice, and fish. World Bank projections as of January 1985 indicate little improvement in coffee prices in constant dollar terms through the rest of the decade (see table 2-5). For the rest of the 1980s, banana prices are projected to show some decline. The prices of both sugar and cotton are projected to rise significantly from their depressed 1982 levels; substantial increases are expected in the price of sugar. The price of tobacco is projected to decline during the rest of the decade, while a substantial recovery is expected in the price of rice. Food prices are projected to remain well below the levels registered during the 1970s, particularly 1970–77.

These projections suggest modest increases during the 1980s in the prices of the agricultural products now exported by Colombia. The country can continue to expand banana exports rapidly and can capture additional shares of the cotton and sugar markets. Significant increases in cattle and beef are not unreasonable to expect, along with efforts to take advantage of the projected recovery in rice prices. The industry believes, with good reason, that a continued expansion in exports of flowers is possible despite the recent increase in U.S. import duties on this category. A tentative review of various agricultural commodities on a product-by-product basis suggests that while coffee exports in constant dollars may increase more than 1 percent a year during 1985–90, noncoffee agricultural exports could increase about

Table 2-5. *Price Projections for Important Agricultural Exports, 1976 and 1981–90*
(1983 constant dollars per metric ton, unless otherwise indicated)

Export commodity	Actual[a]				Projection		
	1976	1981	1982	1983	1984	1985	1990
Coffee[b]	477	271	305	290	324	311	291
Bananas[b]	390	385	370	429	377	420	295
Cotton	256	177	158	185	182	148	173
Sugar	386	359	178	187	117	74	315
Beef	240	237	236	244	231	225	246
Tobacco	2,138	2,253	2,381	2,245	2,035	2,303	2,182
Rice	386	463	289	277	257	230	339
Food[c]	110	89	70	74	75	64	82

a. These are not actual prices of Colombian exports but World Bank estimated average prices of these commodities; they could therefore differ from Colombian prices quoted elsewhere in this book—for coffee, for example.

b. Cents per kilogram.

c. A weighted index, with 1977–79 as base.

Source: World Bank estimates as of July 1985.

5 percent a year. These projections, however, do not account for a faster rate of crawl in the exchange rate than at present, or for the development of nontraditional exports with a favorable export climate in the country.[10] Fruits and vegetables could become significant exports in the future, with improved processing, packaging, and marketing and with the establishment of lasting export relations abroad. The excellent environmental conditions for growth in Colombia and its large reserves of tropical hardwood forests indicate that the country might have a comparative advantage in producing and exporting such tropical hardwood products as lumber and plywood. The low level of present exports in these categories and their decline during the past decade suggest that this possibility should be examined closely.

An effort has been made here to separate out empirically the effects of some primary variables, including the real exchange rate on noncoffee exports, using quarterly data for 1970–81 (see appendix B).[11] While world economic growth has a stronger long-term effect, the findings show that the effect of changes in the level of the real exchange rate on the volume of noncoffee exports is significant.[12] It is also noteworthy, however, that real changes in the exchange rate are needed, which means that in order for a nominal depreciation to be effective, it should not be accompanied by commensurate increases in the domestic price level. Colombia's exports depend strongly on the commercial policies of its trading partners. The protectionist behavior of some industrial countries and neighboring Latin American countries can critically affect the possibilities for expansion of noncoffee exports.

The results suggest that the long-term elasticity of the volume of noncoffee exports in Colombia with respect to the real exchange rate lies between 1.2 and 1.7, which narrows down earlier estimates. The various estimates suggest different behaviors of the lag structure of this elasticity. While some estimates indicate a higher short-run response, others suggest a more nearly even distribution of export response. To arrive at a more definite answer will require additional work.

The long-term elasticity of the volume of Colombian exports with respect to the world level of activity is typically large, ranging from 5 to 9. Even though this is a wide range, it does suggest that to a large extent the recovery of Colombia's external sector will depend on the world economic situation, provided that movements in the Colombian exchange rate match those of other countries that compete for the same markets. These findings indicate that both domestic exchange rate policy and world economic activity will be important to export performance. Finally, the long-term elasticity of exports with respect to the domestic level of activity, holding external activity constant, is, as expected, negative. In most cases its coefficients are not significant, suggesting that changes in Colombian real income do not significantly affect the performance of noncoffee exports.

Regression analysis indicates that a real depreciation of the peso of 10 percent against the U.S. dollar, holding constant the relation of the dollar to the basket, could be expected to increase noncoffee exports in real terms more than 10 percent above what they would otherwise be in the long term. A world economic recovery, without improvements in the Colombian exchange rate, on the other hand, may not ensure a revitalization of Colombian exports in the face of depreciation of the exchange rate by Brazil, Mexico, Chile, and other countries that produce similar exportables.

Addressing the Appreciation of the Peso

While some observers suggest that the appreciation should be corrected by accelerating the rate of depreciation of the crawling peg, others have recommended a once-and-for-all devaluation.[13] These alternative approaches can have quite different effects on factor prices, and they in turn can affect success in achieving a change in the real rate of exchange. In particular, the functions of real wages, expectations, intermediate goods, and the interest rate in determining the effect of changes in the NER on the RER need to be considered.

The Role of Wages

Even if all factor costs were held constant, a higher NER would increase the price of tradables in nominal domestic currency, and the cost of nontradables would be increased to the extent that they would contain tradable input components. The higher the share of these tradable components in nontradable production, the more domestic prices would rise and the less the effect of a higher NER would be in actually raising the RER. More realistically, if prices of factors and inputs were allowed to adjust at least partially, the change in RER would generally be smaller. The importance of wage adjustments would depend on the share of the wage bill in total production costs and in the type of wage negotiations already under way that affect the rate of wage increases in the face of a devaluation.

Interest Rate Effects

Underlying the analysis in appendix C is the recognition that Colombia's is a semiopen economy and that, consequently, both open economy models and closed economy models are inappropriate. Three alternative formulations for the determination of the interest rate in a semiopen economy were developed and tested, using quarterly data for the period 1968–82. The results obtained are remarkably good and indicate that discrepancies between the domestic (nominal) interest rate and the world interest rate plus expected devaluation will be eliminated through time; that in one quarter, between a third and half of a unitary discrepancy between the domestic rate and the world rate plus the expected rate of devaluation will be corrected; that in six quarters an acceleration of the rate of devaluation of the crawling peg will be almost completely translated into an equivalent increase in the domestic rate of interest; and that an excess supply of (real) money will exercise significant negative pressures on the nominal interest rate—that is, that there is a liquidity effect.

Appendix C suggests that an increase in the rate of depreciation of the crawling peg will be quickly translated into an equiproportionate increase in the domestic nominal rate of interest. If this faster rate of crawl, moreover, produces a desired higher real exchange rate, the domestic rate of inflation will increase by less than the acceleration of the peg and will produce an increase in the real interest rate. During the period of the expected acceleration of the crawl, the interest-rate effect can hurt, in particular, nontradable industries such as the construction sector, in addition to industries with high ratios of debt to equity. With respect to the tradable goods sectors, the higher rate of the crawl will produce effects that will then work in the opposite direction. To the extent that a higher crawl results in a higher real exchange rate, on the other hand, the level of activity in these tradable sectors would increase, possibly dominating any depressing effect from the higher interest rate.

The domestic nominal interest rate is observed to move broadly in line with the world interest rate plus the expected devaluation in Colombia (see appendix C). An increase in the rate of the crawl may therefore be expected to produce a higher nominal rate of interest, affecting the cost of capital—that is, the rental rate of capital—and exerting upward pressure on the prices of nontradable goods; to that extent, there will be a tendency for the acceleration of the crawling peg to be less effective. Some observers have taken the view that the rising interest rates will generate a higher rate of inflation through the cost-push mechanism: such an effect is possible in the face of the persistent stickiness of certain costs and prices. An empirical investigation of this issue as it pertains to Colombia needs to be made.

The main aspect of this interest rate problem is that a higher rate of the crawl can affect the expected rate of depreciation and produce higher interest rates during the period of acceleration of the peg. It is possible that a large one-step devaluation, if perceived by the public to be large enough, can remove expectations of higher rates of devaluation, leaving the domestic interest rate unaffected. If the public is not convinced by the magnitude of such a one-step devaluation, however—and it usually has not been in Latin American countries—there may be no such mitigating effect.

Effect of Monetary Disequilibrium

The analysis presented so far has been focused on cost aspects, ignoring demand considerations. The real effect of a nominal devaluation, however, will also depend on, among other things, the behavior of monetary policy. In particular it is expected that an excess supply of money will be translated into an excess demand for nontraded goods, which will then exert an upward pressure on their prices. In that sense the effect of a nominal devaluation on the RER could also be offset by an easy monetary policy that would produce an excess supply of money and an increase in the nominal price of nontradables. In order for a devaluation to affect the RER, special attention must be given to both wages and monetary behavior.

Export Promotion Efforts

Although coffee dominates exports, Colombia sells a wide range of commodities abroad. Manufactured products constitute about twice the value of agrobased commodities, excluding coffee, and the share of these two categories combined in total exports has gradually increased. Colombia exports to a large group of countries. The North American share of Colombian sales declined from about 37 percent in 1970 to 22 percent in 1982, while the European share declined marginally from 49 percent to 48 percent during the same period; these shares have been increasing since 1982, however. Developing countries have been buying ever larger amounts, and by 1982 Central America and the Caribbean claimed 6.5 percent and Asia, including Japan, 4.4 percent of Colombia's exports.

The Function of PROEXPO

PROEXPO, the Export Promotion Agency, following policy guidelines of the National Council of Economic and Social Policy (CONPES), is in charge of export promotion activities. An autonomous institution subsidiary to the Central Bank, PROEXPO is able to maintain independence from most other public institutions; its primary function is the implementation of export promotion policies, particularly those concerned with the provision of export credits. The central executing agency dealing with most trade-related policies, however, is the Foreign Trade Institute (INCOMEX), which directs the execution of government policies concerning imports and exports, through instruments such as the provision of licenses for importing and exporting.

Apart from reimbursements received from its past credits earned in the course of sixteen years of operation, the budget of PROEXPO benefits from a 5 percent import tariff. Its total annual budget is roughly $800 million. About 92 percent of its expenditures consist of the provision of credit for exporters and investments in a variety of activities. A number of services—identification of exporters, exportables, and export markets and the provision of technical assistance—are also offered.

In the administration of PROEXPO better definition of functions and areas of responsibility and improved internal coordination of activities are needed. The agency could make better use of the commercial attachés abroad and reduce its excessive dependence on the Central Bank. Statistical information needs strengthening as well. In general, promotional activities need greater attention; some efforts could be channeled away from pure financing of exports by the government and into export promotion activities. Support of exporters needs to be stepped up through more studies of export potential, a strengthening of relations with the export community, better coordination of Colombia's commercial offices, and a more active share in the development of new export lines by PROEXPO. On the policy side, a gradual elimination of import restrictions, which now constrain the supply of inputs needed for exports, and reduction of effective protection across the board will be needed to sustain rapid export growth. The increase in import restrictions is likely to hurt export activities to some extent despite the import duty drawback provided by Plan Vallejo. In 1983 about half of noncoffee exports did not or could not take advantage of this scheme. A reorientation of the free trade zones toward export promotion and the attraction of foreign investment in export industries would be helpful initiatives.

Foreign Investment

Historically, the development of natural resources has not had much to do with growth despite the country's rich agricultural and mineral base. This lagging development was caused in part by the lack of processing industries, in part by high transport costs, and in part by the authorities' unwillingness to support investment projects of either private or foreign participation in these areas fully. Traditionally, the country has had a lukewarm attitude toward foreign investment. In addition, Colombia was self-sufficient in petroleum until 1976, reducing the need to come to grips with foreign investment in this area. The oil crisis and the need to import petroleum during the second half of the 1970s changed that situation substantially, and Colombia is now seeking development of its hydrocarbon and petrochemical resources, as well as of coal and nonfuel minerals, with significant foreign participation. Recent government policy actions, moreover, particularly those that would allow greater profit remittances across the board and gradually dismantle regulation of private sector borrowing from abroad, signal a policy shift toward allowance of greater foreign participation in the private sector.

Policy Conclusions

Colombia's crawling peg has by and large been successful in the long term, although the real exchange rate remained significantly appreciated during 1983–84. Using 1975 as the base period, the RER index measured against a trade-weighted currency basket stood at 75 in 1983. During 1983–84, the government pursued a policy of accelerated crawl of the exchange rate against the U.S. dollar. Given the appreciation of the U.S. dollar against other major currencies, however, a part of this potential gain has been offset. Nevertheless, a significant real depreciation was achieved in 1984, and this has accelerated in 1985.

The government's policy is now to eliminate the overvaluation of the peso by means of an accelerated crawl. Although the foregoing calculation implies a significant lag to be adjusted for, the real gain in 1984 was nevertheless estimated to be the largest in a single year since 1967, when the crawling peg was established. While the nominal rate of the crawl could be increased even further, its effect on the real rate would depend on the way domestic inflation would be affected and on the behavior of external inflation: the NER is a policy variable, but the RER is only partially so. It is expected that in 1985 more depreciation of the RER than that achieved in 1984 will occur.

In the future, while a depreciation of the U.S. dollar against the major currencies of the world would assist in improving the RER rapidly with respect to the basket, it might nevertheless be important to pay special attention to the real rate of exchange between the peso and the dollar as well: a good part of the exports are denominated in U.S. dollars and the U.S. market may be crucial for the future growth of agricultural and industrial exports from Colombia. In determining future adjustments of the peso, it may be advisable to account also for a gradual phasing out of special export incentives. A direct comparison with exchange rate movements of Colombia's export competitors may also be necessary.

In principle, a nominal depreciation will raise the RER only if there is a price variable such as nominal wage that is not tied to the nominal exchange rate, if the nominal money supply is not fully adjusted to accommodate higher prices, or if there are accompanying reductions in some component of aggregate demand such as government expenditures. Nominal wages are neither rigid nor completely flexible in Colombia. This means that real wages can be flexible, and a nominal depreciation of the peso can, in principle, produce a real depreciation. Negotiations in 1983 brought about an increase of 22 percent in the urban areas and 28 percent by mid 1984 in the rural areas in the nominal minimum wage for 1984, significantly higher than the 1983 rate of inflation and the average for 1984 and ahead of the improvement in productivity, at least as far as the rural wage is concerned. Wages will need to be set with greater cognizance of a possible inflationary effect, unless they are closely tied to increases in productivity. Additionally, since the prices of nontradables are moderately flexible, a reduction in the fiscal deficit would be essential. Such fine tuning to affect the nominal prices of nontradables, while by no means easy, appears to be feasible in Colombia, as shown to some extent by the 1984–85 experience.

With the domestic nominal interest rate estimated to move broadly in line with the world interest rate plus the expected depreciation of the peso, an increase in the rate of the crawl might tend to produce a higher nominal rate of interest domestically. This interest rate complication is a factor that has supported proposals for a one-step devaluation, which, if perceived by the public to be large enough, can remove expectations of higher rates of devaluation, leaving the domestic interest rate unaffected. The government's present preference is for an acceleration of the crawl based in part on its good track record in Colombia and the recent success in depreciating the peso in real terms with this method.

World economic conditions and the RER have significant statistical effects on non-coffee exports. Exports from agriculture have been hit in recent years by low international prices and surplus stocks. Furthermore, penetrating into agricultural markets and crossing trade barriers with a number of important commodities is problematic. At the same time, the country needs to return to more aggressive export promotion efforts. Additional sector work is proposed to examine constraints to domestic policy, institutional and legal frameworks for the rapid increase of exports, and market conditions and impediments to entering new areas on a product-by-product and country-by-country basis. Also needed are a gradual elimination of import restrictions, a reduction of effective protection across sectors, and, as the government has initiated, improvements in the actual functioning and efficiency of Plan Vallejo.

Notes

1. On trade policy and performance, see David Morawetz, *Why the Emperor's New Clothes Are Not Made in Colombia* (New York: Oxford University Press, 1981).

2. Examining normal years means excluding years in which there were unusual commodity prices, oil stocks, or other such special circumstances. Clearly basic changes in the domestic or world economy—such as significant variations in domestic productivity, the availability of a new resource at home, or permanent changes in the terms of trade of a country—can change the equilibrium level. See, for example, John Williamson, *The Exchange Rate System* (Washington, D.C.: Institute for International Economics, September 1983).

3. C. F. Díaz-Alejandro, *Foreign Trade Regimes and Economic Development: Colombia* (New York: Columbia University Press for the National Bureau of Economic Research, 1976).

4. A detailed discussion of the exchange rate and other trade reforms is provided in Jan Peter Wogart and others, "Colombia: Manufacturing Sector Development and Changes in Foreign Trade and Financial Policies," Report no. 4093-CO (Washington, D.C.: World Bank, Latin America and the Caribbean Projects Department, Industrial Development and Finance 2, 1983); and Eduardo Wiesner, "Devaluación y mecanismo de ajuste en Colombia," in *Política economía externa Colombia* (Bogotá, 1978, processed).

5. See Wogart and others, "Colombia: Manufacturing Sector Development."

6. The spectacular performance of some of the East Asian economies in the 1980s is worth mentioning. Growth of GDP in Korea and Singapore ranged from 6 to 10 percent a year during the 1980s, and similar results were obtained in Malaysia and Thailand. Exports from Korea, Thailand, and Singapore have been increasing substantially in real terms during the 1980s.

7. For an earlier study of the subject, see Fernando Montes, "Principales determinantes de comportamiento de las cuenta corriente durante la decada," in *Ensayos sobre política económica*, no. 2 (September 1982).

8. That is, $(1.113 - 1.037)/1.037 = 0.073$. For other studies see Jorge Ospina Sardi and Mauricio Carrizosa Serrana, "Evolución y perspectiva del certificado de abono tributario (CAT)," in *Revista nacional de agricultura*, no. 856 (November 1981); and FEDESARROLLO, *Coyuntura económica*, December 1983.

9. Given the option of investing externally, a broad equivalence has been observed between the Colombian interest rate, adjusted for the expected rate of depreciation of the peso, and U.S. rates.

10. Korea has shown great flexibility in increasing its exports and capturing additional exports markets, even when external conditions have been unfavorable. Between 1979 and 1983, Korean exports are estimated to have increased some 50 percent in constant dollars.

11. On the relation between exports and the exchange rate, see, for example, José Antonio Ocampo, "Política económica bajo condiciones cambiantes del sector external," in *Ensayos sobre política económica*, no. 2 (September 1982), pp. 7–65; Mauricio Carrizosa, "El futuro de la balanza comercial," in *La economíca colombiana en la decada de las ochenta* (Bogotá: FEDESARROLLO, 1979); and Juan José Echavarria, "La evolución de las exportaciones colombianas y sus determinantes," *Revista del Banco de la Republica* (Bogotá, 1980).

12. For the statistical analysis a real exchange rate between the dollar and the peso was used as the relevant explanatory variable, so that the result could be compared with results obtained in earlier studies. If an exchange rate defined in relation to a basket of currencies is used, however, the results are similar.

13. For the former suggestion, see José Antonio Ocampo, "En defensa de la continuidad del régimen cambiario," *Coyuntura económica*, vol.13, no. 1 (March 1983); for the latter, see Armando Montenegro, "La sobrevaluación del peso" (Bogotá: CEDE, University of Los Andes, April 1983, processed).

3

Import Policy for Growth and Stability

THIS CHAPTER concerns changes in Colombian import regimes, focusing on the recent increases in import restrictions and associated economic problems. Import restrictions—consisting mainly of import licensing and tariffs—have periodically been increased in order to protect domestic producers in agriculture and other sectors, to prevent a deterioration of the balance of payments, or for both these purposes. The use of tariff increases as a tool for financing public sector deficits has also influenced import policy: tariffs have been increased to finance the deficits of public sector agencies. On the other hand, additional import restrictions have raised the level of domestic prices, have caused inefficiencies in allocation of resources, and have caused consumers to suffer losses in welfare. In recognition of these problems, a policy of opening up imports has been periodically followed, particularly during periods of high growth.

Following a period of moderate liberalization after 1967, however, there was a drastic increase in restrictions after the third quarter of 1982, raising the level of import controls beyond that which existed before the opening up of 1979. Beginning in early 1983 import licensing and exchange controls were significantly increased, primarily to reduce the loss of international reserves. Even before the 1982–84 measures, roughly a third of imports were subject to prior license, and World Bank estimates of tariff rates showed average levels on items, excluding exemptions, of about 26 percent. A significant decline in imports in 1983–84 hurt production and exports in agriculture and in nonagricultural sectors.[1] On the other hand, these measures partly offset the disadvantages to import-competing sectors from appreciation of the peso.

At this writing import policy has been undergoing further changes. The government is in the process of adopting a more outward-looking strategy than that represented by the changes made in 1982–84. Selective opening up of imports has been initiated, with emphasis first on making available greater quantities of imported inputs for export production. The full effects of such a shift in policy are yet to be assessed.

Long-Term Policy Directions

Major policy tools have been quantitative restrictions consisting of licensing, prior deposit requirements, and import tariffs.[2] The rate of effective protection has been determined not only by the level and coverage of nominal tariffs and other import taxes and the extent and structure of quantitative restrictions within the import license regime, but also by the controls under which foreign exchange is allocated to authorized imports and by the real exchange rate of the peso, which has varied substantially.

Severe import controls used in the 1950s and throughout much of the 1960s were attempts to foster industrialization by giving strong protection to the domestic production of manufactured goods. In 1966 many of the tariff barriers and quantitative controls on imported inputs and investment goods required to produce export goods were reduced or removed. Unfortunately, these measures were not accompanied by improvements in the real exchange rate or the real interest rate, and as a result the balance of payments was hurt and controls were eventually reimposed. Under the two development plans of 1966–70 and 1970–74, a vigorous policy of export promotion, which eventually permitted a reduction in import controls through most of the 1970s, was pursued. The gradual move toward opening the economy favored employment by encouraging labor-intensive exports.[3]

Opening Up of Imports in the 1970s

By the mid 1970s a process of liberalizing and simplifying the import regime had been initiated. Since then, its implementation and effects have varied widely in response to changing economic conditions and constraints imposed by arrangements under the Andean Pact. During 1967–82 as a whole, tariffs were gradually reduced, and a large number of items were moved from the prohibited and prior-license lists to the free imports list. Furthermore, between 1967 and 1982 varying importance was attached to the deposit required prior to receipt of the import permit: the requirement was eliminated in early 1976, reimposed in mid 1976, increased in 1977 and 1979, and reduced in early 1982.[4]

The participation by Colombia in the Andean Pact may have limited its ability to attract foreign investment and, to a lesser extent, to reduce protection. The Andean Pact involves some limits on foreign investment except in major energy and mining projects. There has been foreign investment in the petroleum sector and a few scientific mining projects. On the side of trade restrictions, Colombia's tariffs in many goods had fallen to roughly the average of the Andean Pact's common minimum tariff by 1979. Further reductions in protection were inhibited somewhat by the pact. On the other hand, Colombia did benefit from a rapid expansion of manufactured exports to Venezuela and Ecuador following initiation of the pact, although much of this growth can be attributed to the petroleum boom in the other two countries.

Effect of Import Substitution

In general, import substitution has stimulated the economy when output was depressed below normal levels. Import substitution came into conflict with export promotion, however, particularly as production capacity became more fully used and both sectors began to compete for the same scarce resources and bid up costs and prices. In sum, a general policy for import substitution is responsible for a variety of costs. A reduction in imports, while benefiting a specific import-competing industry, increased costs and prices in other industries that use the import as an input.[5] On balance, import substitution tended to increase prices in the aggregate and to slow the growth of output in the long run. Nontraditional, non-resource-based exports, moreover, have been more labor-intensive in Colombia than import-competing industries. Thus, with growth returning to a normal level along a long-term trend, continued dependence on an import-substitution strategy reduced both the long-run demand for labor and the growth rate more than would a development strategy of concentrating new investment and resources in those industries in which the country has a comparative advantage in exporting or import substitution, as was done in the period 1967–74.

Long-Term Development of Imports

Between 1970 and 1982, Colombian imports of merchandise increased more than sixfold, from $800 million to $5.4 billion. The acceleration was especially pronounced after the mid 1970s (see table SA-9). The growth in imports during the 1970s was significantly greater than that registered during the 1960s; imports expanded 5.7 percent a year during 1970–80, but only 2.7 percent during 1960–70. As a proportion of GDP, legal imports of goods and n.f.s. grew during 1970–82 (see table SA-1). Not included in these official statistics, however, is a substantial amount of contraband. Smuggled imports of textiles in some recent years are estimated to have been as much as 20–25 percent of the value of local production; import smuggling has been estimated to be equal to 10 percent of official imports.[6]

The shares of the broad categories—consumer, intermediate, and capital goods—have not undergone any significant change since 1975. During the period 1980–83 the category of raw materials and intermediate goods constituted about 52 percent of total imports, followed by capital goods (36 percent) and consumer goods (12 percent), which are not significantly at variance with the proportions recorded in 1970 (see table 3-1). It is also estimated that industrial inputs represented some 35 percent and industrial equipment 21 percent of total imports in 1982, while nondu-

Table 3-1. *Imports, by Economic Category, 1970, 1975, and 1980–83*
(percent)

Category	1970	1975	1980	1981	1982	1983
Consumer goods	10.3	11.3	13.3	12.8	12.6	10.8
Raw materials and intermediate goods	43.7	52.2	52.7	52.0	50.6	51.2
Capital goods	44.0	36.1	34.0	35.2	36.8	38.0
Unclassified	2.0	0.4	...	...	...	...
Total[a]	100.0	100.0	100.0	100.0	100.0	100.0

... Zero or negligible.
a. Before balance of payments adjustment.
Source: Table SA-10.

rable consumer goods represented only 6 percent. As will be seen, food and agricultural outputs and inputs have constituted relatively small proportions.

Imports of agricultural commodities as a proportion of agricultural value added are rather small, although they rose from about 2.2 percent in 1970 to about 3.5 percent in 1983. As a proportion of total imports, the share of agricultural imports was more than 5 percent in 1982–83. Imports of certain categories, however, are more important than these aggregate measures suggest: in 1981, roughly 15 percent of the gross value of domestic output of cereals and nearly 10 percent of that of vegetables were imported. Imports of wheat, corn, sorghum, and barley are estimated to have amounted to 467, 120, 82, and 50 thousand tons of imports in 1982. Roughly 90 percent of domestic consumption of wheat is met by imports. Aggregate estimates of agricultural imports, nevertheless, contradict widely held beliefs concerning their relative importance and their effect on the domestic economy.

Nominal tariffs on foods, beverages, vegetables, oil, and livestock products have ranged from 18 percent to 38 percent, which on the average are lower than the rates on nonagricultural commodities. More important, several potential and actual imports are controlled by the Instituto de Mercadeo Agropecuario (IDEMA, the Agricultural Marketing Institute), which has a monopoly on certain agricultural imports, and as a result these products receive higher nominal rates of protection than the tariff rates would imply. As will be elaborated in chapter 4, a combination of import controls and price supports by IDEMA has helped to maintain the domestic prices of several agricultural commodities at levels significantly higher than international levels. IDEMA has been exempt from import tariffs, and it has enjoyed a monopoly on licenses to import certain commodities. It is noteworthy that domestic support prices have been significantly higher than international prices of corn, wheat, and sorghum, in which the country does not seem to have a comparative advantage, while the opposite has been true of rice and barley, which could compete in international markets. Domestic producer prices have been broadly in line with the support prices for these crops, notwithstanding year-to-year variations.

High and rising agricultural production costs have been related to rural real wages and to the cost of agricultural inputs that incur high port-handling and domestic transport costs, in addition to the import tariffs and restrictions on certain inputs. While import tariffs on fertilizer and some other inputs have been low (3–7 percent), other port and transport costs raise domestic prices well above border prices (see chapter 8). Tariffs on transport vehicles have been high, while the incidence of tariffs on agricultural equipment has varied, depending on whether the same products are produced domestically. In evaluating protection for importables, therefore, the effect of increased input costs must be accounted for (see chapter 4).

In the aggregate, a drive to protect agriculture from imports is unlikely to have any significant quantitative effect on the balance of payments or on domestic production, and such an effort will become unnecessary as the real exchange rate is improved. Throughout the long term, the foreign exchange savings from any major import-substitution effort in behalf of principal agricultural imports is likely to be modest. Wheat, corn, sorghum, and soybeans are now imported in significant quantities, but, as shown in table 3-2, while world prices of these commodities are expected to increase from their depressed 1982 levels, they are not expected to exceed 1976 levels in real terms. Continued imports of these commodities at existing levels ought therefore not to be viewed with alarm. One area for import substitution, however, might be forestry products. The trade deficit in all forestry products in 1980 was estimated to be more than $108 million. Most of the deficit was accounted for by pulp and paper imports, which grew to $113 million in 1980 and $157 million in 1981. The possibility of increasing pulp and paper production might be explored under the proposed National Forestry Research Plan (see chapter 8) and the reforestation plan of the Federación Nacional de Cafeteros de Colombia (FEDERACAFE, the Coffee Federation), under its diversification program (see chapter 6).

Table 3-2. *Actual and Projected Prices of Agricultural Imports, 1976 and 1981–90*
(1983 constant dollars per metric ton)

Commodity	Actual[a]				Projected		
	1976	*1981*	*1982*	*1983*	*1984*	*1985*	*1990*
Wheat	226	188	165	170	168	168	153
Corn	170	125	108	136	138	120	113
Grain sorghum	159	121	107	129	121	117	109
Soybean oil	664	486	442	527	737	645	563

a. See table 2-5 for an explanation.
Source: World Bank data as of July 1985.

Recent Developments

The tendency to liberalize imports, observed since 1967, was reversed during 1982–83. In 1982, Resolution 39/82, dated September 7, moved a number of luxury items from the free-imports list to the prior-license list. Decree 3080/82, dated October 28, on the other hand, raised the level of import tariffs on most import items by about 20 percent. The reason for these measures was to protect the domestic industry, both by barring luxury imports and by granting a higher level of protection to domestically produced goods. These measures—together with the increase in export incentives—were intended to compensate in part for the appreciation of the real exchange rate.

On April 19, 1983, by Resolution 015/83, it was decided to move 684 additional items from the free-imports list to the prior-license list. The main difference between this measure and earlier measures—Decree 3080/82 and Resolution 39/82—was that now items were moved from one list to the other not to protect the domestic industry but to reduce the level of total imports. In fact, the items with higher import value were generally the ones moved from the free-imports list to the prior-license list. (There were some exceptions—fertilizer, for example.) The government hoped that these measures would arrest the depletion of international reserves. On May 16, 1983, Resolution 030/83 moved an additional hundred products that were considered luxury items into prior licensing. By this time roughly 56 percent of the positions in the import list, excluding prohibitions, were under prior licensing. In October 1983, another 103 items—most of them intermediate goods in production, such as chemicals—were added to the list. By 1984, more than 90 percent of the items were on prior licensing. In mid 1983, a further tariff increase took place, raising the rates by about 10 percent over the existing levels, followed by a 2 percent increase, a subsequent 25 percent increase in 1984, and an 8 percent surcharge on most imports. The recent changes do not violate agreements under the General Agreement on Tariffs and Trade (GATT) or the Andean Pact.

Import Tariffs

Table 3-3 sets out the weighted average nominal tariffs for twenty-one sections during 1979–83 on the basis of the stated tariff levels applicable to ninety-nine chapters. These levels would, of course, be vastly lower if they were calculated on the basis of the implicit rates applicable to all importers, including all exemptions. In particular, the present calculations exclude certain other duties for PROEXPO and general purposes and do not take into account various exemptions relevant to government imports, to imports from the Andean Group (about 6 percent of imports), to imports from the Asociación Latino Americana de Desarrollo y Integración

Table 3-3. *Weighted Average Nominal Tariff, 1979, 1981, and 1983*
(percent)

Section	Product	Chapters	1979	1981	1983
1.	Live animals and related products	1–5	25.25	22.75	27.25
2.	Vegetables and related goods	6–14	15.93	14.09	16.75
3.	Greases, oils, vegetable oils	15	20.32	18.17	21.03
4.	Foods, beverages, alcoholic beverages, tobacco	16–24	35.77	32.31	38.45
5.	Mineral products	25–27	12.29	11.21	13.28
6.	Chemical products	28–38	17.91	16.41	19.62
7.	Plastics, cellulose, rubber products	39–40	35.78	27.41	32.26
8.	Leathers, furs, luggage	41–43	21.75	22.63	25.49
9.	Timber, cork, vegetable coal	44–46	38.95	35.41	42.89
10.	Paper and related products	47–49	30.55	25.37	28.38
11.	Textiles	50–63	51.55	52.24	63.31
12.	Shoes, hats, artificial flowers	64–67	53.09	53.15	63.78
13.	Stoves, cement, pottery, glass	68–70	38.53	29.69	35.16
14.	Pearls, precious stones, coins	71–72	33.71	34.71	41.66
15.	Common metals	73–83	28.49	25.24	30.05
16.	Machinery and electrical materials	84–85	26.51	22.83	26.80
17.	Transport materials	86–89	45.96	38.50	45.99
18.	Optimal materials, medical materials, music, and television	90–92	22.69	21.98	23.60
19.	Weapons	93	49.13	49.80	59.70
20.	Other products	94–98	44.92	38.73	45.72
21.	Art objects and antiques	99	0.00	0.00	0.00

Sources: Constructed from data obtained from Gonzalo Giraldo Echeverri, "Estructura de la protección arancelaria y para-arancelaria en Colombia despues de las reformas de 1979," *Revista de planeación y desarrollo*, vol. 11 (May–August 1979), pp. 7–47; the DNP; *Arancel de aduanas legis*; and DANE, *Anuario de comercio exterior*, various issues.

(ALADI, the Latin American Association for Development and Integration), and to imports from other groups.

A further weighting of the rates for the economy, excluding all exceptions, indicates that the average nominal tariff in the first quarter of 1979 was 27.62.[7] This rate declined to 26.11 in the second quarter of 1981 before increasing to 29.02 in the first quarter of 1983 and an estimated 32.00 in the third quarter of 1983. This increase in the weighted average tariffs between 1981 and 1983 represented an increase of 4.6 percent in the effect of the tariff, defined as one plus the tariff rate, which—barring changes in quantitative restrictions and transport costs—determines the internal price of importable goods, together with changes in the exchange rate.[8] It was preliminarily estimated that the basic rate increased to about 42.50 in 1984, implying a further increase in the effect of the tariff from 1981 by about 13 percent. An estimate of the average nominal tariff rate at the beginning of 1985 was roughly 50 percent, although the effective rate might have been only about a third of that.

The last generalized tariff reduction was in mid 1979.[9] In 1983 the average tariffs were higher than in 1981 for ninety-six of the ninety-nine chapters of the tariff schedule. Also, for seventy-one of the ninety-nine chapters, nominal tariffs were higher in 1983 than in the first quarter of 1979, when the last major step toward liberalizing the import sector was taken. At this level of aggregation in table 3-3, tariffs increased in twenty of the twenty-one sections between 1981 and 1982; tariffs were higher in fourteen of the twenty-one sections, however, than they were in 1979. These tables show that even though the recent increase in the level of tariffs has been fairly general, affecting most sectors, the magnitude of the tariff increases were modest, although the 1984 changes were significant. Furthermore, the increase in protection is based fundamentally on the increase in the coverage of import licenses, rather than on tariff increases.

EFFECTIVE PROTECTION. A number of studies have been concerned with the degree of protection granted to value added, or effective rates of protection (ERPs). The ERP can be thought of as the subsidy to value added, and takes into account distortions in the output price and in the prices of traded inputs. Even though there is information on the level and structure of effective protection for 1979 through 1981, there is little information readily available for the more recent period. Since data on the historical behavior of ERPs (up to 1981) in Colombia are available in a number of publications and reports, table 3-4 contains only the overall averages, standard deviations, and maximum and minimum rates of ERPs for 1979, 1980, and 1981.[10] The average rate of effective protection declined steadily until 1981 as a result of successive liberalization measures. In 1981, however, its dispersion, measured by the standard deviation, was higher than in 1979 and 1980.

PUBLIC SECTOR IMPORTS. Import tariffs have not applied to most public sector imports—roughly a quarter of all imports including petroleum—in Colombia; there is thus an element of discrimination between the treatment of the public and private

Table 3-4. *Rates of Effective Protection, 1979–81*
(percent)

Statistic	1979	1980	1981
Average	47.55	43.79	38.66
Standard deviation	43.42	40.31	55.26
Maximum rate	397.90	399.51	606.26
Minimum rate	−48.65	−45.78	−60.84

Sources: Giraldo, "Estructura de la protección"; and the DNP.

sectors. This policy has also encouraged the public sector to use a mix of inputs that is heavily based on imports. In practice, however, public sector agencies must apply to the Industrial Division of the DNP for exemption from import duty, and about 30 percent of such applications are rejected, causing some conflicts within the public sector. In principle, according to the policymakers, it would be preferable to eliminate the provision that exempts the public sector from the payment of import tariffs. This step would also help to achieve uniformity in the protective structure.

Import Licenses

Import licenses have traditionally been an important tool for controlling the volume and composition of imports. Between 1974 and mid 1982, as a result of the liberalization process, the number of items subject to prior import licenses declined steadily. In late 1982 and early 1983, however, this tendency was reversed, as many items were moved from the free-imports list into the prior-license list.

The fact that a particular good is in the prior-license list means that any person or agency that wants to import a certain amount of that good has to apply to the Instituto de Comercio Exterior (INCOMEX, the Foreign Trade Institute) for a license. Because INCOMEX does not have recent experience in processing numerous applications, it has taken considerable time for a decision to be reached regarding any given application. The criteria for deciding when to grant a license, to whom, and for what amount have not yet been determined, although some guidelines exist. Given the tight foreign exchange situation, the government has revived the practice of allocating a monthly quota of foreign exchange to INCOMEX, which then decides how to allocate it among various applicants.

Table 3-5 presents information on the proportion of goods within each section of the tariff schedule that was subject to prior licenses in 1979, 1980, and the first quarter of 1983. The principal change in the second quarter of 1983, not shown in the table, is that most of the products in sections 1 through 4 have been moved into prior licensing. In addition, the October change has increased the prior-license coverage, particularly in chapters 29, 39, and 41. These figures have been constructed as weighted averages, the importance of each chapter having been weighted by relative imports to construct the averages. In the agricultural goods sections—section 1, live animals and related products; and section 2, vegetables and related goods—the number of items subject to prior licenses has increased significantly from the number in both 1980 and 1979. This is especially true of section 1, in which 92 percent of imports have been subject to prior licenses since April 1983. The coverage has also increased for processed foods, sections 3 and 4. The change is especially dramatic when the coverage of prior licenses for section 4—food, beverages, alcoholic beverages, and tobacco—in 1980 is compared with 1983.

For the rest of the sections—that is, those that do not include agricultural products or food—the change in the coverage of the prior license system since 1979 is less drastic. It is clear, however, that at present the volume of goods, weighted by

Table 3-5. *Imports, by Regime, 1979–83*[a]

(percentage under licensing, weighted average)

Section	Chapter	1979	1980	April 1983[b]
1	1–5	78	54	92
2	6–14	82	79	90
3	15	71	65	89
4	16–24	51	20	90
5	25–27	72	53	51
6	28–38	74	22	20
7	39–40	45	30	48
8	41–43	68	19	38
9	44–46	99	74	60
10	47–49	53	38	59
11	50–63	45	45	81
12	64–67	68	18	69
13	68–70	28	15	54
14	71–72	74	0	24
15	73–83	51	46	63
16	84–85	50	48	45
17	86–89	80	76	84
18	90–92	22	18	31
19	93	100	100	100
20	94–98	90	62	96
21	99	100	100	100

a. For a description of goods included in each section, see INCOMEX, *Arancel de aduanas legis*.
b. Subsequent changes in May and October 1983 raised the percentage for chapters 1–24 to 100.
Sources: Giraldo, "Estructura de la protección"; Resolution 015/83; and INCOMEX data.

their relative importance, that are subject to prior licenses has increased significantly since 1980. Additional information regarding the distribution of imports by regime is given in table SA-15, which presents disaggregated data at the chapter level for 1979, 1980, and 1983.

Other Restrictions on Trade

In addition to tariffs and licenses, there are a number of taxes on imports that also have the effect of restricting trade. The following are the most important ones.

According to Resolution 2/82 of the Monetary Board, the importation of a number of goods was subject to a prior deposit of 10 percent, payable before the nationalization of a commodity. This deposit did not yield any interest, was not negotiable, and could be used to pay for a portion of the import of that particular good. In some exceptional instances these deposits could be used to pay for imports of other goods (see Resolution 16/82 of the Monetary Board). These restrictions, however, were eliminated in 1983 by Resolution 99, which also eliminated the maximum payment period for imports and prior deposit for transport cost. Subsequently a minimum payment period for some imports has been introduced.

According to article 229 of Decree 444 of 1967 all imports into Colombia are subject to a 5 percent tax over their c.i.f. value. The proceeds of this tax are used to finance PROEXPO. According to article 20 of Decree 688, 1967, all imports into Colombia are subject to an additional tax (currently 2 percent over the c.i.f. value). The proceeds of this tax are used to finance general purposes in the government budget. There is also a stamp tax (3.15 percent) on the f.o.b. value.

Policy Implications of Recent Developments

Toward the end of 1982 there was a clear movement away from the tendencies to open up the economy that had been observed since 1967. Even though until 1983 the increase in the level of nominal tariffs was relatively modest, the coverage of the system of import licenses increased dramatically. Recent plans are to reverse this trend gradually in order to introduce greater efficiency into the structure of production.

Increasing Trade Restrictions

The increases in the level of protection during 1982–84—that is, higher tariffs, more restrictive licenses, or both—have compensated in part for the present overvaluation of the peso and have brought about a higher real effective exchange rate for import-competing goods than otherwise (see chapter 1); to that extent, the degree of competitiveness of this group of goods has increased. When tariffs and licenses are used, however, as in this instance, there is a serious problem in that the recovery of the importable sector takes place partly at the expense of the exportable sector. The higher real effective exchange rate for importables means a lower real effective exchange rate for exporters. This policy of using commercial policy to promote importables is equivalent to imposition of a tax on exportables.[11] Consequently, while tariffs tend to generate an increase in the level of activity of importables, they also tend to produce a decline in the level of activity of noncoffee exportables, especially nontraditional exports.

Furthermore, the increase in protection tends to affect the overall level of activity of the economy. It has been documented that export-promotion economies tend to outperform import-substitution economies in growth, income distribution, and employment.[12] To the extent that the result of the new commercial policies is an implicit tax on exports, a slowdown in overall growth could be expected. The authorities also increased export subsidies during 1982–84. If the increases in tariffs and export subsidies are sufficiently large, this combined policy could generate an effect on relative prices similar to that of a devaluation. This does not seem to have happened during 1982–84, however, because the increased import restrictions have dominated the additional export incentives. This means that the export-tax effect discussed earlier was the likely result of the 1982–84 policies.

Use of Import Licenses

From an economic point of view, the Colombian system of import licenses is similar to a quota, or quantitative restriction, system. The main difference, however, is that in the case of licenses the quantity of any particular good that can be imported in any period of time is not known a priori by the public. Also, this quantity can easily be altered by the authorities, in response to varying circumstances. In a sense then, it may be said that the Colombian system of licenses is equivalent to a flexible quota system. This import-licensing system has two basic economic effects: it restricts the volume of a good that can be imported, and it produces an increase in the domestic peso price of licensed goods above what it would be in the absence of the license. This means that the domestic price of the imported good will exceed the foreign price plus the tariff, transport costs, and other normal adjustments. From the point of view of efficiency, and to the extent that the allocation of licenses is administratively decided by the authorities without the possibility of resale of licenses, this system can lead to corruption and welfare costs exceeding those of an equivalent import tariff. To the extent that the allocation of licenses is arbitrary, moreover, there will be income distribution effects associated with the scheme, because those parties that obtained the quotas would receive related rents, while consumers would incur losses associated with the higher prices they would have to pay.

EFFECT ON IMPORTS. The effects of the 1982–84 increases in the prior-licenses coverage have been to reduce the volume of importable goods available and raise domestic prices. The full medium-term effect of this policy on domestic prices, however, depends on the actual restrictiveness of the licenses, the elasticity of demand for imports of those goods, and the process by which the licenses are allocated.

With respect to the restrictiveness of licenses, the available historical evidence indicates that at least for agricultural goods, licenses have been fairly restrictive and have had a fairly considerable effect on prices. Domestic prices of some agricultural goods have significantly exceeded world prices (corrected for tariffs, taxes, and estimated transport costs). In the absence of import licenses, it is probable that the domestic price of an imported good (P_d) will be equal to the international price adjusted for the tariff and other taxes and domestic transport costs.[13] The difference between the prices observed when import licenses are in effect and P_d can then be attributed to the effect of the import licenses. The available information on the price elasticity of the demand for imports refers to fairly comprehensive categories of goods. Empirical analyses of the subject have found price elasticities of demand for imports that range from -0.17 for capital goods to -1.52 for consumer goods, which would imply that a significant price increase can be caused by additional import restrictions.[14]

TARIFFS VERSUS LICENSES. If it is intended that increased protection should be temporary, it would be desirable to compare the merits of tariffs or licenses as alternative means of achieving it. The disadvantages of licenses—from the point of view of both welfare and administration—are well known. On the basis of pure efficiency, tariffs would be preferred over licenses.[15] In the present situation of Colombia, however, there is an additional consideration: which of the two systems— tariffs or licenses—is more likely to be temporary, or which of these two measures will be easier to reverse once the exchange rate problem has been solved. Licenses are determined by a high-level ministerial advisory committee for the external sector, and a resolution is signed by the minister of economic development. The recommendation for a tariff change is made by a national council on tariff policy to the president and the minister of finance, and a decree is signed by the president. It is not clear which of the two—tariffs or license—is likely to be less permanent on institutional grounds. A point that favors licenses as a temporary protective measure is that by their own nature they would easily become nonbinding if everyone who applied for a license immediately received one.

If licenses were to be applied as a temporary measure, two ways of improving their efficiency could be considered: licenses could be allocated in a way that would reflect the willingness of economic agents to pay for them, possibly by auctioning them, and the resale of licenses in the free market might be allowed. In principle, auctioning could be developed on the basis of bids submitted by interested parties, who would specify the unit price to be offered for different numbers of licenses. The numbers corresponding to each unit price would then be added together to obtain the total demand at each clearing unit price. By equating the aggregate demand with the number of licenses the government wished to supply, a market-clearing unit price could be established.[16]

Policy Conclusions

The primary objective of the 1982–84 changes was to arrest the decline in international reserves, rather than to provide additional protection to the domestic industry. A gradual reversal of the recent restrictive measures would be desirable—as recognized by the government in its most recent actions—from the point of view of the production sectors as export policies begin to take effect. Liberalization is envisaged to proceed in stages in order to reduce the adjustment costs to domestic producers and the short-term employment effects. In particular, a major liberalization while the exchange rate is appreciated could be problematic, and it would need to be tied to a depreciation of the peso to reach an equilibrium level.

In the meantime, it would clearly be desirable to make use of controls that are temporary in nature, easy to apply, and on the whole cost-effective. Studies in other countries have demonstrated that tariffs, if applied with fair uniformity across sectors, are preferable to quantitative restrictions, since tariffs allow the volume of international trade to respond to changes in domestic demand and supply with greater flexibility. At the same time the flexibility of the control instruments ultimately depends on the ease of making changes, given Colombian administrative and legal procedures.

Even though there are no infallible answers, for the present situation in Colombia it seems advisable to reduce import restrictions as the real exchange rate reaches equilibrium and exports respond to improvements in the real exchange rate. In the short term, however, if there is no way to induce quick enough adjustments in the real exchange rate, it may be advisable to undertake a temporary policy of tariffs and export incentives together in addition to depreciation of the exchange rate. If this policy is adopted, it is essential that the newly imposed import policies are temporary and that the public is made clearly aware of the temporary nature of these policies.

It would be normally desirable to rely on a system such as tariffs that maximized the probability that increases in protection would be temporary. If it is decided, however, that licenses are best suited for this purpose, they should be allocated in a way that would capture the willingness of different parties to pay for them. In view of the problem with international reserves, one criterion for licensing at present is the availability and terms of external financing for imports. In general, however, a good number of licenses are allocated more or less arbitrarily, their recipients gaining the implied rents. Auctioning the licenses would increase the efficiency of the system and transfer the rents to the government.

The government could periodically—say, every three months—announce through INCOMEX the auctioning of a certain number of licenses for selected commodities. Interested parties would then submit bids that would specify the unit prices they were willing to pay for different numbers of units of a commodity. These bids would be added up, and the clearing price—consistent with the amount to be auctioned—would be determined. This procedure would allow the central government to capture the rents derived from licenses and would avoid serious problems of income distribution and efficiency. Ideally this scheme could be supplemented with the transaction of licenses in the open market. Additional work would be needed before such a proposal could be put into effect; it might also need to proceed in stages, being focused initially on selected commodities on a pilot basis.

Notes

1. On the benefits of liberalization, see, for example, Anne O. Krueger, *Foreign Trade Regimes and Economic Development: Liberalization Attempts and Consequences* (Washington, D.C.: National Bureau of Economic Research, 1978); Bela Balassa, *The Policy Experience of Twelve Less Developed Countries, 1973–78,* World Bank Staff Working Paper no. 449 (Washington, D.C., 1981); and Jagdish N. Bhagwati and

T. N. Srinivasan, "Trade and Development," in *International Economic Policy: Theory and Evidence*, ed. Rudiger Dornbusch and Jacob A. Frenkel (Baltimore, Md.: Johns Hopkins University Press, 1979). On Colombian policy see Luis Jorge Garay S., "La política de importaciones, 1978–82: Una evaluación" (Bogotá, June 1982, processed).

2. Imports fall under free registration or prior import licensing. Items under the former can be freely imported without quantitative limitations after a procedure of administrative registration has been followed. Quantitative restrictions are imposed through the latter, which requires specific approval for each import permit. INCOMEX, the foreign trade institute, is responsible for administering these controls, and in practice, uses its discretion to exercise control even over commodities in the free registration category.

3. See Miguel Urrutia, *Winners and Losers in Colombia's Economic Growth of the 1970s* (New York: Oxford University Press, 1985); and Francisco Thoumi, "International Trade Strategies."

4. See Sergio Clavijo Vergara, "Los depósitos previos de importación," *Ensayos sobre política económica*, no. 1 (March 1982).

5. See World Bank, *Colombia*.

6. More accurate estimates need to be developed.

7. The concept of weighted average tariff is tricky because the higher the tariff the less of a good imported and thus the lower its weight. In the extreme case a prohibitive tariff would have a weight of zero.

8. $PM = PM^* (1 + t)e$, where PM is the domestic price, PM^* is a world price, $(1 + t)$ is the effect of the tariff, and e is the nominal exchange rate.

9. Gonzalo Giraldo Echeverri, "Estructura de la protección arancelaria y para-arancelaria en Colombia despues de las reformas de 1979," *Revista de planeación y desarrollo*. vol.11, no.2 (May-August 1979).

10. See, for example, Thomas L. Hutcheson and Daniel M. Schidlowsky, "Colombia," in *Development Strategies in Semi-Industrial Economies*, ed. Bela Balassa and associates (Baltimore: Johns Hopkins University Press, 1982); Giraldo, "Estructura"; and Ocampo, "Politica económica bajo condiciones cambiantes de sector externo."

11. The symmetry between import tariffs and export taxes holds in both a world with nontradable goods and one without.

12. At this stage the evidence suggesting that in growth the extent to which liberalized export-oriented economies outperform inward-looking economies is overwhelming. See Krueger, *Foreign Trade Regimes*; Bhagwati and Srinivasan, "Trade and Development"; and Ian M. D. Little, Tibor Scitowsky, and M. Scott, *Industry and Trade in Developing Countries* (New York: Oxford University Press, 1970).

13. $P_d = P^*[(1 + t) + T] + r$, where P^* is the world price c.i.f., t is the tariff, T is other taxes, and r is domestic transport costs.

14. See, for example, Kanta Marwah, "An Econometric Model of Colombia: A Prototype Devaluation View," *Econometrica*, vol. 37, no. 2 (April 1969), pp. 228-51; Alberto R. Musalem, *Dinero, inflation y balanza de pagos: La experiencia de Colombia* (Bogotá: Banco de la Republica, 1971); Mohsin S. Khan, "Import and Export Demand in Developing Countries," *IMF Staff Papers* (Washington, D.C., 1974).

15. See, for example, Krueger, *Foreign Trade Regimes*, and J. N. Bhagwati, *Anatomy and Consequences of Exchange Control Regimes* (Cambridge, Mass.: Ballinger, 1978). Tariffs are particularly superior when licenses cannot be resold.

16. See, for example, Jagdish N. Bhagwati and T. N. Srinivasan, *Lectures in International Economics* (Cambridge, Mass.: MIT Press, 1983); P. Engelbrecht-Wiggans, "Auctions and Bidding Models: A Survey," *Management Science*, vol. 26 (February 1980), pp. 119–43; and C. A. Holt, Jr., "Competitive Bidding for Contracts under Alternative Auction Procedures," *Journal of Political Economy*, vol. 88 (June 1980), pp. 433-45.

Part Two

Agricultural Price Policy

4

Price Interventions,
Competitiveness, and Incentives

THE FOCUS OF this chapter is on sectoral incentives that are the result of macroeconomic policies and sectoral price interventions and on their effects on profitability,
and efficiency in agriculture.[1] As observed in chapter 1, from the mid 1970s until
1983 the effect of macroeconomic policies on noncoffee agriculture was on balance
negative, while coffee benefited from a price boom during 1976–80. Sectoral policies, on the other hand, were intended to directly boost agricultural production and
income. These policies include price supports, import protection and export subsidies, and nonprice inducements through agricultural investments of the government, input supply, research, extension, and transfer of technology. These interventions favored agriculture, and, with varying degrees of efficiency, offset some of
the (unintended) disincentives from macroeconomic policies.

A significant intervention is the protection of importables, effected by a combination of import controls and price supports. The levels of protection in Colombia
have been high, given international distortions, and tended to more than offset the
appreciation of the exchange rate. Only about 10 percent of agricultural output is
thus protected, however, and the degree of protection would not be considered
pervasive. The levels of protection declined somewhat during the first half of the
1970s and increased thereafter, so during the 1970s as a whole no significant trend
can be observed. The competitiveness of import-competing products as well as export items is influenced also by changes in the exchange rate and the rate of inflation.

More generally, incentives in agriculture as a whole are influenced by the levels
and changes in the prices of agricultural products—consisting not only of exportables and importables but also of the large group of domestic products that constitute 30 percent of agricultural output—in relation to the rest of the economy.
These relative prices are affected by government interventions as well as by market
forces. The discussion of price supports and import restrictions will therefore be
complemented by analyses of measures of competitiveness and relative prices in
agriculture and the extent to which government policies may be significant in these
respects.

Government Interventions in Agriculture

Four types of direct government intervention can be distinguished in Colombian agriculture, the first two operating in the external sector, the other two in the domestic agricultural sector: agricultural trade restrictions, including import tariffs, and import-export licensing; agricultural export subsidies, and in the case of coffee, export taxes; output price supports; and price fixing in output and input markets. Direct price controls are set by the Ministry of Agriculture (MoA) on cocoa, sugar, and sisal and on fertilizers and pesticides, although the ministry—through IDEMA, the Agricultural Marketing Institute—intervenes directly in the market to buy or sell only sisal and some sugar. Producer price supports for wheat, barley, corn, soybeans, sorghum, sesame, beans, and rice are set by IDEMA and the ministry.

Price support policy is closely linked to import licensing. Imports of food crops are controlled by INCOMEX, the Foreign Trade Institute. Permission to import is granted after INCOMEX is satisfied that a deficit for the crop exists at the prevailing price level. Thus, the support price can in principle be maintained without a subsidy, even when the international price may be lower. Other than coffee, the major agricultural exports from Colombia include sugar, flowers, bananas, cotton, rice, and tobacco, each of which is eligible to receive the subsidized PROEXPO credit. In addition, several products now receive CERT, the tax-reimbursement certificate, of 20–25 percent—25 percent for rice and livestock, for example, and 20 percent for cotton.[2] As a member of the Sugar Exporters' Association, Colombia faces a quota on its exports of sugar. The domestic price of sugar is fixed by the MoA after negotiations with the Productores de Caña (PROCAÑA, the Sugar Growers' Association) and the Asociación de Cultivadores de Caña de Azúcar de Colombia (ASOCAÑA, the Sugar Mills Association). This price takes into account the cost of production and the level of international prices. Cotton and rice now receive a variable export incentive over and above CERT, depending on the level of international prices.

The main instruments of protection for agriculture are tariffs and quantitative restrictions on imports and incentives for exports. In Colombia, exports of agricultural products have usually been subjected to a quota, with the exception of flowers, bananas, and tobacco. First priority has been given to supplying the domestic market; when this requirement has been satisfied and a surplus remains, permission to export has been granted. For coffee, export quotas have been set in recent years by the International Coffee Organization (see chapter 6). Domestic producers and consumers of cotton have been obliged to reach an agreement on both quantity and price before the government decides on export permits; as would be expected, this provides more leverage to domestic consumers—that is, to the textile industry—than to producers. Rice export permits have been granted only if a production surplus is expected. Most import licenses are purchased by IDEMA, and INCOMEX normally does not grant an import license without prior consultation with IDEMA and the MoA. As a result, the protection granted to the production of a particular product does not constitute the legal tariff rate or export incentive alone, but may be significantly greater. The combined effect of tariffs and quantitative restrictions is nevertheless reflected by nominal rates of protection measured by a comparison of domestic and international prices.

IDEMA's Policy

The main functions of IDEMA are to buy, sell, and distribute certain agricultural products; to maintain adequate operating stocks; to import and export certain other products; and to intervene in the marketing of strategic agricultural commodities. One of IDEMA's main tools has been the provision of support prices for wheat, barley, corn, sorghum, sesame, beans, and rice. The purpose of the price supports—announced twice a year at the beginning of the planting seasons—has been to guarantee that domestic producers can recover production costs or realize a minimum level of income per unit of output.[3] Price-support and import policies have been closely related, and IDEMA attempts to supply short-term deficits by imports and to build up stocks to tide over periods of short supply.

In addition, an effort has been made through import policy at least to equate prices of the imported products with the support prices plus distribution costs.[4] Most of IDEMA's imports and sales involve raw materials and intermediate inputs in production. Various reasons are given for this emphasis: domestic production of raw materials falls short of domestic consumption in the case of wheat, sorghum, corn, soybean cake, and milk, all of which IDEMA imports; the market structure for raw materials is imperfect; and the share of imported raw materials in the production costs of food for direct human consumption is high. More significant perhaps, IDEMA's interventions in general help the government to appropriate economic rents from import controls, which otherwise would go to private industry, and also help to protect the domestic producers of agricultural raw materials.[5]

Level of Price Support

In principle, price supports take into account estimated farm production costs and international prices. In practice, imports are kept under prior licensing, with global import quotas, by product and by semester, and buyers of the products imported by IDEMA continue to pay IDEMA the full difference between the domestic support price and the cost of importing. Support prices have increased at a rate approximately equal to the rate of inflation from a base determined in the early 1970s, and the real value of support prices has not changed on the average (see tables 4-1 and SA-13). The real peso value of price supports—with the exception of rice—declined after 1975, however, following steady increases in the value of the index during 1970–75. In the second half of the 1970s, the general intervention

Table 4-1. *Price Comparisons and IDEMA Purchases, Semesters 1 and 2, 1980–84*
(pesos per ton)

Commodity and price	1980		1981		1982		1983		1984	
	1	2	1	2	1	2	1	2	1	2
Wheat										
Support price	12,000	14,000	15,500	17,500	19,000	20,600	22,500	24,750	26,730	29,500
Market price	n.a.	13,500	14,986	15,960	18,381	19,037	20,534	22,340	n.a.	n.a.
IDEMA purchase price	11,925	14,744	15,887	17,825	19,129	21,401	23,114	25,425	n.a.	n.a.
IDEMA purchases[a]	85.6	29.4	49.5	41.7	91.7	50.1	80.7	n.a.	n.a.	n.a.
Corn[b]										
Support price	9,600	11,680	14,040	15,986	18,250	20,246	22,965	23,980	26,380	27,700
Market price	n.a.	13,825	13,465	14,200	16,354	19,172	21,144	23,810	n.a.	n.a.
IDEMA purchase price	8,950	11,480	13,525	14,958	17,642	18,863	21,997	22,709	n.a.	n.a.
IDEMA purchases[a]	0.3	2.8	2.1	3.2	3.5	6.6	3.5	n.a.	n.a.	n.a.
Soya										
Support price	14,930	16,000	21,200	24,000	27,600	30,300	33,000	35,475	39,400	43,340
Market price	n.a.	19,150	21,300	24,000	27,634	31,194	34,000	37,213	n.a.	n.a.
IDEMA purchase price	n.a.	n.a.	20,325	23,625	27,168	30,245	30,449	35,504	n.a.	n.a.
IDEMA purchases[a]	n.a.	n.a.	0.1	6.7	2.0	0.2	0.1	n.a.	n.a.	n.a.
Sorghum										
Support price	8,645	9,800	11,500	13,200	15,000	16,700	17,900	19,240	20,780	22,440
Market price	n.a.	11,436	12,228	13,269	14,181	16,971	17,585	19,320	n.a.	n.a.
IDEMA purchase price	8,289	9,568	11,182	12,624	14,730	16,189	17,463	18,611	n.a.	n.a.
IDEMA purchases[a]	3.3	2.0	7.5	1.2	19.7	8.6	6.7	n.a.	n.a.	n.a.

Sesame									
Support price	29,820	29,820	29,820	31,000	32,000	35,000	38,200	42,020	46,220	58,240
Market price	n.a.	29,800	24,500	28,000	30,500	40,000	40,000	44,600	n.a.	n.a.
IDEMA purchase price	29,554	29,651	29,539	30,611	31,568	34,275	37,310	41,406	n.a.	n.a.
IDEMA purchases[a]	93.9	18.1	89.5	10.3	33.4	4.4	3.8	n.a.	n.a.	n.a.
Beans									
Support price	30,000	37,500	40,500	45,000	46,000	52,000	58,300	64,130	69,900	85,000
Market price	n.a.	40,000	44,000	52,500	60,800	63,500	67,700	69,540	n.a.	n.a.
IDEMA purchase price	n.a.	n.a.	30,666	36,173	n.a.	n.a.	41,580	63,442	n.a.	n.a.
IDEMA purchases[a]	n.a.	n.a.	2.1	0.2	n.a.	n.a.	0.3	n.a.	n.a.	n.a.
Rice[c]									
Support price	9,957	11,777	12,720	14,500	16,200	18,100	19,900	21,700	24,180	25,390
Market price	n.a.	n.a.	10,860	13,250	14,790	14,550	17,137	17,605	n.a.	n.a.
IDEMA purchase price	9,247	10,418	10,647	12,097	13,460	14,882	16,344	17,649	n.a.	n.a.
IDEMA purchases[a]	5.4	10.9	0.2	1.9	1.4	17.1	10.1	n.a.	n.a.	n.a.
Barley									
Support price	9,800	10,500	13,000	15,000	16,800	18,600	20,100	22,500	24,750	29,500
Market price	n.a.	12,500	14,150	14,000	15,438	17,450	18,500	21,500	n.a.	n.a.
IDEMA purchase price	n.a.	n.a.	n.a.	n.a.	n.a.	15,750	n.a.	19,840	n.a.	n.a.
IDEMA purchases[a]	n.a.	n.a.	n.a.	n.a.	n.a.	2.1	n.a.	n.a.	n.a.	n.a.

n.a. Not available.

Note: The support price is set for a certain grade of the crop, usually a superior grade, so that the average price paid by IDEMA is typically lower. The market price is the national average farmgate price.

a. As a percentage of total production.

b. Weighted average price of white and yellow corn.

c. Average price of CICA 7, 8, and 9 and Metica and Oryzica rice.

Source: IDEMA.

also declined except for sesame and wheat. This reduced level of intervention was in part the result of the precarious financial situation of IDEMA as a result of the huge losses that it incurred during the period 1970–74 and continued to accumulate in the years following.

The 1983 increases in price supports were nearly uniform and corresponded to inflation levels. The increases announced for semester 1 of 1983, for example, ranged from 7 percent to 9 percent for all crops. Similarly, while IDEMA claims to be concerned with stock levels, the 1983 semester 2 support price of rice was increased 9 percent, even though IDEMA had large stocks of rice from the preceding year that it could not profitably export and, according to IDEMA's own estimates, costs of production increased only 5 percent during the semester. Thus it appears that changes in IDEMA's support prices have been based primarily on the rate of inflation. This implies an attempt to ensure that farmers' returns on a crop do not drop below previous levels in real terms rather than an attempt to alter the production mix.

Effect of Policy

IDEMA's support price is offered for a certain grade that is usually higher than average, and the support price is therefore typically higher that the average price actually paid by IDEMA (see table 4-1). The support price of a commodity is uniform across the country. Both the announced support price and the average price actually paid by IDEMA are usually higher than the market price would have been in areas located far from consumption centers but lower than the average open market price in the country and close to estimated producer prices (see table SA-14). Consequently, IDEMA manages to purchase only a small fraction of the output of most crops. In general the total value of IDEMA's purchases does not exceed 1–3 percent of the total value of agricultural output in noncoffee agriculture. The principal exceptions are wheat and sesame, of which IDEMA has purchased 49 percent and 43 percent respectively of the total annual production during the last three years. Therefore, while IDEMA has had a strong influence in stimulating production and increasing farm incomes for some products in some regions, its price support function is not an important policy tool for stimulating production throughout the country.

Protection and Efficiency in Agriculture

A comparison of domestic prices and international prices provides a measure of the extent to which domestic production is protected from external competition. In table SA-15 the f.o.b. prices of major traded commodities are compared with Colombian prices at the official exchange rate during 1970–82. Admittedly, these comparisons are rough. In many instances international prices are the result of subsidies provided by exporting countries. No quality adjustments are made in comparing external and internal prices. The use of the official exchange rate does not account for the overvaluation of the peso that has occurred since the mid 1970s. As a result, any implicit tax on exports—that is, a domestic price lower than the external price—would be underestimated, and protection of imports—that is, an external price lower than the domestic price—would be overestimated. Finally, a more nearly correct price comparison for import-competing commodities would be between the farmgate price and the Colombia import price c.i.f. plus port and transport charges to the consumption center, less transport cost from the farm to the consumption center. The Colombia f.o.b. price of exports would be compared to the farmgate price plus all transport and port charges. The present comparisons can be used only to suggest broad differences in the treatment of imports and exports, and general secular trends.

Exports versus Import-Competing Products

Export agriculture in general has been taxed implicitly, and import-competing agriculture has been protected. For most export commodities—rice, coffee, bananas, tobacco, cotton, and sugar—the ratio of domestic to international prices (f.o.b.) has been significantly less than one, no matter whether the export crop is food, such as rice, or is not a food item—cotton, for example.[6] Even after adding international transport costs to the Colombian prices of most of these commodities, price ratios would appear to be less than one. In the case of import-competing crops—barley, corn, wheat, sorghum, soybeans, and butter—the ratio of the domestic to the international price (f.o.b.) has been significantly higher than one, suggesting that one government objective is to achieve self-sufficiency in food, although this aim may not be expected to be realized for each specific crop.

Self-sufficiency in food, however, has been pursued at a high cost with respect to many import-competing products, as the nominal protection granted these products—corn, wheat, and sorghum, for example—has at times reached levels between 50 percent and 100 percent. The implied cost of protection, moreover, has increased in recent years as levels of protection have gone up significantly. There appears to be some measure of protection of animal products, such as beef and milk, and particularly butter. The rates of nominal protection of beef and milk, however, must be interpreted with particular care, since the domestic price of beef seems to be the average of different qualities of meat, while the international price is for meat of only the best quality. The international price used in the price comparison for milk is the U.S. producer price, as supplied by the Central Bank, for lack of a better indicator, while the quality of U.S. milk and Colombian milk is quite different.

The pattern of protection during 1970–83 as a whole was rather stable, even after accounting for the growing overvaluation of the peso since the mid 1970s. Export crops remained implicitly taxed, while import-competing food crops were being protected at the official exchange rate. One export crop that exhibits wide variability in its index of nominal protection is sugar; at times it appears heavily taxed, while at others it seems to be heavily protected. The reason for such volatility rests on the goal of keeping prices in the internal market relatively stable in the face of highly volatile international prices.

Protection and Efficiency

The levels of nominal protection have been related positively to the inefficiency in production of a small group of food crops, such as wheat, corn, sorghum, and soybeans. This conclusion is based on comparisons of average production costs with their international peso prices, although unadjusted for production subsidies provided abroad (see table SA-16). Production of corn and wheat appear to be inefficient by international standards, and the levels of nominal protection received barely serve to cover the high costs of production. The production of soybeans and sorghum is less inefficient when compared with international standards, and the corresponding levels of nominal protection of these products are smaller than for wheat and corn. Cotton and rice seem to be competitive but historically they have been implicitly taxed and subject to export controls; recently increased CERTS—tax credit certificates—and a variable subsidy are efforts that have been made to offset the disincentives from an appreciated exchange rate and declining domestic competitiveness.

Historically, it appears that crops which can be developed as exports and which can compete successfully in international markets have not been stimulated but have been implicitly taxed. Only when export crops develop problems in external markets have support measures been devised and implemented, as they have for cotton. On the other hand, import-competing crops that do not stand up to external competition have received protection, but not much increase in their output has been achieved. Most of the protection granted to import-competing crops has gone to food crops in general, particularly cereals.[7]

A More Precise Estimate of Protection

Strictly speaking, the farmgate price of importables should be compared to the c.i.f. import price plus port and transport charges to the consumption point less transport charges from the farm to the consumption point. Data on port and transport charges, however, are not readily available. If it were assumed that the sum of port charges and transport costs from the port to the consumption point is equal to the transport costs from the farm to the consumption point, a direct comparison of the c.i.f. price with the farmgate price would be possible. Since port charges in Colombia are high, this simplifying assumption would lead to an overestimation of the nominal rate of protection. In a sense, the resultant estimate gives a measure of protection both from policies of import restrictions, including tariffs, and from natural protection in the form of high port charges. The nominal rates of protection thus calculated for five principal import crops are given in table 4-2. The high nomi-

Table 4-2. *Nominal Rates of Protection for Selected Importable Crops, 1980–82*
(percent)

Crop	1980	1981	1982
Wheat	36	45	91
Corn	87	67	79
Soybeans	37	46	85
Sorghum	67	57	110

Note: These rates are measures of the percentage differences of farmgate prices over international prices c.i.f. Colombian ports.
Sources: IDEMA, DNP, and estimates made by Mateen Thobani.

nal rates of protection imply that the bulk of the importable crops receive a production subsidy in the sense that they could have been imported more cheaply. The rates of protection impose an implicit consumption tax, since retail prices are based on markups from the protected farmgate prices. The distortion suggests the possibility of gains from lowering import restrictions.

Calculating nominal rates of protection for Colombia's exportable crops is difficult for two reasons: first, the comparison must now be made between the Colombian f.o.b. price and the farmgate price plus the sum of transport costs to the port and port charges—the earlier simplifying assumption on transport and port charges can no longer be made; second, Colombia's exportables, such as sugar, cotton, rice, flowers, and tobacco, unlike the importables, cannot be exported before significant processing costs have been incurred. One way to circumvent these problems is to compare the f.o.b. price to the domestic wholesale price, on the assumption that the wholesale price approximates the farmgate price plus processing and transport costs. The problem with port charges remains, however, as do the differences in quality between domestically consumed exportables and actual exports. For these reasons a more precise estimate of protection rates for exportables has not been attempted. Nominal rates of protection for exportables are expected to be significantly lower than for importables, however, and may be negative, at least for some crops, in several years.

Turning to the effective rate of protection (ERP), since agricultural inputs in Colombia receive lower rates of protection than do importable outputs, the ERP of the latter would exceed the nominal rates given earlier.[8] Therefore, importables unambiguously receive high rates of protection. The ERP of exportables, however, is more difficult to determine for the same reasons mentioned in respect to nominal rates.

Evaluating Protection: The Case of Wheat

The stated purpose of wheat protection is not so much to stimulate domestic production—in which IDEMA has had limited success, since about 90 percent of Colombian consumption of wheat is still imported—as to increase farm incomes in certain regions. The concerns are net losses of efficiency and the effect of this policy on farm incomes, consumer welfare, and government revenues. In evaluating a reduction of the high rate of protection given to wheat, consideration should also be given to the substitutes or complements for wheat in either consumption or production. Removing wheat alone would lead to the movement of resources into the production of a protected substitute: a second best policy might be to reduce the ERP of wheat to that of its substitutes. The welfare gain from eliminating wheat protection alone is likely to be small, while the principal substitutes for wheat in production and consumption are also protected at fairly high rates. The more interesting case might be to calculate the potential welfare gain if IDEMA were to lower its support prices for all imported cereals.

The welfare effect on consumers, producers, and the government that would be associated with lowering wheat protection by 10 percent, 15 percent, and 20 percent has nevertheless been measured.[9] Based on an analysis of producer and consumer surplus, the results show that it is the consumer who would stand to gain most from the policy, and the government and IDEMA would lose the most. The net gain in efficiency from such a wheat policy above varies from Col$163 million to Col$226 million. This net gain in efficiency is modest compared to the value of consumption, which would be less than 1 percent. Even when the elasticity of supply was increased from a short-run value of 0.6 used in the analysis to a long-run elasticity of 1.2, the gain in efficiency as a percentage of the value of wheat consumption increases to only slightly more than 1 percent in the 10 percent distortion case.

Interventions by IDEMA

The elements and the pattern of protection for import-competing cereals have varied since 1970. While the ratio of support to international prices declined in 1970–75, it increased in 1976–83. The reason is that during 1970–75, the increase in costs that had to be covered by higher support prices was smaller than the rise in the peso value of the international price; thus was the double objective of making agriculture more efficient and of increasing the real incentives to domestic agricultural production accomplished; the opposite behavior of costs and the peso value of international prices occurred during 1976–83, and it is for this reason that a higher level of protection was required. As for commodities in which the country seems to enjoy a comparative advantage and for which IDEMA's support prices are lower than international prices, the reasons for IDEMA to intervene are to build up working stocks and to support producers when bumper crops are harvested at the regional level.

In certain regions there may be an effect on production, but it is not significant nationally. Only in the case of paddy rice and wheat were support prices higher than average nationwide producer prices during 1970–82; for all other products—

sesame, barley, beans, corn, sorghum, and soybeans—average nationwide producer prices have in general been higher than support prices. Thus only in the case of wheat and sesame have price supports possibly been an effective incentive to boost output, both because support prices are higher than producer prices or international prices and because the participation of IDEMA in the market for these products is rather large. It is doubtful whether intervention for the rest of the products has any significant effect either in increasing production or in guaranteeing a minimum return to the producer: the intervention of the institute in these cases is to be looked on rather as a help to producers at times when problems of excess production arise at the regional level or when stocks need to be built up to complement the function of the institute as a distribution entity and to diminish risks.

Support prices higher than international prices of most importables can be maintained because imports are restricted. INCOMEX must approve the import of every crop whose price is supported by IDEMA. It grants a license only after consulting with IDEMA and the MoA and after confirming that a deficit for the crop exists. This is to ensure that consumer prices do not fall below IDEMA's support prices. IDEMA may import the commodity without paying any tariffs, whereas other importers must pay between 15.5 percent and 24.5 percent. While IDEMA's domestic purchase price may be higher than its import purchase price, the price at which IDEMA subsequently sells is based on its domestic purchase price.[10] Thus IDEMA obtains all the rents from the system of tariffs and licenses. The farmgate price of wheat in 1982, for example, was 91 percent higher than its price c.i.f. Even after accounting for differences in the costs of transport from the port to Bogotá, instead of from Pasto, the principal wheat-growing region, to Bogotá, the farmgate price remains about 70 percent higher than its import parity price. Since tariffs on wheat in 1982 were only 16.5 percent until October, when they were raised to 18.5 percent, and IDEMA does not pay tariffs anyway, the difference of 70 percent constitutes rent to IDEMA and port charges. Port charges have been estimated to be very high in Colombia and are likely to contain elements of rent.

Production Incentives for Major Commodities

Despite the protection for importables and increases in the levels of protection during the second half of the 1970s, production incentives of Colombia's traded agricultural commodities—that is, both exports and import-competing commodities—have on the average declined since 1975. Evidence is provided by an index of the real peso value of international prices for selected agricultural commodities (see table SA-18). This index is the product of the international price in dollars and the average exchange rate for each year, divided by the implicit gross domestic product (GDP) price deflator for that year, thus combining the conditions prevailing in international markets with domestic economic policies and conditions.

Protection and Competitiveness

To the extent that the GDP deflator reflects trends in domestic production costs, this index indicates broad patterns in international competitiveness of Colombian agriculture. For the majority of the fifteen products chosen for the exercise, the index fell 25 percent to 50 percent between 1975 and 1983, and for two of these products, butter and beef, no clear trend exists. This behavior differs remarkably from that experienced during the years 1970–75, when the index rose for most of the products, showing rather substantial margins in some instances.

Among the products chosen, the country produces and imports butter, barley, corn, wheat, palm oil, and soybeans. The index for butter varied moderately during 1975–83 and no clear trend can be deduced. The 1982 value of the index for barley was 35 percent lower that in 1975, but the index had reached a bottom level in 1978 and recovered thereafter. The index for wheat, corn, soybeans, and palm oil has been falling sharply. Among export products the index for beef, rice, sugar, coffee, bananas, tobacco, and cotton has decreased significantly since 1975. In the case of cotton, the loss of international competitiveness was so great that the area planted and the output fell to a third their size after 1975.

External and Internal Factors

International economic conditions, particularly low international prices, have undoubtedly had an effect on the trend and the level of the index for several products. It is worth noticing, however, that the international price of products such as coffee, bananas, beef, and tobacco was higher in real terms during 1981–83 than it was in 1975 (see tables 1-3 and 4-3). If domestic conditions had remained unchanged—that is, if prices and the exchange rate had remained constant—the index of the real peso value of international prices of agricultural exports of these products should have been higher in 1982 than in 1975. High rates of inflation and a deteriorating—that is, appreciating—real exchange rate have been important reasons for the loss of competitiveness of agricultural exports. In addition, this decline is substantial when the index of international prices—which is the index of the real peso value of international prices with stable prices and stable exchange rates—is compared to the actual index of the real peso value of international prices.

The same conclusions are obtained when the index of competitiveness is generated on the basis of the ratio of the peso value of the international price to the average production costs for some selected agricultural commodities—rice, corn, sorghum, soybean, wheat, and cotton (see tables 4-4 and SA-19). The pattern observed is similar to that of the previous index, although the levels vary somewhat. Using the index that incorporates production costs, it will be seen that rice, corn, sorghum, and soybeans have suffered a greater loss in international competitiveness

Table 4-3. *International Prices of Selected Agricultural Exports, 1970–83*
(constant prices; 1975 = 100)

Year	Cotton[a]	Sugar[b]	Bananas[c]	Rice[d]	Beef[e]	Tobacco[f]
1970	110.1	36.8	137.2	91.5	172.3	157.0
1971	119.2	41.4	106.9	85.4	192.7	132.1
1972	116.3	60.9	112.2	88.1	226.9	131.1
1973	166.7	66.5	95.9	134.9	260.8	114.7
1974	139.5	166.4	85.5	150.7	245.5	104.5
1975	100.0	100.0	100.0	100.0	100.0	100.0
1976	143.5	56.0	103.7	72.4	104.3	100.1
1977	121.7	36.2	101.1	72.1	123.3	100.5
1978	104.3	29.7	90.0	73.3	104.0	91.9
1979	100.2	32.8	91.6	62.8	154.1	89.5
1980	112.5	89.7	97.5	75.4	159.5	87.5
1981	105.7	55.6	106.0	90.2	144.6	103.3
1982	93.2	28.0	104.4	59.7	112.4	120.1
1983	104.8	27.3	115.9	59.7	n.a.	118.2

n.a. Not available.

Note: Constant prices are nominal prices divided by the index of manufacturing unit value (MUV), taken from World Bank data of January 1985. For coffee see table 1-3.

a. Liverpool index.
b. Caribbean (New York).
c. Latin America (U.S. ports).
d. United States (New Orleans).
e. Argentina (frozen).
f. United States (all markets).

Sources: IFS and estimates compiled by J. García-García.

than have cotton and wheat. The general trend observed in all of these commodities, however, is the same: following a period of substantial gains, 1970–75, there has been a loss of international competitiveness in agricultural production in Colombia since 1975.

Trends in Relative Prices of Agricultural Products

The internal relative prices of agricultural production have varied significantly since 1970.[11] As shown in table 4-5, the domestic prices of agricultural output rose in relation to those in the rest of the economy during the early 1970s, fell during the mid 1970s, recovered again briefly between 1976 and 1977, and declined continuously thereafter. The direction of change in these price movements for agriculture as a whole has been connected with price changes in commodities internationally traded by Colombia. Comparing the terms of trade—that is, the ratio of

Table 4-4. *International Prices of Selected Agricultural Imports, 1970–83*
(constant prices; 1975 = 100)

Year	Wheat[a]	Corn[b]	Barley[c]	Sorghum[d]	Soybeans[d]	Butter[e]	Palm oil[f]
1970	68.8	98.6	87.5	100.2	107.5	93.7	122.4
1971	77.1	91.0	75.0	88.6	108.9	122.0	113.6
1972	79.6	79.8	119.2	86.1	108.2	127.9	86.3
1973	133.8	116.5	126.4	126.1	188.4	87.5	125.3
1974	137.7	126.0	95.5	128.4	143.1	83.6	177.2
1975	100.0	100.0	100.0	100.0	100.0	100.0	100.0
1976	87.5	92.4	85.1	91.9	103.1	104.2	93.1
1977	62.7	72.4	79.0	71.6	115.0	105.9	113.8
1978	65.8	65.0	56.7	66.2	93.7	116.8	107.6
1979	74.0	66.9	79.9	72.5	93.0	124.9	105.0
1980	73.6	67.0	74.5	84.2	85.9	133.7	86.5
1981	78.3	73.1	102.3	86.0	87.5	130.5	88.8
1982	77.6	62.7	97.4	75.0	76.0	123.5	70.8
1983	80.9	76.3	60.9	n.a.	84.7	102.2	67.4

n.a. Not available.

Note: Constant prices are nominal prices divided by the index of manufacturing unit value (MUV), taken from World Bank data of January 1985.

a. United States (U.S. Gulf ports).
b. Yellow no. 2 (U.S. Gulf ports).
c. C.i.f. Colombia, from DANE.
d. United States (Rotterdam).
e. New Zealand (London).
f. Malaysia (Europe).

Sources: Same as for table 4-3.

implicit price deflators of peso exports to peso imports, both in agriculture and in the economy as a whole (see table 4-6)—with producer prices of agricultural commodities in relation to prices in the rest of the economy, a fairly close correlation in the directions of change can be observed.

The movements in Colombia's terms of trade have been dominated by coffee prices, and changes in producer prices in agriculture in relation to prices in the rest of the economy have been stronger for coffee than for noncoffee agriculture. As a result of the sharp fluctuations in the international price of coffee, and its dominance in the terms of trade and the domestic prices of agricultural output in relation to those of the rest of the economy, however, a clear distinction must be made between coffee and noncoffee agriculture. The domestic price of coffee in relation to prices in the rest of the economy has followed the same pattern as that of the terms of trade for coffee: both reached a peak in 1977 and declined continuously thereafter. Variations in domestic relative prices of coffee have been less pronounced than variations in the terms of trade, which will be further elaborated upon in chapter 6.

Table 4-5. *Producer Prices in Agriculture in Relation to Prices in the Rest of the Economy, 1970–83*

(index of price ratios: 1975 = 100)

Year	Total agriculture[a]	Coffee[b]	Noncoffee agriculture[c]
1970	98.1	112.4	92.8
1971	94.4	95.8	93.9
1972	99.4	105.4	97.4
1973	109.1	120.3	105.1
1974	105.8	103.0	106.8
1975	100.0	100.0	100.0
1976	111.1	150.8	98.0
1977	126.1	201.3	103.4
1978	109.4	149.0	93.9
1979	96.1	112.3	88.9
1980	92.3	106.8	85.8
1981	82.8	82.6	83.3
1982	82.7	82.0	82.9
1983	81.7	79.8	82.5

Note: Gross value of output deflators were used; the comparison in each column is with the entire nonagriculture sector of the economy.

a. Broad definition; see text.

b. Consisting of pergamino and processed coffee.

c. Sectors 02 and 03 plus sector 12.

Source: García-García, "Aspects of Agricultural Development," which is based on DANE data.

The terms of trade for noncoffee exports as a whole have varied relatively little since the mid 1970s, and their levels in 1982–83 were hardly different from those in 1974–75. Within the agricultural sector also, the terms of trade for noncoffee exports have fluctuated less than those for coffee, but since the mid 1970s—with some exceptions—a downward trend can be observed. International price variations have differed significantly from product to product, as will be discussed in the following section; what is indicated in table 4-6 is only an aggregate picture. The declining terms of trade for Colombia's noncoffee agricultural exports can be discerned from international price trends. With efforts to hold the country's competitiveness, export performance could have been better, despite this decline in international prices. Within the domestic economy the decline in the price of noncoffee agricultural products in relation to other prices has been stronger than the decline in the terms of trade.

Two subperiods emerge with clear trends: 1970–74 and 1975–83. During the first there was an improvement in the internal relative price of noncoffee agricultural products, but no clear trend appeared for coffee. On the other hand, there was no defined pattern in the external terms of trade either for coffee or for noncoffee agricultural products during 1970–74. The improvement in domestic terms of

Table 4-6. *Prices of Exports in Relation to Prices of Imports, 1970–83*
(1975 = 100)

Year	Exports	Coffee exports	Noncoffee exports	Agricultural exports[a]	Noncoffee agricultural exports
1970	107.3	135.0	82.6	176.8	132.5
1971	99.0	115.9	84.6	137.1	93.5
1972	109.4	132.9	93.2	155.3	110.8
1973	122.1	150.1	103.6	128.7	117.0
1974	113.3	111.4	114.8	90.9	122.5
1975	100.0	100.0	100.0	100.0	100.0
1976	131.3	179.7	98.6	171.3	91.7
1977	164.8	286.7	101.7	234.2	101.4
1978	144.5	197.1	102.5	271.4	87.7
1979	123.5	141.3	105.8	154.3	87.5
1980	127.7	139.6	116.7	142.8	101.2
1981	109.7	103.5	115.1	119.6	97.3
1982	112.9	116.9	110.4	107.8	83.9
1983	113.9	114.4	113.6	108.2	90.8

Note: The comparison is with prices of all imports except in the case of agricultural exports, prices of which are compared with those of broad agricultural imports.

a. Broad definition, including sectors 01, 02, 03, 08, and 12 in the DANE classification.

Source: Same as for table 4-5.

trade for noncoffee agricultural products can be explained by a move to liberalize trade and promote exports that took place between 1970 and 1974 in the form of lower nominal tariffs and lesser quantitative restrictions. These permitted an increase in the real exchange rate which was then transmitted to the noncoffee agricultural sector.[12] During 1975–83, the trend in domestic relative prices has been one of deterioration for noncoffee agriculture, with the exception of 1977, when a serious shortfall of domestic production pushed prices of agricultural products upward. Besides movements in the external terms of trade, domestic factors also significantly explain the decline in the internal relative price of noncoffee agricultural products since 1975. Some of these considerations were analyzed in chapter 1—improvements in the terms of trade for coffee, a lag in the exchange-rate adjustment, a growing fiscal deficit, and inadequate use of import policy to offset inflationary pressures.

Policy Conclusions

An important sectoral intervention—in addition to credit subsidy (see chapter 8)—is represented by import restrictions complemented by IDEMA's price supports, provided mostly to cereals and other food crops, which, with the exception of rice, do not generally appear to enjoy a comparative advantage. The import-competing component is a relatively small part, so despite substantial levels of protection of this segment, the competitiveness and production incentives have been diminishing since the mid 1970s. The policy inference is not that the levels of import protection should be raised further: levels of protection are already high, and protection imposes a cost on consumers, while it has, on the whole, been ineffective in stimulating production. Exports of agricultural products, on the other hand, have in the past been subject to a quota depending on estimated surpluses, with the possible exception of flowers, bananas, and tobacco. In 1984, a shift in policy in favor of removal of export restrictions has been initiated. It would be advisable to maintain such a policy direction for an extended period in order to guarantee producers that they would not face impediments to exporting.

If the objective of IDEMA is to protect domestic producers of importables, import restrictions might achieve that goal without price supports, unless the market is completely monopolistic. Even if some price supports are to be provided, a reduction of the support prices in areas farther removed from consumption centers to take into account increases in transport costs would be desirable for the sake of efficiency. On the other hand, income distribution goals might be particularly important in such removed areas, and alternative redistributive mechanisms might need to be devised. Reforms of IDEMA's seasonal price stabilization and a separation of price support operations from storage functions would be helpful.

While the benefits from import controls and price supports have been small, their economic costs are more complex to estimate. In a partial and static analysis these costs do not appear large compared to the value of sectoral GDP. The losses in allocative efficiency caused by policy are not very large in the case of wheat. Nevertheless, these interventions bear a significant financial cost, particularly in comparison with the public sector operations in agriculture. At least from this point of view, improvements in efficiency in pricing policy would merit attention. Furthermore, there may be benefits from providing greater incentives to reallocation of resources and to dynamic efficiency. Also, gains from liberalization of trade, if measured in the framework of general equilibrium, are likely to be more significant.

International conditions have undoubtedly contributed to the problems of Colombian agriculture: the terms of trade for noncoffee agricultural exports have declined since the mid 1970s, as international prices for these products in real terms have declined. The country could have maintained greater competitiveness abroad, however, with more adequate macroeconomic policies. Despite low and declining protection, as measured by domestic and external price ratios for traded commodities, the international competitiveness of Colombia's noncoffee agricultural products was stronger during 1970–75 than in the post-1975 period. Declining competitiveness since 1975, despite rising protection, has been at least in part the result of high rates of domestic inflation and an appreciating exchange rate. In general terms, the emphasis of policy for the 1980s could be on establishing a more neutral macroeconomic framework, which would not prejudice incentives to agriculture. In addition, export promotion could replace import protection as a development strategy. A favorable export climate within Colombia would be essential in order to regain external markets and to restore the confidence of exporters in the government's intentions concerning export promotion. The macroeconomic adjustments under way (see chapter 9) are in the right direction from these points of view.

The range of price distortions in Colombia during the 1970s, including protection to agriculture and manufacturing and the pricing of capital and labor, has been judged moderate in comparison to groups of high-, moderate-, and low-distortion countries.[13] Coefficients of protection during the 1970s have been moderate for agricultural products as a whole, high for corn, moderate for cocoa, and low for rice and beef. The fact that agricultural prices have not been unduly distorted during the last decade has also been related to the sector's good long-term record.[14] Consistent with these observations, the needed shifts in agricultural pricing policies for growth and employment supported in this book are relatively modest.

Notes

1. Earlier discussions include Roberto Junguito Bonett, "Agricultural Incentives in Colombia" (Bogotá, 1982, processed); Eduardo Sarmiento Palacio, *Inflación, producción y comercio internacional* (Bogotá: FEDESARROLLO, 1982).

2. Although many of the differences have been reduced, the degree to which exports of various agricultural products benefit from these incentives varies. Flower exports to the United States, for instance, receive only a 1 percent CERT on account of objections by the United States, while those to other countries receive 20 percent.

3. L. F. Londoño Capurro, *Política agropecuario, 1981–1982* (Bogotá, 1982), p. 26; IDEMA, "Filosofía de los precios de sustentación (Bogotá, November 1982, processed), p. 4; and Eduardo Sarmiento Palacio, "Objetivos del IDEMA" (Bogotá: n.p., n.d.), pp. 8 and 84.

4. A. Ramírez Ramírez, *IDEMA: Dos años de labores, 1980–1981* (Bogotá, 1982, processed), p. 31.

5. IDEMA, "La intervencion del IDEMA en el mercado de alimentos y materias primas" (Bogotá, January 1983, processed), p. 8.

6. Beef seems to be protected, as shown in table SA-15. The difference between the domestic and international price, however, is probably absorbed by the marketing margin from producer to wholesaler.

7. On the matter of comparative advantage and domestic resources costs see "Ventajas comparativas de productos agropecuarios en Colombia," vol. 1 (October 1982), a report prepared for the DNP by Econometria.

8. See Edward Tower, "Understanding Shadow Prices, Second-Best Tariffs, the Effective Rate of Protection and Domestic Resource Cost from the Perspective of Simple General Equilibrium Models" (Washington, D.C.: World Bank, July 1983, processed).

9. Mateen Thobani, "Welfare Impact of Reducing Import Restrictions on Wheat" (Washington, D.C.: World Bank, Country Policy Department, April 1984, processed).

10. IDEMA's selling price is much higher than its import price plus transport and handling costs and is only feasible because of a government policy of restricting imports through licensing. Thus the support price policy and import restrictions policy go hand in hand.

11. The relative prices of two activities means the ratio of the implicit price deflator of gross output for these activities. When no mention is made to the contrary, the term "relative price" refers to domestic relative prices. In these measures agriculture is defined to include sectors 01, 02, 03, 08, and 12 in the

DANE classification of national accounts. The rest of the economy comprises sectors 04, 05, 06, 07, 09, 10, 11, and 13–35.

12. The average nominal tariff was reduced from 70 percent in 1970 to 30 percent in 1974. See Roberto Junguito and Carlos Caballero, *Problemas y perspectivas del proceso de integración andina* (Bogotá: FEDESARROLLO, 1974). The liberalization process between 1970 and 1974 is documented by Jorge García García in *The Effects of Exchange Rates and Commercial Policies on Agricultural Incentives in Colombia: 1953–1978*, International Food Policy Research Institute Research Report no. 24 (Washington D.C.: IFPRI, June 1981), chapter 6.

13. World Bank, *World Development Report 1983* (New York: Oxford University Press, 1983); Ramgopal Agarwala, *Price Distortions and Growth in Developing Countries*, World Bank Staff Working Paper no. 575 (Washington, D.C., 1983).

14. Urrutia, *Winners and Losers in Colombia's Economic Growth of the 1970s.*

5

Price Stabilization in Agriculture

INSTABILITY OF DOMESTIC PRICES is considered by sources in and out of the government as a serious problem for producers and consumers of agricultural commodities in Colombia. Greater price stability is often recommended on various grounds, and some policies have been put into effect and others proposed for this purpose. Policies connected with stabilization concern two distinct but interrelated aspects: year-to-year price variation and seasonal price fluctuations. These two types of price instability will be discussed in turn, and related macroeconomic and sectoral policies and other alternatives will be evaluated.

FEDERACAFE (the Coffee Federation) reduces domestic price changes of coffee in the face of volatile variations in international markets. The Oficina de Planeación del Sector Agropecuario (OPSA, the planning office of the Ministry of Agriculture) sets producer prices, usually once a year, for sugar, cocoa, sisal, and fiber, and intervenes between producers and cotton manufacturers in the negotiation of cotton prices. The agency may not be an effective price stabilizer, however, since it does not actually buy or sell any of these products. IDEMA sets support prices for producers and influences consumer prices through its sales and imports of staples such as rice, wheat, corn, barley, beans, sorghum, and soya. Many of these are seasonal crops; the agency's purchase, import, storage, and sale policies therefore affect seasonal variations in price. In addition, the government policy of subsidized credit for storage has important implications, which will be discussed later. IDEMA's nationwide contribution to seasonal and annual price stabilization may be limited, however, since—in view of its financial constraints—it intervenes substantially only in a few markets, as is shown in table 5-1.

Some Basic Considerations

A concern of policymakers is that high seasonal prices of food items hurt poor consumers who spend a large share of their income on food. This notion confounds

Table 5-1. *IDEMA's Purchases as Percentage of National Production of Each Crop, 1980–84*

Crop	1980–81	1981–82	1982–83	1983–84
Beans	0.6	n.a.	2.0	n.a.
Corn	2.3	5.2	5.4	7.6
Rice (paddy)	4.4	10.3	10.8	2.7
Sesame	64.7	22.9	3.0	0.7
Sorghum	4.2	14.7	6.5	3.7
Soybeans	0.9	1.1	0.0	n.a.
Wheat	41.6	60.1	52.1	35.7
Barley	n.a.	2.1	0.3	n.a.

n.a. Not available.
Source: IDEMA.

the conceptually distinct issues of the average price level and the variations of the price during the year. Stabilizing the price would imply prices lower in some seasons and higher in others than any present prices. Consumers are clearly better off in the former seasons and worse off in the latter than under a regime of unstable prices. On balance, consumer welfare may actually be reduced throughout all seasons by price stabilization.[1]

It is believed by some observers that price uncertainty leads producers to make wrong production decisions. Producers, uncertain about the future price, base decisions on the current price, thereby causing alternate booms and busts. If producers were to learn from experience, however, they would find that high prices one year tend to be followed by low prices the next year, and they would make the appropriate adjustment in planning decisions, leading to a leveling off of prices. Where IDEMA is effective, it is difficult to understand why producers would base planting decisions on current prices when IDEMA publishes future support prices far enough in advance to base plans on them. Another consideration is that reduction of agricultural risks could be expected to promote investments, expand production, and reduce consumer prices.

Concerns regarding the macroeconomic effects of price instability are based on the assumption that consumers and producers have different marginal propensities to consume.[2] Thus, it is often argued that when fluctuations in agricultural prices and production cause shifts in income between the two groups, the demand for individual products—and aggregate demand—also fluctuate, destabilizing the rest of the economy. It should be noted, however, that if incomes of producers of different crops are not highly correlated, large shifts of income from agricultural producers as a group to consumers or vice versa would be rare, since the shifts in some crops in a given year would tend to be offset by the opposite shifts in other crops.

It is seldom clear in discussions of stabilization whether the objective of actual or proposed policy is to stabilize prices, incomes, or some other variable. Additionally, sometimes the task involves insulating domestic markets from variations in international prices, whereas in other instances the source of variation is instability in domestic production. In all instances, the effect of government intervention per se and its costs have been inadequately evaluated. The only effort being made in this study is to initiate an analysis of these issues, and the findings offered in the rest of this chapter on seasonal and annual variations in prices will need to be further analyzed.

Indexes of variability and of differences between realized and predicted values of three variables for different crops have been computed: prices, profit—net income per ton and gross income per ton, if annual cost figures were unavailable—and annual return on land investment. Domestic prices at the producer and consumer levels are more stable and predictable than are international prices for the crops considered, namely, coffee, rice, sugar, wheat, cotton, corn, barley, and potatoes. It is not clear whether on the average this finding is obtained from government intervention, or is the consequence of farmers' and traders' own storage and other efforts, or both. For coffee, the stabilization program of FEDERACAFE has had a significant effect. There may also be some additional fragmentary evidence on the price stabilization effects of government policy: with respect to potatoes, with little or no government intervention, the variability of domestic prices has not been much less than the international variation, whereas in the other cases, as already noted, variation in prices is less domestically than internationally.

On the other hand, price is perhaps not as good an indicator of risk or uncertainty as income and profitability. It is well known that stabilizing prices does not necessarily stabilize income or profitability. An example is a product with random production and a demand elasticity of unity. In such an instance, although production fluctuates from year to year, low production is offset by high prices and vice versa, so income is stable in the market without any intervention. On the other hand, if the price in this instance is stabilized by an external agency, the income of producers fluctuates with production, and price stabilization destabilizes income. For potatoes, total income and income per hectare seem to be more stable in domestic prices than in international prices by about the same amount as other crops. Judged by these criteria, therefore, little credit can be attributed to government programs in stabilizing farm income.

In any event, for all crops, including potatoes but excepting cotton, producer prices and incomes vary less if they are evaluated at domestic prices than at international prices. In selected instances, such as coffee, domestic price stabilization can be attributed to policy, but such a relation is less clear in other instances. Furthermore, income stabilization appears to be achieved, at least in respect to potatoes, with much less price stabilization than in other instances. It appears that with or without government intervention, domestic variables tend to be less volatile and, to a lesser extent, more predictable than international variables. It is not clear why this should be true, though a study in Malaysia found that producer prices were naturally buffered from external fluctuations because middleman margins were positively correlated with these prices.

Addressing Year-to-Year Instability

Any plan that solves the microeconomic problem of production risk by breaking the link between the income of producers and the expenditures of consumers may exacerbate the macroeconomic destabilization problem. With no stabilization plan, agricultural production and price shifts cause transfers of income between producers and consumers of agricultural commodities. In years when producers' incomes and their expenditures on nonagricultural commodities are low, consumers' expenditures on agricultural products are also low, and their expenditures on nonagricultural commodities are high. Thus the overall demand for the nonagricultural commodities tends to stay at a constant level, although it may fluctuate somewhat because of differences between agricultural producers and consumers in marginal propensities to consume. But suppose the link between producer income and consumer expenditure were to be broken—in a case in which producer income is stabilized by the provision of countercyclical credit, for example, with concessionary credit made available to producers in bad years. Consumers' expenditures on nonagricultural products would be high, as before, but they would no longer be offset by a decline in producers' expenditures on these products. Shifts in total expenditures would be more pronounced, and the net effect of stabilizing producers' income would be destabilization of nonagricultural demand. It can also be shown that in general there is no presumption that a buffer-stock scheme would stabilize nonagricultural demand; it might well destabilize it.

Export Price Stabilization

For internationally traded crops, domestic prices can be stabilized by import or export taxes or subsidies without breaking the link between producers' income and consumers' expenditures. A law approved by the congress facilitates the use of variable export incentives to stabilize domestic prices of exportables. With the CAT system, changes in an export subsidy rate were made administratively, but only once a year. Under the new system, CERT, the rates—five levels, with a maximum of 25 percent, announced by Decree 637 of 1984—are expected to be changed more often, greatly increasing the flexibility of the system. When the world price of a product increases, its rate can be decreased quickly, thus preventing its domestic price from rising very much; the opposite can take place when its world price falls. As noted, this kind of plan has the advantage that consumers' expenditures are still linked to producers' incomes, avoiding the macroeconomic side effects of some other stabilization plans. It is also probably less burdensome to the economy than many other possible plans, such as direct import management by the government and quotas.

One limitation, however, is that its scope of coverage is limited to exports. It is, of course, possible to expand the coverage to importables, as the European Community (EC) does with its variable levies, but in any event it cannot be used for nontraded items. A second limitation is that the size of the export subsidies is limited by GATT. (In fact, the main purpose of the flexible plan is to allow incentives to be changed quickly if other signatories to GATT complain; the price stabilization function is secondary.) As a practical matter, this may not be very important for some crops, but may be a real limitation on the ability to stabilize the prices of others.

One disadvantage of this sort of plan is that there is a temptation to use it to increase distortions of production incentives beyond what they would be otherwise. The EC has used its variable levy system not only for stabilization, for example, but also for protection. Certainly, it is possible to stabilize prices without increasing average protection of a good beyond existing levels, but it is probably difficult politically. For an import that is not protected now, this would involve taxing imports in years of low world prices and subsidizing them when world prices are high. It may be quite difficult to subsidize imports in the face of the opposition of domestic producers. If the stabilization efforts should produce greater protection from foreign competition, the economic costs may be high.

A second disadvantage is the economic inefficiency involved in failing to react to world market signals. Economic efficiency demands, for example, that an export product be produced and exported at a level such that its marginal cost is equal to its price. But if producers are insulated from world prices, the price on which they base production decisions is not the price that reflects the true social value of the product. If producer prices are stabilized, a country will not export enough of an export product when world prices are high to take full advantage of the good prices, and it will export too much when world prices are low. Rough estimates of this kind of efficiency or welfare cost—defined as the sum of loss in producer and consumer surpluses in comparison with a situation without interventions—are presented in table 5-2 for several crops. While the annual costs for any single crop are not overwhelming, the cumulative value of these costs carried into the indefinite future can be substantial. It should be noted, however, that these are welfare losses from perfect price stabilization. To the extent that a price stabilization scheme does not make the price perfectly stable, the costs will be correspondingly less.

A third disadvantage is that the plan requires government officials to make judgments about whether observed world price movements are transitory or part of a long-run trend. If the movements are part of a trend, but are thought to be transitory, the rate will be adjusted in the expectation that it will be readjusted when the price returns to its previous level. Since the price will never return to this level, the adjustment becomes a permanent change in protection of the good. This disadvantage could be mitigated to some extent by basing the CERT adjustment on the deviation from the long-run price. This long-run price would be recomputed each year as a moving average of previous years. When the price moved to a new level as part of

Table 5-2. *Welfare Cost of Domestic Price Stabilization for Some Import and Export Crops*
(million 1975 pesos)

Crop	Annual welfare cost	Net present value of cost[a]
Wheat	59.4	848.6
Corn	60.9	870.0
Barley	0.9	12.9
Rice	231.7	3,310.0
Cotton	108.6	1,551.4
Potatoes	126.3	1,804.3

a. Net present value of an infinite stream of the annual cost, evaluated using a real interest rate of 7 percent.
Source: See appendix E.

a long-run trend, this would at first appear to be a large deviation, leading to a large compensating adjustment in the rate. But as the price remained at its new level, it would be seen as less and less of a deviation, and the adjustment would become smaller each year.

Futures Market

Colombia might consider diminishing the risks involved in agricultural production and processing by allowing producers and processors access to futures markets. Hedging in futures markets does not stabilize incomes, but it does eliminate uncertainty about price, which is one of the problems about which the government is justifiably concerned. Eliminating risk in this manner can be, by and large, without cost to the government, and it is free of any efficiency costs as well, differing in both respects from the support price policy of IDEMA and such price stabilization plans as CERT.

HEDGING FOR RISK REDUCTION. Hedging involves the buying and selling of futures contracts in such a way that movements in the value of the contracts offset the movements in the price of the commodity that the hedger will buy or sell in the future. An idealized hedging transaction might proceed as follows:[3] An importer of wheat who will need to buy wheat on December 1 buys a futures contract on a U.S. commodity exchange calling for delivery of wheat on that date, paying $150 a ton. The contract is an enforceable agreement, and if he wanted, the importer could accept delivery of the wheat. But, for any of several reasons, the importer may not wish to buy the wheat through the futures market and need not accept delivery to relieve himself of the risk of paying a price different from $150. Suppose, for example, that on November 30, the spot price of wheat—that is, the price for immediate delivery—is $160 a ton. Then his futures contract, which on this date is essentially a contract for immediate delivery, is worth $160. The importer could sell his contract for $160, making a profit of $10 on his transaction in the futures market. He could then apply this profit to buying wheat from another source for $160, paying $10 more than he expected to pay. He would finally have paid, in effect, a price of $150. (Note that if the price of wheat from this source is not $160, then the final price he has in effect paid is not exactly $150. But as long as the prices of wheat asked by his source are well correlated with prices in the U.S. market, the profits or losses in futures market transactions will tend to offset movements in his prices and decrease his risk accordingly.)

Similarly, an exporter of, say, cotton could reduce his risk by hedging. If the exporter wished to sell cotton on December 1 at an assured price, he could sell a futures contract for delivery on that date at the going price for such a contract—say, eighty cents a pound. On December 1, if the actual price he received for his crop was seventy cents a pound, he would nevertheless receive in effect a price of eighty cents, because he could liquidate his position in the futures market—that is, buy back the contracts he sold for eighty cents—at a price of seventy cents, thereby making a profit of ten cents a pound.

OTHER ADVANTAGES. In addition to the advantage of giving importers and exporters the opportunity to reduce risk from price fluctuations, participation in futures markets would have an important concomitant advantage.[4] The spread between the current spot price and the futures contract price provides valuable information on the way the market expects the price to move, since the futures contract price is a good predictor of the spot price that will prevail on the date the contract matures. This kind of information is valuable in making decisions about storage and inventory control. One analyst argues that this function of futures markets is of greater value than the reduction of price uncertainty.[5]

POLICY PROBLEMS. While the value of futures markets, especially as they relate to reduction of risk, has been widely recognized by academic and government sources, their use by Colombians has been rare. In fact, it appears that only three economic agents have used futures markets—for several reasons.[6] First, and perhaps foremost, government exchange controls have made participation difficult. The government has, to some extent, been reluctant to authorize the use of foreign exchange for this purpose for fear that hedgers will begin to speculate and require large quantities of foreign exchange to pay their losses. Even in those instances in which it is willing to do so, the licensing procedure is time-consuming and does not allow hedgers much flexibility in the timing of purchases and sales of contracts.

Second, strict controls on imports decrease the usefulness of hedging. As implied by the foregoing examples, for maximum reduction of risk the physical commodity must be purchased in the same market as the futures contract. Otherwise, even on the contract maturation date, the value of the contract may differ from the value of the commodity. Import controls make the purchase of commodities in world markets more difficult. Of course, some reduction of risk is still possible, to the extent that world and domestic prices are well correlated, but the effectiveness of hedging is reduced. Similarly, for goods imported by IDEMA, or imports of which are licensed by IDEMA, hedging is made less effective in reducing risk by the fact that decisions are made a very short time before the importation actually occurs.

Third, the unpredictability of government trade policy makes hedging riskier. If an importer hedges in the futures market, planning to import a commodity, for example, and the government then places that import on the prior-license list, the importer is in effect changed from a hedger to a pure speculator, and his risk has increased manifold. Fourth, for some agents hedging is not very useful because prices are controlled by the government, a policy that makes prices on the whole predictable. This is true of producers of crops whose future support prices are fixed and are announced before planting time. It is also true of export crops to the extent that their domestic prices are fixed by the CERT plan. This factor appears to have had much to do with the decision of one cloth manufacturer to stop hedging after the government began fixing domestic cotton prices. Finally, inadequate information about the value of futures markets may also help explain why they are rarely used.

Some of these problems would be mitigated by the development of a domestic futures market. In the long run, it is possible that the Bolsa Agropecuaria will develop into a domestic futures market. In fact, contracts are now available through the Bolsa which call for delivery—in 150 days—of crops that are nonexistent when the contract is signed. But since these contracts are not tradable, the transfer of risk to speculators is not possible. The Bolsa also has quite limited market participation—only about 2 percent of Colombia's agricultural output is sold through the Bolsa—and is completely dominated by IDEMA, which participates in 70–80 percent of all the transactions—73 percent in 1982. The Bolsa is still young and is struggling to work out a number of problems that prevent it from attracting greater participation. In time, it may succeed in attracting a sufficient number of participants to make IDEMA a relatively small part of the Bolsa and to develop the economies of scale that are necessary if a futures market is to function efficiently, but until this comes about, there is little chance that it can function effectively as a futures market.[7] In the meantime the government might remove obstacles to participation in international futures markets.

Seasonal Price Fluctuations

One objective of the government is to ensure that food prices do not rise unduly in the periods between harvests. Such seasonal stabilization can in principle be facilitated by varying the timing and quantities of imports and exports of agricultural products. In practice the country's internal storage system is equally important in assuring adequate supplies and moderating prices in the nonharvest months. This section will be concerned with the effects of storage policies, with particular attention to two issues: first, whether the existing system of subsidized loans for storage, the bonos de prenda (BP), is desirable and efficient, and second, whether IDEMA's sales policies tend to discourage private storage activities.

Considerable storage capacity is owned by IDEMA, industrial processors, producers' associations, and twelve general facilities, called Almacenes Generales de Depósito (AGD), which are subsidiaries of private banks.[8] Identifiable on-farm storage capacity (excluding coffee plantations) in 1977 was only 0.91 percent of the total.[9] This figure is probably an understatement of the available capacity, but field observations suggest that on-farm capacity may be limited. Most individual storers use rented space in AGDs, which are generally owned by the banks with which those storers do business. Since some banks specialize, for example, by catering to the needs of growers of particular crops, these banks also specialize in the storage of particular commodities. When someone stores a commodity in an AGD, he receives a deposit certificate, or Certificado de Depósito (CD), specifying the quality and quantity of the merchandise. This certificate then becomes a title to the property and can be bought and sold in the market. It may be returned to the bank as collateral for a loan under the BP system, which will be described below.

Subsidized Credit for Storage

Under the bonos de prenda system, a bank may make a loan at a subsidized interest rate, using the CD as collateral, and rediscount part of the loan through the Central Bank. Only certain crops qualify for loans under this system, but the list is fairly extensive: African palm oil, sesame, cotton fiber, cottonseed, anise, paddy rice, cocoa, coffee, barley, sisal, beans, powdered milk, corn, potatoes, sorghum, soybeans, tobacco, wheat, and products for export. A serious limitation is that only growers, processors, and IDEMA are eligible for loans under this system, thus excluding wholesalers and other middlemen. In general, the loans can be for as much as 80 percent of the value of the stored crop, evaluated according to a basic price established by the Monetary Board.[10] This share is known as the discount margin.

The subsidy element in the BP loans can be substantial and has changed quite a bit since the system was established, as shown in table 5-3. Of course, the "subsidy" is not measured strictly by the difference between the market rate and the BP rate, because the subsidized loan is made on only 80 percent of the value, based on the basic price, which may deviate substantially from the market value. That is, to use the BP system is as if a storer incurred all the normal storage costs, but received a rebate in the amount of $0.8\ P_bQ(r_m - r_s)$ a year, where P_b is the basic price, Q is the quantity stored, r_m is the real market interest rate, and r_s is the real subsidized rate.[11] This subsidy element depends as much on P_b as it does on the difference between r_m and r_s. The value P_b may vary with the passage of time and with different crops; therefore, the subsidy element is different in different years and

Table 5-3. *Market Interest Rates and Bonos de Prenda Rates, 1970–81*
(percent)

Year	Market interest[a]	Rate of inflation[b]	Real market interest (ex post)	Interest rate bonos de prenda	
				Nominal[c]	Real (ex post)
1970	13.3	7.2	6.1	10.0	2.8
1971	16.4	12.6	3.8	10.0	– 2.6
1972	15.6	14.1	1.5	10.0	– 4.1
1973	20.3	22.1	– 1.8	10.0	– 12.1
1974	30.4	25.2	5.2	15.0	– 10.2
1975	23.8	17.5	6.3	17.0	– 0.5
1976	22.4	25.4	– 3.0	17.0	– 8.4
1977	22.9	27.5	– 4.6	17.0	– 10.5
1978	25.9	19.7	6.2	17.0	– 2.7
1979	36.5	26.5	10.0	17.0	– 9.5
1980	41.5	24.5	17.0	24.0	– 0.5
1981	52.5	25.6	26.9	28.8	3.2

a. CAT, 120-day maturity, average annual rate.
b. Consumer price index.
c. Average discount rate.
Sources: Calculations by the DNP, based on Banco de la Republica, *Resoluciones de la Junta Monetaria*, various issues, and the Asociación Bancaria (Asobancaria, the banking association).

with different crops. Table SA-20 shows the evolution of the ratio P_b/P_m for different crops, where P_m is the market-producer price of the product. The subsidy can be written as a fraction of the market value of the crop.[12]

Table 5-4 shows the value of the subsidy element as a percentage of market value for several crops in 1980 and 1981, the last years for which full information was readily available. (Where appropriate, the 0.80 has been adjusted to 0.70 or 0.75.) These figures are expressed as annual percentages and are thus directly comparable to the financial cost of storage. Storing barley with a subsidy of 12.05 percent and a market interest rate of 41.5 percent, for example, is exactly as costly as storing barley at a market interest rate of 29.45 percent (= 41.5 percent – 12.05 percent), with no subsidy given. So from the point of view of storers the BP system in 1980 and 1981 can be considered equivalent to a reduction in the market interest rate by the amounts shown in table 5-2. The subsidy rates vary from a low of 5.12 percent (palm oil in 1980) to a high of 17.26 percent (barley in 1981), with unweighted averages of 9.65 percent and 13.55 percent for the two years.

Both the discount margin and the interest rate charged on the rediscount are set by the Monetary Board. As of July 29, 1981, the discount margin was 40 percent and the interest rate on the rediscount was 25 percent. At the same time, the discount rate on the BP was 30 percent and the margin of discount was 80 percent for most crops; that is, for every $100 worth of stored crops, evaluated at the official

Table 5-4. *Value of Subsidy to Storers as Percentage of Market Value of Stored Crops, 1980–81*
(percent)

Crop	Subsidy[a]	
	1980	1981
Barley	12.05	17.26
Beans	6.41	11.35
Cocoa	10.91	13.43
Corn	7.17	12.86
Cotton fiber	14.32	14.28
Cotton seed	10.30	14.09
Palm oil	5.12	14.53
Rice (paddy)	10.29	12.45
Sesame	13.23	13.27
Sorghum	8.44	12.14
Soybeans	8.47	15.67
Wheat	8.98	11.32
Unweighted average	9.64	13.55

a. $S = 0.8(P_b/P_m)(r_m - r_s)$, where

S = annual subsidy,
P_b = basic price,
P_m = market price,
r_m = market interest rate,
r_s = subsidized *bonos de prenda* discount rate.

For wheat and palm oil, 0.8 in this formula was replaced with 0.7.
Sources: Computed from tables 5-3, SA-20, and SA-21.

basic prices, a storer could borrow $80 from the commercial bank at an interest rate of 30 percent; the bank could then rediscount $32 (40 percent of $80) at the Central Bank at an interest rate of 25 percent. The bank's effective rate of return on its loan can be computed as $[0.30 - (0.25)(0.40)] / (1 - 0.40) = 0.33$. It is clear that in recent years the incentive for banks to make loans through BP rather than through normal market channels has declined, contributing to the decline in the real volume of BP loans.

Costs of Subsidized Credit

First, it is costly to the government and to lending institutions to subsidize loans to storers. Table SA-22 shows the total cost of the program for each major product in 1981 and how the cost is divided between banks and the government.[13] Although the exact ratio varies from crop to crop, depending on the ratio of discounts to rediscounts, in general private banks bear at least as much of the cost of subsidizing crop storage as does the government and much more of the cost of subsidizing manufactured and export goods.

The main recipients of the subsidy are a few large firms in concentrated industries. In 1978, the last year for which these data were readily available, one firm used 18.6 percent of the total loans rediscounted, the largest four firms used 46.6 percent, and the largest eight firms 59.1 percent.[14] This tendency is even more striking in certain industries: in cotton fiber, barley, tobacco, and cocoa, four firms used between 85 percent and 100 percent of the loans rediscounted. The use of the subsidy by growers, including growers' associations, was only 1 percent of the total.

If the banking system is more or less competitive, the portion of the cost borne by it—half or more—would ultimately be passed on to savers (in the form of lower interest on deposits) and to borrowers (in the form of higher interest charged on loans). It was not possible to estimate the relative magnitudes of these burdens without a detailed analysis of elasticities of supply and demand for lendable funds. The portion of the cost paid in the first instance by the government is ultimately financed by an "inflation tax." The rediscounts of the BP by the Central Bank are financed by the creation of money. This can cause a rise in the general price level, in effect taxing the holders of cash balances and transferring purchasing power from holders of cash balances to the recipients of the subsidy. In general, the inflation tax would be expected to be regressive; that is, the rate of taxation—as a percentage of wealth—declines with the absolute level of wealth, because the poor hold a larger share of their wealth in the form of cash. On balance, therefore, the BP system operates to transfer resources from savers, investors, and holders of cash to a relatively small number of industrial firms.

The second type of cost involved concerns efficiency. The system subsidizes firms' storage activities, and by doing so, it encourages the diversion of investment from other activities to storage, to such an extent that the true social marginal value of the storage is less than the marginal value of alternative investments. It is difficult to estimate the magnitude of the efficiency loss without a detailed analysis of elasticities. The size of the distortion is certainly large enough to create a large loss, however, especially for certain crops (see table 5-2). It is, of course, possible that the subsidy to storage could be optimal in the presence of other distortions. This does not seem likely, however, because the type of distortion that would make this subsidy optimal—subsidies of a similar size for other investment activities of the firm—are not generally present.

Reforms of the System

First, if the government desires to encourage agricultural storage, it could do so in a way that would benefit all storage activity. There does not seem to be any legitimate reason for excluding middlemen from the subsidy, especially since the principal alternative beneficiaries at present are large processing firms.

Second, the subsidy should be divorced from the money supply function of the

Central Bank. This linkage between rediscount of BP and the expansion of the monetary base has two peculiar effects. One is that seasonal increases and decreases in agricultural production and the consequent demand for storage to some extent tend to reduce control of the supply by the monetary authorities on a year-to-year basis and introduce a seasonality into the monetary base. This problem could be serious if the rediscount formed an important part of the monetary base, although that part was only around 1.8 percent in 1984. The effect on monetary stability is actually greater than this figure would imply, however, because changes in BP rediscounts are reflected, peso for peso, in changes in the monetary base. Changes in the base, in turn, change the money supply through a multiplier effect. Thus, for each peso by which BP rediscounts vary, the money supply changes by several pesos. If BP rediscounts should ever again form a significant share of the monetary base—8.4 percent, for example, as in 1974—this would be a source of concern.

The more serious linkage runs the other way: changes in monetary policy tend to have a direct effect on storage activity. In periods of tight monetary policy, the rediscounts available for BP tend to be contracted, discouraging storage. In one sense, this is as it should be; tight money always raises interest rates, raising the cost of storage. When monetary policy affects storage through its intermediate effect on interest rates, however, it also affects other competing investment activities, both private and public, in the same way. Given the way in which the BP system is set up, it is not possible to assure this result; BP rediscounts may be affected to a greater or lesser extent with respect to alternative investments by monetary changes, depending on political decisions.

Perhaps a better system would be to include interest subsidies for storage as a line item in each year's budget. A person taking out the type of loan currently eligible for BP would be charged a nonsubsidized rate of interest by the bank but would then be reimbursed directly by the government for some part of the interest cost, perhaps using the bank as an administrative agent. Presumably the fraction would remain constant for several years. In this way, storage would always be given the same advantage as other investments, but its cost would rise or fall as it should along with the cost of other investments as monetary or real factors in the economy caused the interest rate to rise or fall. An additional advantage is that it would finance the government's share of the subsidy from general revenues, rather than by the creation of money, thus avoiding the possibly regressive inflation tax. The share of the subsidy now financed by the banks could be taken over by the government—perhaps financed by a tax on the banks—or could be left with the banks by mandating that they give storers a rate higher than the current discount rate (since banks would no longer be partially reimbursed by subsidized rediscounts) but below the market rate.

Third, the mechanism for allocating credit among various crops might be changed. At present the amount of credit available to a storer depends on the basic price set for each crop by the Monetary Board. This price is used to establish a value for the physical quantity stored, and this value is the basis for the size of the subsidized loan available. These basic prices have little connection to market prices but rather, to a large extent, are set on the basis of political considerations. As might be expected, the basic prices are the subject of lobbying efforts by producers' associations.[15] Consequently, the ratio of basic prices to market prices—and the subsidy element—vary widely among products, and the products with weak producers' associations generally lose out. The contrast between the subsidies available for cotton, with a strong producers' association, and beans, an important food crop with a relatively weak producers' association, can be seen in table 5-2. This distortion tends to cause inefficiency by encouraging storage of some crops more than of others, with no apparent rationale.

As table 5-2 demonstrates, the size of the bias tends to change in time. When the ratio of basic prices to market prices of cotton and beans, for example, is compared, cotton always has an advantage, but the magnitude of the advantage varies from 1 percent (in 1976) to 223 percent (in 1980). This bias could be eliminated by setting the ratio of basic price to market price at the same level for all crops. The overall ratio could be adjusted each year as a means of controlling the demand for subsidized credit. Alternatively, the ratio could be set at unity every year, and the credit could be rationed by changing the rediscount interest rate or the margin of rediscount. Of course, this rationing would all be unnecessary if the whole scheme were revised in such a way that basic prices would be set at the same level as market prices each year, and the demand for storage loans each year would be determined by a uniformly subsidized interest rate. The average demand for several years, of course, would be determined by the size of the subsidy offered.

IDEMA's Function in Storage

IDEMA is the single most important agricultural storage agent in Colombia. It is full owner of 10.7 percent of total storage capacity, is partial owner of another 5.6 percent (Almagrario and Almapopular), and sometimes rents space from privately owned AGDS.[16] It is much more important in the storage of some crops—especially rice, wheat, corn, and sorghum—than others. As indicated by table 5-5, in some products, IDEMA's storage and sales policies can have a significant effect on market conditions, including incentives for private storage. The profitability of storage is determined by the difference between the purchase price of a commodity and the sale price after storage compared to storage costs.[17] In a competitive storage industry, storage each year would be sufficient to ensure that, for the marginal firm or the marginal units, the expected price spread was just sufficient to cover the costs. The policies of IDEMA affect the price spread.

GOALS AND POLICIES OF IDEMA. The pricing policies of IDEMA are rooted in two of its perceived goals, in addition to supporting producer prices: to keep consumer prices low and to aid the government in its fight against inflation. In the past, these goals have caused IDEMA to pursue unrealistic pricing policies. After buying and

Table 5-5. *IDEMA's Share of Total Stocks of Selected Crops, 1979–81*
(percent)

Year	Month	White rice	Wheat	Imported corn and sorghum
1979	June	32	89	21
	December	22	16	19
1980	June	29	42	11
	December	39	32	59
1981	June	38	56	51
	December	14	52	47

Source: Computed from *IDEMA: Dos años de labores, 1980–81* (Bogotá: IDEMA, 1982), cuadro no. 12, p. 42.

storing commodities, IDEMA would sell them for little if anything more than it paid, thereby failing to cover its own storage costs. Its recent policy has been an attempt to operate on a financially sounder basis, while still meeting the same goals. It comprises the following three operational rules: (1) the selling price is not to exceed an amount equal to the purchase price plus carrying cost of 3.5 percent a month; (2) the selling price is not to rise more than 20 percent a year, in any event; (3) if market conditions at any time are such that the market price is lower than the price that would be indicated by rule 1, IDEMA is to sell at the prevailing market price. Rule 1 reflects the goal of financial responsibility, rule 2 reflects the goal of fighting inflation, since 20 percent is the government's inflation target, and rule 3 reflects the goal of assuring low consumer prices.

EFFECTS OF IDEMA'S POLICIES. To the extent that the policy outlined above is effective, it is likely to have a negative effect on private storage, although the analysis would have to be revised if the actual policy were to function differently in practice. First, even if prices always rose 3.5 percent a month, this would be insufficient to cover private storage costs. IDEMA calculated the cost of storage as 3.5 percent by using the subsidized BP rate of interest as the financial cost of storage, then adding its other costs, such as physical spoilage. BP loans are only available, however, to cover 80 percent or less of the value of the stored crops evaluated using the basic prices. The remaining 20 percent must be financed at the market rate. In addition, since the ratio of the basic price to the market price is less than 1 for almost all crops and differs substantially among crops, the true financial cost of storage is always higher than the BP rate and differs from crop to crop. It also changes with variations in the market interest rate.

Table 5-3 showed the direct interest subsidy equivalents of the BP system in 1980 and 1981. That is, with the schedule of basic prices in those years, and market and BP rates as shown in tables 5-3, SA-21, and SA-22, the effective financial cost of storage was reduced by the amount shown in table 5-3 for each crop. The effective simple annual financial storage cost of rice, for example, with a subsidy equivalent of 10.29 percent, was 31.21 percent (41.5 percent – 10.29 percent) in 1980, or, since the interest is compounded bimonthly, a true cost of about 36 percent a year or 3 percent per month. IDEMA sources suggest that when the BP rate is 24 percent, as it was in 1980, the financial cost of storage might be 2.31 percent a month. This may be a substantial underestimate of the true cost, and the underestimate is even more serious for crops whose subsidy equivalent is smaller. Obviously, the magnitude of the underestimate becomes smaller as the market interest rate approaches the BP rate, but it would always be an underestimate unless the two were equal. In addition, the 3.5 percent figure seems to be an estimate of IDEMA's marginal cost; that is, it does not include fixed costs, such as the cost of construction of storage facilities, nor does it adequately cover other nonfinancial costs, which are estimated to be significant.[18] Consequently, storage would be uneconomical for private storers—and, indeed, for IDEMA also—if IDEMA succeeded in limiting the price increase to 3.5 percent a month.

Second, the 20 percent a year ceiling on price increases would make storage for a fairly long term uneconomical in a period of 20 percent general inflation. (And, presumably, it is because inflation is expected to be 20 percent or greater that the 20 percent ceiling was chosen as an anti-inflation tool.) The fundamental reason for this is that the price of the stored crop must rise in *real* terms—that is, at a rate greater than the rate of inflation—in order to cover the cost of storage. Consider the case most favorable to a policy of limited price increases, a hypothetical crop that is harvested almost the year round and has to be stored for consumption for only a short time; even so, a 20 percent ceiling is insufficient. Suppose, for example, that the harvest is spread nearly evenly over nine months of the year, so that consumption must come from storage for only three months. In a period of 20 percent annual inflation, the price of the crop would rise during the nine months of harvest by about 15 percent because of the general inflation. After the end of the harvest, when consumption must come from stocks, suppose that IDEMA regulates its stocks so that the price rises 3.5 percent a month. At the end of one month and one week of storage, the price will be 20 percent higher than it was at the beginning of the harvest about ten months earlier. If IDEMA then holds the price constant, storage will be a losing proposition for the rest of the year.

In general, if the underlying rate of inflation were about 20 percent, the price would rise 20 percent from the beginning of one harvest to the beginning of a harvest one year later. But this does not mean that the price during the year should not rise to a level higher than 20 percent above the original price. It must rise to a higher level in order to make it profitable to carry stocks, even though it will fall when the new harvest begins. That is to say, on average the price would behave as shown by the solid line in figure 5-1. If marginal consumption must come out of storage beginning at $t_0 + 9$, storers must be reimbursed for the real costs of carrying stocks—real interest costs, physical losses, and so on—over and above the nominal

Figure 5-1. *Inflation, Seasonal Price Rise, and Storers' Profits*

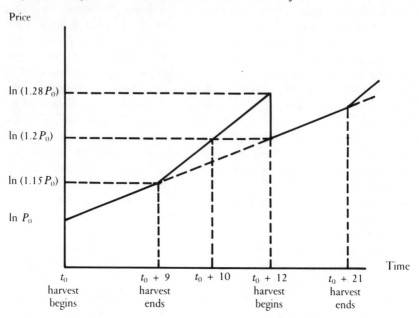

Price

$\ln (1.28 P_0)$

$\ln (1.2 P_0)$

$\ln (1.15 P_0)$

$\ln P_0$

t_0
harvest
begins

$t_0 + 9$
harvest
ends

$t_0 + 10$

$t_0 + 12$
harvest
begins

$t_0 + 21$
harvest
ends

Time

Source: Estimate based on price analysis for 1982.

gains in the value of their stocks caused by inflation. To place a 20 percent ceiling on price increases is to make storage for the last two months of the year unprofitable.

Finally, the interaction of rules 1 and 3 tend to make storage unprofitable on the average. The fact that profits from storage are stochastic is ignored. Storage decisions are normally based on expectations about the prices at which the stored crop will be sold in the future. When the crop is actually taken out of storage and sold, the price may be higher than expected, in which case profits are made, or the price may be lower, in which case losses are incurred. In a competitive market, the profits in some years balance the losses in other years, so on the average, costs of the marginal firm or marginal unit are just covered. But IDEMA's rule 1 guarantees that the price will not rise rapidly enough to do more than cover costs, even in the best of times. And rule 3 guarantees that in times when prices are lower than a firm expected them to be, it would lose money. There is fairly convincing prima facie evidence that IDEMA has suppressed the rate of price increase in at least one crop— rice—below what it must be to make private storage profitable. Castillo Niño examined the evidence from 1978 to 1982 and concluded that prices after harvest had frequently risen at a rate such that private storage would not generally have been profitable.[19]

Reform of IDEMA's policies in a variety of ways is now being studied and beginning to be executed, particularly in an effort to increase private-sector storage. In the future, to avoid displacement of private storage, the financial cost of storage could be calculated more realistically along the lines suggested here. So long as the BP loans are based on basic prices, the true financial cost will be different for each crop, and this should be reflected in a different pricing policy for each. Second, IDEMA should not try to act as an anti-inflationary tool, since it cannot suppress inflation by its pricing policies, and its attempts to do so will only distort its pricing decisions. Finally, if it is desirable to subsidize consumer prices, this might be done by lowering prices equally in all seasons rather than by decreasing the rate of price increase between harvests, in order to avoid long-term distortion of storage decisions and consumption patterns.

Policy Conclusions

The government has been considering ways and means of introducing greater price stability, particularly for internationally traded commodities. A variable export incentive scheme, CERT, is now in effect, and an export price stabilization fund to be financed by the private sector is now being studied.

An alternative and more efficient price-stabilizing scheme is that of allowing hedging in international futures markets, which would reduce price uncertainty for several imported products and some exported products. If importers and exporters could be encouraged to use international futures markets, it would provide the benefits of risk reduction directly to them and indirectly to domestic producers and consumers, to the extent that domestic prices move with international prices. In the absence of a viable domestic futures market, the government might consider taking steps to remove the obstacles to participation in international futures markets.

First, legitimate hedging might be exempted in certain ways from rules governing other foreign exchange transactions. So long as the futures market activity is truly hedging—that is, is coupled with a transaction for the physical commodity—the possibility of significant losses in foreign exchange are remote. General rules could be developed for this purpose to ensure that futures markets were not used for speculation but to leave potential users sufficient flexibility to hedge effectively. Such rules might limit the exemption from exchange controls to agents who actually deal in the commodity, limit futures market transactions to one set (buying and selling) per transaction in the physical commodity, and limit the size of the futures market transaction to the size of the transaction in the physical commodity.

Second, a commitment might be needed to exempt hedging from changes in trade policy during the period of the transaction. This step would eliminate the risk that a policy change would prevent a hedger from consummating the part of the transaction involving the physical commodity, changing the position of the hedger to that of a pure speculator. Third, futures market activity might be substituted for government control of domestic prices for reducing the uncertainty of producers. While prices guaranteed by the government remove the incentives for hedging, guaranteed prices are less efficient and more costly to the government, and they are perhaps no more effective in reducing uncertainty for producers. Fourth, import restrictions on agricultural commodities might be gradually eliminated, and hedging in more commodities might thereby be encouraged.

Storage permits the transfer of consumption from periods of low marginal value—that is, low price—to periods of high marginal value. Storage is costly, however, and the optimal amount of storage is therefore less than that required to make prices constant throughout the year. The optimal storage should, in fact, be much less than this in an economic environment such as that of Colombia, where the economic cost of storage is high because of the high returns on alternative investments. In general, market signals would be sufficient to give incentives for the optimal level of storage, and storage subsidies, such as the bonos de prenda, the subsidized credit system, are likely to be unnecessary.

The bonos de prenda system has subsidized storage of different crops at unequal rates, with no apparent economic rationale for the differences other than special circumstances and problems of individual products and the disparate ability of various beneficiaries to exert political pressure. The system causes transfers of income from savers, investors, and holders of cash to a relatively small number of large producers and creates an undesirable linkage between storage and the monetary base. If it were necessary to give a subsidy to storage, it would be better to include it as a line item in the federal budget and administer it as a direct rebate to anyone—producer, distributor, or manufacturer—who stores agricultural commodities. The amount of the rebate could be determined as some fixed fraction of the financial cost of storage—the opportunity cost of funds tied up in the stored commodity, for example—based on the true market value of the crop at the time of storage and the market rate of interest.

In the past, IDEMA has been expected to carry out such widely divergent and conflicting objectives as assuring high prices for producers and low prices for consumers, holding price increases over the course of the year to the target rate of inflation, making private storage profitable, and supporting itself financially. Its function is now being redefined to emphasize those goals that are consistent. If IDEMA's primary goal is to support producer prices, this goal might be more efficiently met through import adjustments alone rather than through the elaborate additional purchasing program now being used; if the aim is to improve the distribution of income through price support—which may not be an efficient instrument for this purpose—such an effect might be evaluated, explicitly recognized, and financed separately by the government.

IDEMA is in the process of reforming its policies so that for the medium term, the private sector will increase its participation in storage and marketing and the institution's financial burden will be reduced. In this connection, policies regarding price increases between harvest periods need to be changed if private storage is to become financially feasible on a larger scale and if IDEMA's financial losses are to be controlled. First, IDEMA should not be expected to help control inflation through its pricing policies, not only because of the inefficiencies generated but also because inflation is for the most part a macroeconomic phenomenon. Second, IDEMA should retain its goal of allowing prices to rise at a rate sufficient to cover storage costs, but its estimates of these costs need to be reconsidered. It would appear that the costs, both financial and nonfinancial, of storage are significantly underestimated at present. Probably the best guide to true storage costs would be the average historical rates of price increase during periods of minimal outside intervention. These figures for different crops could be considered along with direct cost estimates to decide upon more realistic target rates of price increase.

Notes

1. B. F. Massell, "Price Stabilization and Welfare," *Quarterly Journal of Economics*, vol. 83 (May 1969), pp. 285–98.

2. See, for instance, Yesid Castro Forero, "Precios agrícolas y su incidencia económica," *Revista nacional de agricultura*, no. 861 (February 1983).

3. A more detailed discussion is contained in Alfredo Fuentes Hernández, "Participación de Colombia en los mercados de futuros," *Revista nacional de agricultura*, no. 863 (June 1983), pp. 97–106.

4. Other agents, such as producers and consumers in domestic markets, could also reduce risks by hedging in international futures markets, to the extent that domestic prices are correlated with international prices, or by hedging in a domestic futures market.

5. Holbrook Working, "Futures Trading and Hedging," *American Economic Review*, vol.43, no. 3 (June 1953), pp. 314–43.

6. See Fuentes Hernández, "Participación de Colombia en los mercados de futuros," part 2, *Revista nacional de agricultura*, no. 864 (August 1983), pp. 109–20.

7. One of the necessary conditions for the smooth functioning of a futures market is that it be cheap to purchase and sell contracts, thus encouraging sufficient buying and selling to establish a legitimate market price at all times. This, in turn, means that brokers' commissions must be low. Unless market participation is quite heavy, brokers will not receive a competitive return on their labor, commissions will be increased, participation will decline further, and so on, until the market collapses. In addition, participation must be heavy enough to support a large number of brokers, so that collusion will be impossible and the operation of the market will be competitive.

8. Exceptions are Almagrario and Almapopular, which are also such general facilities but are partially owned by IDEMA and consequently are considered semiofficial rather than private. Almacafe is also an exception since it is owned by FEDERACAFE and not by a private bank.

9. According to a report of the Division de Regulación Técnica of the Ministry of Agriculture, "Capacidad instalada de almacenamiento y secamiento en bodegas y silos."

10. This share is 70 percent, rather than 80 percent, for palm oil, sisal, and wheat and 75 percent for export products.

11. Obviously, for the crops eligible for only a 70 percent or a 75 percent loan, the 0.8 should be replaced accordingly.

12. $[0.8 \, P_b \, Q \, (r_m - r_s)]/ P_m Q = 0.8 \, (P_b/ P_m)(r_m - r_s)$. Throughout this analysis, computations are based on the assumption that the interest rate is the rate paid on the full amount of the loan; that is, it is assumed that a rate of interest of 25 percent means the borrower pays $25 interest on a $100 loan. On some Colombian loans, the interest is taken out of the principal, so the interest rate is an understatement

of the true rate. On a loan at 25 percent, for example, the borrower would receive only $75 ($100 – $25), leading to a true rate of 33 percent (25/75). Computation of interest in this way would not alter the qualitative results of the analysis, although it would change the numbers. If interest is computed in this way, for example, the subsidy as a fraction of market value should be the following:

$$0.8 \ (P_b/P_m)(r_m - r_s)/(1 - r_m)(1 - r_s).$$

13. The cost in table SA-22 may be a slight underestimate for the following reason: the interest rate used as a market rate is the rate in the CAT market and is thus essentially a risk-free rate of interest. To the extent that BP loans are risky, the true market rate for them would be higher and the computed subsidy greater. Since these loans are well secured, however, it is doubtful that the risk premium on them would be very large in a free market.

14. Alvaro Silva, R. Monsalvo, and Gabriel Montes, "El almacenamiento de productos agropecuarios en Colombia," *Revista de planeación y desarrollo*, vol. 11, no. 3 (September–December 1979), p. 100. The four largest firms, not including IDEMA, used 43.0 percent of the total.

15. Silva and others, "El almacenamiento," pp. 92–93.

16. Figures are for 1979, the most recent year for which information is readily available; source: "Informe estadistico sobre la capacidad instalada en Colombia para almacenamiento de productos agrícolas" (Bogotá: OPSA, July 1980).

17. If goods are stored by the producer, not by a third party who purchases them for resale later, the purchase price is to be interpreted as the market price at the time the goods are placed in storage—that is, the opportunity cost.

18. John Nash, "Non-Financial Costs of Storage" (Washington, D.C.: World Bank, Latin America and the Caribbean Country Programs, Colombia Division, April 1984, processed).

19. Alvaro Castillo Niño, "Inestabilidad de los precios agrícolas" (Bogotá, 1983, processed).

6

Coffee Policy under Changing Prices and Technology

WHILE COFFEE has been to a large extent responsible for Colombia's economic advances during the 1970s, the difficulties of the coffee sector in the first half of the 1980s have included the buildup of stocks and related financial and economic policy dilemmas. Although overproduction may not necessarily continue indefinitely, developments in the early 1980s suggest the need for adjustments in domestic incentives and in supporting infrastructure in order to encourage an increase in the movement of certain resources into noncoffee activities. This chapter contains a review of price and nonprice policy options being considered by the authorities to address these current issues while protecting the long-term performance of the coffee economy.

Colombia's Coffee Economy

Coffee has represented a significant share of Colombian GDP and an overwhelming proportion of exports (see table 6-1). Coffee is grown on one million out of a total 4.5 million hectares of cultivated land. Nearly 50 percent of the coffee farms are less than 4 hectares. Coffee cultivation employs some 35 percent of the agricultural labor force on a full-time or part-time basis, while approximately 10 percent of the total population are considered to depend directly on production, processing, and primary marketing of coffee for their livelihood. Coffee has also been a significant source of government revenue. Between 1975 and 1979 the ad valorem export tax on coffee contributed about 9 percent of the annual current revenue of the national government before declining to about 6.6 percent in 1980 and 3.4 percent in 1981, owing to a decline both in coffee prices and in the tax rate itself.

During the 1970s coffee production expanded faster than the average rate of growth of agriculture, but no clear difference emerges once the 1980s are included in the analysis.[1] Coffee has accounted for an estimated fifth of the incremental

Table 6-1. *Trends in the Share of Coffee in GDP and Exports, 1970–82*
(ratio of values in current prices)

Year	GDP[a]	Exports[b]	Agricultural GDP[c]	Agricultural exports[d]
1970	6.5	63.5	23.9	82.2
1971	5.0	58.0	19.6	79.2
1972	5.3	49.7	20.2	73.5
1973	5.7	50.8	21.3	78.2
1974	4.2	43.9	16.0	73.0
1975	5.0	45.9	18.7	67.2
1976	7.5	55.4	27.2	78.3
1977	9.6	61.3	32.5	80.9
1978	7.7	65.9	29.1	85.4
1979	6.7	60.8	25.3	84.0
1980	5.8	59.8	25.2	78.6
1981	3.8	48.1	18.7	70.7
1982	3.6	50.5	18.1	76.0

Note: Only the direct contribution of coffee within the agricultural sector is included.

a. Based on table SA-5, using DANE data on GDP at current market prices.

b. Based on table SA-8, using export figures in current U.S. dollars.

c. From table SA-5; using DANE's categories, agriculture in this column is defined to include pergamino coffee (01), other agriculture (02), livestock (03), coffee processing (08), and sugar (12).

d. From table SA-8; agricultural exports are defined to include coffee, livestock, bananas, sugar, flowers, cotton, tobacco, and rice.

Sources: DANE, *Cuentas nacionales de Colombia*, revision 3, 1970–82; Banco de la Republica; and FEDERACAFE.

growth of the agricultural sector since 1970. The greater part of this contribution has stemmed from improvements in yield, since (according to official statistics) there was no net increase in total land under cultivation during this period. The value of coffee exports also expanded in real terms at a rate slightly higher than the average for all agricultural exports. Coffee has represented an average of some 77 percent of agricultural exports since 1970; in the economy as a whole this share of coffee in the value of exports averaged about 55 percent.

Coffee Technology

Three main techniques are practiced in Colombia: traditional technology (primarily for *tipica*), shade technology, and sun technology. The latter two are used in cultivation of the *caturra* variety, which became commercially available in Colombia around the mid 1970s and was increasingly adopted as coffee prices rose during the second half of the 1970s. Yields vary significantly among the three techniques. A FEDERACAFE survey suggests that the shade and sun methods increase yields on the average by 2 and 2.83 times, respectively, over the traditional technology. In density of planting, whereas traditional coffee plantings average 1,800 trees per hectare, the new *caturra* varieties average 4,000 trees per hectare under shade and 4,500 trees per hectare under sun technology.[2] Under shade, the available light is reduced so that coffee trees are planted at a wider spacing, with fewer trees per hectare. Both the new shade plantings and the traditional plantings are in most instances grown under the shade of trees and banana plants, frequently a source of additional revenue. Another important difference between the technologies is that whereas traditional plantings are seldom fertilized, *caturra* coffee in the sun uses about 1,500 kilograms of fertilizer per hectare, and in the shade about 910 kilograms per hectare. The *caturra* plantings use more man-days per hectare than traditional plantings. On a man-days per kilo of coffee basis, however, the sun technology uses slightly more and the shade technology slightly less labor than does traditional.

Estimates of labor requirements given in table 6-2 mask considerable variations among farms that use the same techniques but differ in planting densities and are at different stages of the production cycle. One hectare of *caturra* grown in sun at a density of 5,000 trees per hectare, for example, may require as little as 96 man-days in the second year after planting, or as many as 402 man-days in its fourth year, when it reaches peak production. While the shift from traditional technology to the new would increase total labor requirements per hectare, the effect on total labor use may *not* be positive—and might even be marginally negative—when the higher yields of the new techniques in the face of an output constraint have been taken into account. The new technology is also likely to make labor use more seasonal, compounding the problems of a large migrant labor force. Each hectare converted from traditional technology to the new shade method increases labor use for cultivation by only 31 man-days but increases labor use during the harvest periods by 60 man-days. These problems could be mitigated by diversification in the coffee-

Table 6-2. *Labor Use, by Type of Planting*
(man-days per hectare a year)

	Technology		
Labor	*Traditional*	Caturra *shade*	Caturra *sun*
Cultivation	34	65	83
Harvest	65	125	180
Total	99	190	263

Note: FEDERACAFE quotes different estimates of labor use, depending on the farm models considered. The measures given here indicate only a broad order of magnitude. In the face of a constraint on output, man-days per bag of coffee, which may decline somewhat with the new technologies (see text), might be a more appropriate unit of measurement.

Source: FEDERACAFE.

growing areas to crops that require labor when labor demand for coffee harvesting is low.

More than a third of the coffee-growing areas are planted in the new varieties, about evenly divided between sun and shade technologies (see table 6-3). This area is estimated to produce less than two-thirds of total output. There is little information available regarding the type of farmer who has adopted the new technology, although field observations suggest that the larger farmers with better education and better access to capital more readily adopt the new techniques than do others. This is especially true of the new sun technology, which requires much more fertilizer and other inputs than traditional technology. Since FEDERACAFE-subsidized loans have been available for conversion, however, many small producers also appear to have switched. In assessing the long-term effect of this revolution in production technology, it would be useful to have the benefit of a detailed study of the farmers who have switched to the new varieties.

Changing Fortunes of Coffee

The effect of coffee on the national economy was particularly strong during 1976–80 as a result of price increases and technological advances. World coffee prices began to increase in 1976, peaked in 1977, remained high in 1978–79, and declined after 1980 (see table 6-4). The higher prices were mainly responsible for increased export values in 1967–77. By 1978 export volumes began to respond to the price boom and, combined with higher prices, produced record sales receipts in 1978–80. During 1981–83 the export volume declined from its 1978–80 levels

Table 6-3. *Coffee Production under Traditional and New Technologies, 1980/81–1981/82*

	Area				Production, 1980/81[a]	
	1980/81		1981/82			
Technology	Thousand hectares	Percent	Thousand hectares	Percent	Thousand 125-kilo- gram bags	Percent
Traditional	665.8	66.0	651.2	64.0	3,381.2	43.2
New[b]	343.7	34.0	362.5	36.0	4,442.1	56.8
Total	1,009.5	100.0	1,013.7	100.0	7,823.3	100.0

Note: The coffee year runs from October 1 through September 30.

a. Detail for 1981/82 by technology is not readily available.

b. Includes both sun and shade techniques.

Source: FEDERACAFE, *Informe del Gerente General al ILI Congreso Nacional de Café*, Annex 2 (Bogotá, 1982).

Table 6-4. *Trends in Coffee Exports, 1970–83*
(1975 = 100)

Year	Value[a]	Price[b]	Volume[c]
1970	63.9	80.3	79.6
1971	56.5	70.3	80.3
1972	68.3	85.1	78.9
1973	84.3	101.9	82.7
1974	85.6	101.3	84.5
1975	100.0	100.0	100.0
1976	144.6	188.0	76.9
1977	228.8	350.3	65.1
1978	268.2	242.8	110.5
1979	278.8	204.7	136.1
1980	312.1	230.0	135.8
1981	246.2	222.2	110.8
1982	237.6	219.2	108.4
1983	250.8	222.5	112.7

a. Based on foreign exchange surrendered at the Central Bank.
b. Derived from value and volume.
c. Volume exported, based on declarations of exports.
Source: FEDERACAFE.

and stabilized at levels that were still higher than the 1970–75 averages. The 1981–83 price was significantly lower than the 1977–80 level but in real terms was comparable to the 1970–75 level. The share of coffee in total exports rose in 1976–80 but subsequently fell to the average levels for 1970–75 (see table 6-1).

Domestic production, at some 13 million sixty-kilogram bags of green coffee a year, was higher during 1980–83; the average was about 11.5 million during 1978–80.[3] Exports, on the other hand, fell to about 9 million bags in 1980–83 from a peak of 11–12 million bags in 1979–80. Historically Colombia had maintained a share of world stocks well below its share in exports. This pattern continued until the crop year 1980/81, although between 1977/78 and 1980/81 the stock share reached levels broadly similar to the export share. In 1981/82 this pattern began to change, and, as shown in table 6-5, Colombia was estimated to have held more than 19 percent of world stocks at the beginning of 1983/84, a figure based on stock estimates derived from estimated production, domestic consumption, and exports; its export share in total world exports was 14 percent. On the basis of verified stock estimates of the International Coffee Organization (ICO), however, Colombia's share in stocks changed to more than 21 percent on October 1, 1982, and 20 percent on October 1, 1983. Policymakers realize that it would be advantageous for Colombia to supply its export commitment with a lower level of stocks, as long as the level is sufficient to ensure steady sales even in the face of unexpected upswings in demand.

Table 6-5. *Colombia's Changing Shares in World Exports and Stocks of Coffee, Selected Years*
(percent)

Coffee year[a]	Production[b]	Exports[c]	Stocks[d]
1961/62[e]	10.8	14.2	n.a.
1964/65	15.0	14.0	3.8
1970/71	13.4	11.9	9.4
1976/77	15.6	10.1	6.9
1977/78	15.2	14.9	13.0
1978/79	14.8	18.0	17.5
1979/80	15.4	19.1	15.6
1980/81	16.0	15.2	11.6
1981/82	13.2	14.2	18.3
1982/83	15.8	14.1	18.9
1983/84[f]	14.9	14.2	19.4

n.a. Not available.

a. The coffee year runs from October 1 through September 30.

b. USDA, *Foreign Agriculture Circular: Coffee*; and FEDERACAFE.

c. Based on ICO data concerning exports to all destinations.

d. Initial stocks; the ICO estimate, based on verified stocks, is more than 21 percent.

e. Refers to calendar year 1962.

f. Preliminary estimate.

Sources: FEDERACAFE, the International Coffee Organization (ICO), and the U.S. Department of Agriculture (USDA).

The Federation of Coffee Growers

For more than fifty years the National Federation of Coffee Growers (FEDERA-CAFE), a private association of coffee producers, has been charged by the government with administering coffee policy and has received remuneration from the latter for its services. The federation's most important task has been to support incomes of coffee growers by facilitating the marketing of coffee at a guaranteed minimum price. With this policy it has acted as a regulator of domestic coffee prices in the face of wide variations in international coffee prices.

The federation's presence is strong in the coffee zone, reaching down to the village level through its many projects, some of which, such as health, education, and rural electrification, are not directly related to the production of coffee. It provides rural infrastructure and technical assistance for the coffee sector, controls domestic and export marketing, and advises the government, working with it to determine domestic prices and taxes on coffee. The federation manages the National Coffee Fund (NCF) and has considerable freedom in managing the coffee economy and advising the government on policies in this subsector. The NCF was originally created, in 1940, in anticipation of the need to finance surplus stocks that would arise from the international export quota arrangement under the International Coffee Agreement (ICA) introduced in that year. The functions of the fund have subsequently increased in scope as coffee revenues accumulated and various investment activities such as shipping (through Flota Gran Colombiana), banking (Banco Cafetero), and so on, were undertaken. Recently the finances of the fund have come under considerable pressure as world coffee prices declined and Colombia's coffee stocks accumulated. This situation is reversing itself in 1985 as the rate of peso depreciation has been in excess of the internal price increases accorded to coffee producers (see below).

Adjustments in the Coffee Economy

A large part of the export price has been siphoned off through price interventions such that the domestic farmgate price offered by the federation ranged from 38 to 63 percent of the external price during 1970–83 (see table 6-6). Comparing the end years of the period, the farmer's share of the export price has hardly varied, al-

Table 6-6. *Price Stabilization in Coffee, 1970–83*

Year	World real price[a] (1975 = 100)	Internal real price[b] (1975 = 100)	Internal price in relation to peso export price[c]
1970	124.8	114.8	0.58
1971	102.6	98.3	0.59
1972	107.2	103.9	0.57
1973	120.2	110.0	0.53
1974	105.8	100.0	0.51
1975	100.0	100.0	0.50
1976	190.3	169.2	0.47
1977	263.8	162.9	0.38
1978	176.7	142.0	0.47
1979	154.1	113.2	0.43
1980	137.4	106.1	0.48
1981	97.4	90.5	0.63
1982	109.9	85.6	0.58
1983	104.8	83.3	0.59

a. From table 1–3. These indexes are based on quoted prices, not actual sales prices of Colombia.

b. Purchase price of coffee produced to the federation's quality specifications, deflated by the consumer price index for workers, from DANE.

c. This is the ratio of the nominal domestic price paid by the federation for pergamino to coffee farmers, divided by the nominal world price of green coffee, equivalent to 0.719 pergamino in weight, converted to pesos at the official exchange rate.

Source: FEDERACAFE.

though since 1981 the trend has been downward. The real domestic price of coffee
has almost always moved in the same direction as the real world price of coffee, but
the absolute changes in the former have generally been about half those of the
latter. The domestic price variation during the coffee boom has, nonetheless, had
significant effects on substitutions of *caturra*, which by now have reached prime
bearing age. Since that time, the number of new plantings has declined, but the
substitution of the new varieties for the old has continued. The result has been a
dramatic increase in production, causing Colombia's export capacity to exceed its
sales quota under the ICO by 2–3 million bags and obliging FEDERACAFE to accumulate an all-time high stock level of some 12.2 million bags as of the end of September 1984, exceeding annual export needs.

While little new land is now being planted in coffee—only 2,110 hectares during
the first semester of 1981/82—about 10,000 hectares of coffee were replanted
during the first semester of 1981/82. The federation is not at present making loans
for new planting or replantings. Most, if not all, of the replanting replaces traditional varieties with *caturra*. Each hectare thus replanted increases the long-run
coffee yield: if this increase is about 18.7 sixty-kilogram bags, it would imply that
replanting of 20,000 hectares a year could eventually increase production by
374,000 bags a year, adding to stocks.[4] If exportable production declined and stabilized at a level of about 11.5 million bags and the country's exports remained at the
increased 1983/84 level, on the other hand, the stock buildup could be stopped.

Further buildup of stocks from present levels would incur costs with perhaps little
benefit. FEDERACAFE has estimated storage costs at $44 a ton; at this rate it would
cost about $40 million a year to hold the stocks of 12.2 million bags estimated to
have accumulated by the end of 1983/84 (see table 6-7). In this situation, the

Table 6-7. *Production, Exports, and Stocks of Coffee, 1958/59–1983/84*
(thousand sixty-kilogram bags, unless otherwise indicated)

Coffee year	Production	Total exports	Year-end stocks	Year-end stocks as percentage of exports
1958/59	7,442	6,431	114	1.8
1960/61	7,500	6,043	1,081	1.8
1964/65	8,547	5,743	3,589	62.5
1969/70	8,266	6,874	5,583	81.2
1974/75	7,981	7,542	2,400	31.8
1978/79	12,300	11,431	4,870	42.6
1979/80	11,848	11,540	3,450	29.9
1980/81	13,037	9,031	5,978	66.2
1981/82	12,893	8,990	8,289	92.2
1982/83	12,810	9,174	10,230	111.5
1983/84	13,464	9,966	12,175	122.2

Source: Table SA-23.

financial requirements of purchasing coffee that cannot be exported have turned out to be a burden on the NCF.

Circumstances under which such large stocks could become fully useful—such as severe crop damage in Brazil—seem somewhat unlikely, although there is considerable speculation concerning the true level of estimated world stocks. Even at the peak of the boom that followed the mid 1970s frost, Colombia exported only 11.5 million sixty-kilogram bags. Alternatives to a reduction of stocks do not seem promising. Brazil has destroyed coffee in the past, but to do so may not be politically feasible in Colombia. Increasing domestic consumption to any significant extent does not seem possible. Illegal exports to ICO members cannot be an official policy.[5]

On the other hand, crop disease has already begun to affect Colombian coffee production: a strain of coffee leaf rust, *roya*, which has attacked most coffee-producing countries in Central and South America, attacked a few farms in the Department of Caldas in 1983 and had spread to about seventy-five municipalities by the end of 1984, affecting 4.5 percent of the coffee-producing area. In the past the federation has spent considerable resources to prevent appearance of *roya* in Colombia and to study ways of preventing its spread, should it gain entry. In particular, a new variety of coffee tree has been developed—variety *Colombia*—which is actually a mixture of several strains and supposedly resistant to *roya*. Seed for the new variety is now in commercial production, but replanting with it is still rather limited. Existing stocks of coffee are sufficient to maintain present levels of export, and even to make up for any reduction in national production because of *roya*—which could reduce production by as much as 15–20 percent, depending on climatic conditions and the effectiveness of efforts to control it—while replanting with disease-resistant varieties is taking place. Since there is now a campaign to keep the disease under control, the final effect on production is yet to be determined.

One of the main reasons for the recent stock buildup was the sharp increase in production following record prices and the adoption of new technology during the second half of the 1970s. The stock buildup is also a result of the country's participation in the ICO strategy of holding back sales in order to maintain a certain level of prices. It should also be noted that an ICO exporter's quota is determined in part by that country's share in total stocks held by all exporting countries. A basic ICO quota is determined for ICO countries that export more than 400,000 sixty-kilogram bags. In 1983/84 this quota totaled 53.633 million bags, which was apportioned among exporting countries in this category. (A separate quota, which in 1983/84 totaled 2.567 million bags, is established for small exporters.) About 70 percent of the total basic quota is assigned among the members on the basis of their past exports to ICO members, while the remaining 30 percent is in theory apportioned according to their shares in total stocks held by all exporting nations. Thus, in theory, an increase of 1 million bags in Colombia's stock level, holding other countries' stocks constant, could imply an increase of 200,000–300,000 bags in Colombia's export quota.[6] Such a benefit would be unlikely in practice, because, among other reasons, it is not realistic to assume that there would be no changes in the stocks of other countries. In any event, even if such a benefit were to be realized, it should still be compared with the cost of a stock buildup and the financial and economic costs of the additional production that is not sold.

Coffee Price Policy

FEDERACAFE and the government jointly set a buying price for a certain quality of coffee—a weighted average of Col$15,499 per 125-kilogram bag of pergamino in 1984—at which FEDERACAFE will buy all the coffee of the prescribed quality offered, which it will then export, sell domestically, or store. Establishment of this guaranteed price is perhaps the most important price policy in coffee. Private exporters can and do buy coffee from farmers primarily for export, but in so doing they must pay an ad valorem tax on the value of exports and a retention coffee quota and must sell to the government an amount of *pasilla*—low-grade coffee—and *ripio* (waste) parchment, all of which are determined by the government in consultation with the federation.[7] The retention quota and the *pasilla* and *ripio* "taxes" are generally paid in kind, the exporters physically turning over part of the coffee to the federation as tax. Changes in the federation's guaranteed price often require changing one of the taxes if private exporters' incentives are not to be affected, and the retention quota has been the variable most frequently changed for this purpose. This quota was changed thirteen times during the period 1979–82, while there were only three changes in the ad valorem tax. The quota has ranged from a high of 85 percent in June 1976 to a low of 15 percent in 1980–81 and stood at a weighted average of 66.1 percent during 1984.

Price Policy and Exports

Given the export receipts that an exporter must deposit at the Central Bank (on the basis of their export volumes and average prices assumed for the period by the Central Bank) and given the domestic taxes on coffee, there would be a maximum price an exporter would be willing to pay the coffee farmer. The amount that private exporters would actually buy would then depend on the way their offer price compared with the minimum purchase price guaranteed to farmers by FEDERACAFE. Thus both the price interventions of the federation in the domestic market and the taxes it levies determine the volumes that private exporters find it profitable to purchase and export. Actual exports are also carefully monitored through licenses, provided by INCOMEX, which specify the buyer and destination in conformity with the arrangements negotiated under the ICA. The coffee must also be certified by the federation, weighed on the docks, and cleared of all the taxes and payments before shipping. This close supervision ensures that all actual sales by the exporters are registered; the federation supplements these quantities by its own sales in order to meet Colombia's ICO export quota and non-ICO demand.

To illustrate the effect of prices and taxes on exporters' margins, we begin with the exporters' obligation to the Central Bank. In mid 1983 an estimated $191 had to be turned in at the Bank—*reintegro minimo*, "the minimum surrender," the level of which was a weighted average of $205.95 during 1984—by the exporter for the sale of a seventy-kilogram bag of *excelso* (export quality) coffee. This would be based on a New York price of $204 per seventy-kilogram bag, less an estimated $13 a bag for transfer cost from the Colombian port to New York—that is, $1.32 a pound at New York. Once the *reintegro* has been fixed, the exporter bears the risk of external price variations. In this example it is assumed that the *reintegro* corresponds to the actual world price received by the exporters. A 9 percent ad valorem export tax— reduced to 6.5 percent in 1984—meant that the exporter would receive in pesos the equivalent of $174 per seventy-kilogram bag—that is, $191 less 9 percent, or $17—which would be about Col$13,050 per seventy kilograms at that time. Subtracting an estimated Col$700 per seventy kilograms for the internal cost of converting pergamino into excelso, a net receipt of Col$12,350 per seventy kilograms for excelso is obtained for the exporter. For every seventy kilograms of excelso, ninety kilograms of pergamino is required, and 40 percent—66.1 percent in 1984—of pergamino purchases, or thirty kilograms, had to be turned over to the federation as the retention tax. Thus, with Col$12,350, the exporter must buy 126 kilograms of pergamino, implying an offer price of Col$98 a kilogram. In comparison the federation's guaranteed price at mid 1983 was Col$102 a kilogram. This example is not necessarily indicative of actual price comparisons at present.

The Col$700 "internal cost" must include the exporter's profit margin. Since most of his other costs are fixed by government tax rates, this profit margin can be squeezed by a decline in the world price of coffee below $204, assuming no change in the *reintegro*, or by an increase in the federation's guaranteed purchase price, which would increase the competitive farmgate price, or by an increase in tax rates. Any of these events can decrease, sometimes drastically, the percentage of production purchased by private exporters. On the other hand, if the world price rises while the *reintegro* remains constant and the peso depreciates, exporters' profits increase. In practice, the *reintegro* is adjusted to follow the world price movements with some lag, so in periods of rising world prices exporters' profits increase, and in periods of declining world prices their profits decline.

Price Policy and Revenues

Variations in these prices and taxes during 1975–84 are set forth in table 6-8. The minimum surrender has followed the international price, with some lag. The federation's guaranteed price in real terms—which has been well below international prices—has followed the direction of the latter with a lag, although the spread between the two prices has varied in the course of time. The ad valorem tax has been reduced steadily, and the retention quota has been the main instrument of tax policy; *pasilla* and *ripio* taxes are minor. Total taxes have been as high as 60 percent

Table 6-8. *Trends in Prices and Taxes on Coffee, 1975–84*
(percent, unless indicated otherwise)

Year	Reintegro minimo (U.S. dollars per 70 kilograms)[a]	Federation's guaranteed price (pesos per 125 kilograms)[b]	Ad valorem tax[a]	Retention quota[a]	Coffee taxes ÷ value of production	Private exports ÷ total exports
1975	107.87	2,730	19.0	32.8	34.3	60.0
1976	208.16	5,532	18.0	33.8	41.3	79.0
1977	366.08	7,179	17.0	30.0	48.6	70.0
1978	275.15	7,300	16.0	30.0	59.6	36.0
1979	234.14	7,270	16.0	50.4	60.0	23.0
1980	255.06	8,663	15.9	51.8	50.4	2.0
1981	187.60	9,453	12.7	20.8	19.4	38.0
1982	208.75	11,171	11.3	37.0	28.0	43.4
1983	193.74	13,010	8.7	40.6	26.3	42.7
1984[c]	204.50	14,439	6.5	60.0	n.a.	n.a.

n.a. Not available.

Note: These prices, taxes, and the retention quota are changed several times during the year; the figures given are yearly averages.

a. Yearly averages, weighted by export sales in different months.

b. Yearly averages, weighted by the federation's purchases.

c. January–March estimates.

Source: FEDERACAFE.

of the value of production during times of high coffee prices. At such times of high taxes, the share of private exporters in total exports tends to fall, the federation undertaking the bulk of the exports.

The principal recipient of the coffee taxes is the NCF, since it receives the entire retention tax and a part—36 percent at present—of the ad valorem tax.[8] In 1974, the NCF received 63 percent of total coffee taxes, estimated at Col$6,064 million, while in 1982 it received 84 percent out of Col$34,143 million. The national government receives a good part of the ad valorem tax—56 percent today—while departmental committees of the federation receive about 8 percent.

NCF Finances

Following is an illustrative and partial calculation of inflows and outflows of NCF funds for 1982/83, focused on only those annual receipts and expenditures associated with annual coffee purchases and sales by the federation. The federation's receipts come from two sources—its own sales of coffee and the share of the National Coffee Fund from ad valorem taxes on all coffee exported, both privately and by the federation. In 1982/83, the federation is estimated to have exported 5.1

million sixty-kilogram bags of excelso coffee and surrendered, at $168.57 per sixty kilograms, a total of $859.7 million to the Central Bank. Deducting an estimated 8.8 percent for 1982/83 ad valorem tax and using an average exchange rate of Col$74.4, a value of Col$58,334 million is obtained as revenue from coffee sales. The receipts of the NCF from ad valorem taxes on all coffee exports can be estimated as follows: total exports were about 9.2 million sixty-kilogram bags, with total *reintegro* of $1,541 million, or Col$114,650.4 million. The Coffee Fund receives 3.2 percent of this, or Col$3,669 million. Total receipts of the federation from both sources would then be about Col$62,003 million. In 1982/83, the federation purchased about 4.5 million bags of 125-kilogram pergamino at an average price of Col$12,464 per 125 kilograms, implying an outlay of about Col$55,702 million. These measurements are, to be sure, rough and partial. On the receipt side the value of domestic sales and on the cost side the transport, packaging, and storage expenses have been ignored.[9] It has also been assumed that all FEDERACAFE exports are to ICO members. Receipts and costs of all other operations of the NCF and those from earlier debts and investments have likewise not been considered. On an annual operating basis and excluding these factors, a broadly break-even situation is indicated for 1982/83.

Technology and Yields

To resolve the stock-accumulation problem, one approach might be to discourage replacement of traditional plantings with *caturra*, a step that could eliminate production increases—374,000 bags a year at current rates of substitution in the example given earlier. The traditional planters are generally the poorer coffee growers, however, and should perhaps not be denied the benefit of using technological advances to improve their incomes from coffee. Furthermore, the traditional method is also a relatively high-cost way—per unit of harvested coffee—of producing coffee under many circumstances, as indicated by the rapid adoption of the new technologies. Recognizing these conflicting interests, the federation is employing other measures to discourage further increases in production.

Stumping

Another long-term strategy could be to encourage the stumping, or pruning, of all *caturra* trees every six years, the time at which their production begins to decline.[10] This puts them out of production for about fourteen to eighteen months, after which time they begin to bear again. Their growth then follows the pattern of a newly planted tree, beginning to slow down after another cycle of five to seven years, at which time they could be stumped again. If incentives, possibly in the form of low-cost loans to cover the direct costs of pruning, were provided to farmers to stump systematically, this would reduce annual production. One plan under discussion by the authorities was to seek the stumping of 80,000 hectares of *caturra* trees in rotation, so that at any given time, 80,000 hectares of coffee land would be out of production, implying production forgone of 2.46 million sixty-kilogram bags a year, at least in the initial years of the program. Eventually, however, a tree produces more in its third and fourth years *after* stumping than it would without. Thus, the increased productivity of previously stumped trees might compensate for the production forgone from the currently stumped trees, unless they were stumped again.

FEDERACAFE indicates that stumping is good husbandry and essential to protect long-term yields, and that farmers might prune even without special incentives. Many producers do indeed already follow this practice, although not on a scale that reduces output significantly in the short term; the federation's incentives would at best expedite the process. Loans from the Fondo Financiero Agropecuario (FFAP, the agricultural fund) have been available for pruning under the Ley 5ª program, and a growing number of FFAP loans for coffee renovation have been given for renovating *caturra* by pruning rather than for replanting traditional holdings with more of the same. While the resources of the FFAP appeared sufficient to provide loans for the existing demand for stumping, additional funds would be necessary if a larger program were to be envisaged and implemented.

Planting of Shade Trees

An additional scheme could encourage the planting of shade trees among the pruned coffee trees, thereby converting plots from the sun technology to the shade technology. The shade method uses less fertilizer and produces a smaller yield—12.59 cargas per hectare, rather than 16.84, or 531 kilograms per hectare less—but a better quality of coffee. Since it is proposed to prune 80,000 hectares of *caturra*, on half of which sun technology is probably practiced, the conversion of some 40,000 hectares from sun technology to shade could decrease output by about 354,000 sixty-kilogram bags. One possible way of achieving this aim is to require a farmer to convert his plot from sun technology to shade in order to be eligible for subsidized loans for pruning. Incentives could also be offered for conversion to shade without linking it to the incentives for pruning. Some farmers are already adopting shade technology because it is less fertilizer-intensive and therefore requires less working capital.[11] Stronger incentives could be expected to accelerate this trend.

Coffee Diversification

The continuing coffee diversification program, implemented through the NCF credit program and free technical advice of the Programa de Diversificación y Desarrollo de Zonas Cafeteras (PRODESARROLLO, a part of FEDERACAFE) and through FFAP-subsidized loans under the Ley 5ª program, is seen as both an alternative and a complement to the objective of stabilizing coffee production. The interest rate charge on Ley 5ª loans was about 23 percent during 1983/84, whereas NCF loans were available at 21 percent and the current inflation rate is about 18–20 percent. A farmer typically obtains some credit under the Ley 5ª program and finances the remainder of his diversification plans with an NCF loan. From the second half of 1980 through the first half of 1982, 20,684 hectares were financed for diversification—partly for eradication of coffee, but mainly for renovating or expanding the acreage planted in other crops in coffee-growing areas. Of the 20,684 hectares affected, about 3,225 hectares involved eradication of coffee.

Social Benefits versus Private Benefits

In evaluating the possible social benefits of coffee substitution, it may be assumed in a first illustrative example that additional production of coffee above current demand levels has zero marginal social benefit at present, since every extra bag produced will presumably be stored indefinitely. This assumption should be qualified in a more detailed analysis.[12] At the margin, the annual net social benefit of substituting another crop for coffee can be considered to equal the net present value of the variable cost of coffee production and maintenance not incurred, plus the costs of storage avoided, plus the net value of the alternative crop, minus the cost of the eradication of coffee, and minus other real costs of the efforts that make diversification possible.[13]

BENEFITS. The estimates are as follows: The variable cost of producing coffee was estimated to average around $1,487 a hectare.[14] The coffee production forgone at 0.77 ton per hectare of excelso coffee, at an annual storage cost of $44 a ton would imply a stream of storage costs avoided of about $34 a hectare initially and increasing by $34 a hectare each year. This gives an annualized present value of storage costs avoided of $523.[15] Estimates for the *net* value—that is, gross value less production costs—of alternative crops vary a great deal by crop, but one relatively popular alternative is cocoa, with an annualized net value of about $514 a hectare annually. Cocoa is chosen purely for illustrative purposes. Other alternatives should be evaluated, particularly since cocoa might face some of the same problems as coffee in international markets. Total annual benefits calculated in the case of cocoa are about $2,524 a hectare.

COSTS. The estimated costs are as follows: Reduction of coffee was estimated to cost about $284 a hectare; this would be equivalent to a yearly cost of about $20 a hectare, using a real interest rate of 7 percent. The real opportunity cost, assumed to be 7 percent, of loans totaling about $14,576,708, or $1,020,370 a year for 3,225 hectares eradicated under the program—that is, $316 a hectare—evaluated using a real interest rate of 7 percent, can be considered a cost of carrying out this program. Furthermore, the cost of the free technical assistance might be considered, on the grounds that in the initial years it is necessary to promote diversification; if it is assumed to be equal to its value in the private sector, this would cost about $291,534 a year, or $90 a hectare. Total costs were thus around $426 a hectare a year.

Annual net benefits would be about $2,098 a hectare (2,524 minus 426), the benefit–cost ratio would be about 5.9, and the program would seem socially advantageous in the foregoing example. The most significant modification to this example would occur if the assumption were made that additional stocks have nonzero marginal value. As explained earlier, the strategic value of stocks in influencing exports cannot be ignored. In recent ico negotiations the level of stocks may have affected export quotas in an ad hoc way, although a formal instrument—30 percent of export quota on the basis of a country's share in stocks—has existed since 1976. It is not easy to predict the effect of incremental stocks on export quotas in the future because it will depend on the behavior of other countries, and presumably many other factors. If it depended only on Colombia's behavior and if the formula relating stocks and exports were strictly enforced, the value of additional stocks can be readily seen (see footnote 6) lowering the benefit–cost ratio of diversification.

Private Benefits and Costs

The private producer sees the benefits and costs quite differently than does society. First, a producer sells the crop to the federation or to a private exporter. From the producer's viewpoint, these are revenues that would be lost if coffee were not produced and so should be deducted from the benefits of coffee reduction. Assuming a yield of 0.99 tons of pergamino per hectare (equivalent to 0.77 tons of green coffee), a guaranteed price of Col$12,100 per 125 kilograms of pergamino (the price in early 1983), and an average exchange rate of Col$74 to the dollar, these revenues forgone come to $1,295 a hectare. The producer does not incur storage costs, so from his point of view storage costs forgone of US$523 cannot be considered a benefit. From the example given in note 13, the private cost of coffee production is slightly lower than the social cost, but the difference is only $34. Making these adjustments reduces the benefits to $672. If it is assumed that from the private point of view only half the real interest costs are relevant and since technical assistance is free, costs are reduced to $158 a hectare. The annual private net benefit from diversification would be only $514. Comparing the risks connected with marketing crops other than coffee to those connected with coffee may make the net benefit even lower.[16] It should also be noted that many coffee growers have yields in excess of 0.99 tons per hectare; for them, the benefits from diversification would be correspondingly lower. From the federation's point of view, however, the benefits of diversification are great. The reason is that diversification relieves the federation of buying coffee at the guaranteed price and again incurring further storage costs.

Policy Conclusions

Colombia's efficiency in capitalizing on favorable world prices of coffee has contributed enormously to the generation of Colombian exports, incomes, and employment. More than a fifth of agricultural growth since 1970 can be attributed to this commodity. With the recent problem of stock buildup, however, the focus has shifted to finding ways and means of minimizing the social cost of supplying the country's export quota under the ICA and any additional sales. More work is needed to determine whether the stock buildup would continue under present policies and under alternative assumptions about the life cycle of the existing trees, incentives for increased production, and projections of world demand. At the same time, policies to support the long-term performance of the *caturra* variety also need further study.

While most of the needed adjustments in cropping patterns in the future may be expected to be initiated by the coffee producers, compliance with the ICA nevertheless implies that domestic prices must be kept substantially below international levels to stabilize production. Taking into account transitory changes versus more enduring changes in international prices, price policy would also need to continue to avoid translating temporary increases in international prices into higher domestic prices, particularly since the latter are not easily reversible.[17] If the demand for coffee should recover, reasonable additions to Colombia's export quota might still be met without increasing production.

The federation might also provide—as it does now to varying degrees—nonprice encouragement to reduce the growth of coffee production and to develop commodities other than coffee. In this chapter several options have been reviewed—discouragement of new technology in coffee production, stumping of coffee trees, planting of shade trees, and diversification of coffee. Stumping somewhat postpones output and is considered essential for protecting long-term *caturra* yields. The obstacles to diversification are partly psychological—producers are reluctant to forsake their tried-and-true coffee crops for other activities which to them are yet unproven. They are also partly based on the farmers' inadequate knowledge of cultivation techniques and markets for noncoffee products, such as fresh fruits and vegetables. Most important, the federation's assured market for coffee at a guaranteed price makes other alternatives less attractive, particularly for the small farmer. While the social benefit–cost ratio of diversification is large, the ratio from the private farmer's point of view is significantly less attractive, given the alternative of an assured coffee price.

FEDERACAFE is acutely aware of the emerging difficulties and is financing a diversification program. The program has been less successful in inducing coffee reduction than in encouraging other crops. At the same time, since the decline in the real internal price of coffee has made coffee production only marginally profitable in relation to other activities in some areas, this might be a propitious time to encourage some coffee substitution. The recent outbreak of the disease *roya* has made coffee production riskier, which might make diversification more attractive. More of the funds might be used to provide incentives for the replacement of old coffee trees, particularly in the medium-size and larger farms, by other crops, and to promote marketing and processing, thereby creating greater price assurance for the noncoffee commodities. New loans or grants under the program might be linked to stumping and coffee substitution; alternatively, farmers might be reimbursed for the value of perhaps one year of coffee output postponed.

The structure of incentives governing the distribution of funds to the regional committees of FEDERACAFE might also be reconsidered. At present, the share of the budget to each committee for improving its region is determined by the share of that region in coffee production. It may not be in the interest of an individual committee to give its full cooperation to a program such as coffee substitution in its region, because to do so would decrease the ensuing budget allocations made from the Coffee Fund. Finally, the federation's practice of providing subsidized fertilizer for coffee growers could be abandoned; such a process was begun in 1984.

Even if production were to be stabilized at current levels, given the ICA, stocks might accumulate, unless a sizable increase in world coffee prices and world shortages were to materialize. If not, reduction of production would seem to be needed, and the federation's objective, stated at the 1984 Coffee Congress, is to bring the output down gradually in the coming years. The options, such as pruning and diversification, for production reduction while sustaining long-term yields retain adequate flexibility for farmers to increase coffee yields and output when it is required.

Finally, greater attention might continue to be given to increasing total exports of coffee. Colombia has little control over world demand, however, and only limited control over its quota share under the ICA. The issue of increasing its exports to nonmember importing countries might be handled within an agreement among member exporters.

Notes

1. See tables SA-5 through SA-7 for details of the participation of coffee in the economy.

2. FEDERACAFE, *Censo cafetero, 1980* (Bogotá, 1981). These are averages; a wide range of planting densities is practiced on various farms for all three types of production technology.

3. FEDERACAFE, *Economía cafetera* (Bogotá, various issues); see also table SA-23.

4. The figure of an incremental yield of 18.7 bags per hectare from replanting is based on the difference in average yields for traditional and *caturra* varieties. It is slightly below the estimated incremental yield of 19.2 bags used in ICO, *Coffee in Colombia 1979/80* (London, September 1980), p. 44. Using the ICO's estimate would reinforce the conclusions of the present analysis.

5. It was reported by the U.S. Foreign Agricultural Service, however, that 200,000 bags of contraband coffee were smuggled out of Colombia in 1981–82. One practice is to secure a license to export it

to a country that is not a member of the ico, then transship it to the United States through another producing ico member country. (This last step is necessary because ico consumer members are obliged to purchase only from ico producers.) Much of the contraband was discovered when it was noticed that sales to members of the ico from the country of transshipment were exceeding the quota assigned to that country.

6. The following is an illustrative example of the effect on an export quota if the stocks were in practice considered a factor. In 1983/84, 70 percent of the initial basic quota of 53.633 million bags— that is, 37,543 million bags—would have been distributed among the ico exporters on the basis of their share of past exports to ico members. If a 15 percent export share is assumed for Colombia, the resultant export quota, on this basis alone, would be 5.631 million bags. (The issue of the starting point for calculating a country's historical share of exports is a source of contention among ico exporters. It would be in the best interest of the relatively new producers, for example, to compute the export shares on the basis of recent experience.) The remaining 30 percent of the basic quota, or 16.09 million bags, would be distributed according to the stock shares. The formula used to determine this variable part, QV, is $QV = 0.3 \, S_c \cdot D_w$, where S_c is Colombia's share in the preceding year's stocks and D_w is the projected ico import demand. A 19 percent stock share for Colombia, assuming world stocks of some 54 million bags and Colombian stocks of 10.2 million bags, would imply an additional export quota of 3.057 million bags. The total quota for Colombia in this example is 8.688 million bags, which turns out to be about 16 percent of the basic quota. An additional million bags of Colombian stocks can, other things being equal, increase the country's stock share to about 20.5 percent, which in principle increases the stock-based part of Colombia's export quota by some 241,000 bags, in addition to the original ico allocation of 5.631 million bags.

7. See appendix F for a fuller description of the various mechanisms by which coffee is taxed and subsidized.

8. The ncf receives a portion of the ad valorem tax equal to 3.2 percent of the *total* value of exports (*reintegro*), another 0.8 percent going to departmental committees of the federation, to be spent on projects in the coffee zone. Since the ad valorem tax rate changes from year to year, this 4 percent of total exports represents a variable fraction of the ad valorem tax receipts.

9. The value of the retention tax that the ncf receives may also appear to have been ignored, but this factor is actually included. The retention tax is paid in kind—that is, in bags of coffee. These bags are only of value in 1982/83 to the extent they are sold, not stored, and their sales value was included in the federation's total sales receipts. Storage costs are not easy to estimate without knowing the pattern of stock accumulation. If stocks had accumulated at a steady rate throughout the year, beginning with 8.289 million bags and ending with 10.230 million bags, storage costs would have been about Col$1,811 million. Packaging and internal transport cost are estimated at Col$2,700 per ton, so for 5.1 million bags of FEDERACAFE's purchases, these costs would be about Col$826 million.

10. Stumping is done only on *caturra*, not on traditional plantings. Pruning increases the yield, because *caturra* trees are so densely planted that they eventually compete for light, which reduces the yield. Traditional plantings, being much less dense, do not benefit from pruning.

11. *Informe del Gerente General al XLI Congreso Nacional de Cafeteros*, Anexo 2, November 1982, p. 29.

12. First, there is the possibility that some stocks will be needed in the future. Second, additional stocks can have some strategic or economic value because of the way in which ico quotas are established.

13. The following figures are based on estimates provided by FEDERACAFE. The assumption underlying the production figure is that fields using traditional, sun, and shade technologies are taken out of production in the same proportions as the proportions of total coffee area they represent and that land taken out of production would otherwise produce its current level of production. The variable cost of production, using social costs for inputs, was estimated by the ico in 1976 to be about Col$13,516 per hectare using traditional methods and Col$59,568 using modern methods. Converted to dollars at the 1976 exchange rate and then converted to 1983 dollars, these figures equal $688 and $3,034, respectively. The area-weighted average variable cost of production is $1,487. The comparative figure at market prices is almost the same, at $1,453. Using 1982 estimated production cost figures from Caja

Agraria—Col$66,707 with traditional techniques and Col$137,691 with modern techniques—the weighted average cost at market prices is $1,211 a hectare.

14. The incidence of the disease *roya* may increase costs significantly if it becomes sufficiently widespread to necessitate yearly fumigation in all growing regions. This would add to estimated production costs about Col$1 per coffee tree, or approximately $50–55 a hectare for the *caturra* plantings or $25 a hectare for traditional plantings, at average planting densities.

15. This assumes that each year's production will be stored indefinitely. Thus, without diversification, storage costs would be $34 the first year, $68 the second—$34 for the first year's crop still in storage, plus $34 to store the new crop—$102 the third, and so on. The net present value of such a stream is $7,473. Its annualized net present value is $(7,473)(0.07) = 523, using a real interest rate of 7 percent.

16. FEDERACAFE is trying to set up marketing programs for crops other than coffee to minimize the risk of diversification. It is clear, however, that the risk in these other crops is, and probably always will be, much greater than in coffee, which is tried and known.

17. A continuing analysis has suggested that real producer prices during the period 1985–95 may have to be more than 10 percent lower than 1982 prices if a significant reduction in production is to be achieved; see Takamasa Akiyama, "Analysis of Coffee Policy Instruments and Supply Response in Colombia" (Washington, D.C.: World Bank, Economic Analysis and Projections Department, February 1985).

Part Three

Production Policy
in Agriculture

7

Investment in Agriculture

THIS CHAPTER deals with sector-level issues of the size, pattern, and efficiency of investment in agriculture and their possible effect on performance.[1] Most agriculture-related expenditures are made by the private sector, with strong producer associations proposing policy measures to the government and providing support services to their members. The main contribution of the government to agriculture has been in defining the policy framework. In agricultural investment, moreover, the government's contribution has also been significant in selected areas such as infrastructure development, including rural roads; irrigation and land development; research and extension; and provision of credit.

In this chapter are developed some preliminary estimates of efforts of the private sector in agricultural investment. Severe data constraints, however, limit this analysis. Important issues connected with activities of the private sector concern the government's policy interventions and the production environment: the deterioration in security in the countryside has contributed to the cautiousness of private initiatives in recent years. An analysis of the effect of the sociopolitical factors behind the investment climate, however, is beyond the scope of this chapter. The bulk of the discussion concerns the function of the public sector in agricultural investment. Differences in the definition and classification of expenditures by various agencies, and considerable overlap in their ascribed functions, have severely constrained this analysis as well.

Public Sector Expenditures

During the past decade, even as agriculture benefited from favorable international prices, public expenditures in the sector have, according to official data, decreased steadily in real terms (see table 7-1).[2] As a proportion of total allocations under the national budget, they are estimated to have fallen, which is in contrast to growth in total budgetary expenditures of 8.3 percent during the decade. These estimates of agricultural expenditures, however, exclude the substantial and peri-

Table 7-1. *A Tentative Measure of the Direct Share of Agriculture in Public Expenditure, 1970–82*

Year	Agricultural expenditures (million 1970 pesos)	Share of agriculture in the total (percent)[a]
1970	5,187	25.1
1971	4,762	21.2
1972	4,940	20.4
1973	5,211	21.1
1974	4,497	17.1
1975	2,978	11.7
1976	4,481	14.9
1977	4,862	14.8
1978	3,963	9.7
1979	3,748	8.8
1980	4,041	8.5
1981	3,788	7.6
1982[b]	3,975	7.1

a. Excluding indirect expenditures that benefit the sector.
b. Preliminary estimate.
Source: Table SA-24.

odic financing by the government of debts incurred by Caja Agraria and IDEMA, which appear under budget allocations for public debt repayments.[3] They also exclude expenditures on such categories as rural roads and electrification which indirectly support agriculture. There may also have been some reclassification of functions at one time or another that make comparisons difficult. Nevertheless, a disaggregation of the principal agencies also reveals the declining trend, although its exact magnitude may be hard to establish.

The bulk of public expenditures have been on commercial—that is, marketing—services and physical infrastructure (see table 7-2). This line is constituted in part by IDEMA's own resources generated from its marketing operations and from the credit it raises domestically, such as the bonos de prenda obtained from the Central Bank against goods in bonded warehouses. The Instituto Colombiano Agropecuario (ICA) also generates its own resources from fees charged on the quarantine facilities it operates, from the sale of agricultural products produced at research stations, and from the sale of other services.

Transfers and debt services, on both internal and external credit, compose another large item in public sector expenditures. The magnitude of this item suggests an increase in ad hoc additional allocations made during the year to particular agencies for special projects—for example, to the Corporación Financiera de Fomento Agropecuario y de Exportaciones (COFIAGRO) in one year and to IDEMA in another for constructing wholesale markets. The final disbursements made by the agencies

Table 7-2. *Principal Categories of Public Sector Expenditure in Agriculture, 1976–81*

(percent)

Category of expenditure	1976	1977	1978	1979	1980	1981
Commercial services and phys- ical facilities	50.8	46.1	33.2	23.3	33.8	21.6
Debt service and transfers	22.1	25.1	34.5	39.9	30.4	32.2
Recurrent capital	10.3	8.6	10.3	11.5	11.3	13.0
Research and extension	7.0	5.4	6.3	7.7	6.3	8.7
Design and operation of irriga- tion and drainage	1.1	3.0	2.3	3.6	3.1	4.5
Infrastructure	3.1	2.5	5.1	3.9	4.8	6.9
Agro-livestock credit	3.2	5.1	3.0	3.3	3.8	4.0
Other	2.4	4.2	5.3	6.8	6.5	9.1
Total	100.0	100.0	100.0	100.0	100.0	100.0

Source: Estimates based on Ministry of Agriculture data.

could thus be rather different from their initial allocations and portfolio of projects. While this could be a useful trend toward greater flexibility of investment in the public sector, one serious criticism has been the difficulty of tracing cross-transfers to ensure that appropriated funds are actually spent on those items for which they are designated and that they do not get lost in the recurrent expenditures of the implementing host agencies. It becomes difficult to analyze investment policy when categories of expenditure are not always comparable. The remaining public expenditures are evenly distributed among investments such as research, extension, drainage and irrigation, and social services.

Fiscal Problems

Taking the expenditure pattern of the four main public agencies ascribed to the Ministry of Agriculture as an indicator of public investment in agriculture, the ratios of budgetary allocations to own resources of these agencies increased during the period 1976–82, although a significant reversal of this trend was estimated for 1983 (see table 7-3).[4] These proportions could in fact be larger, given the fact that own resources do not necessarily mean revenues that are generated from the service or commercial operations of the agencies. In fact, "own resources" appears to be simply a convenient classification for funds other than direct budgetary allocations. Thus, for example, INCORA's own resources are largely from loan recoveries. In another example, until 1975 ICA received tax credits of 2 percent directly from CAT, which were considered own resources. In 1976 these were eliminated, so ICA's own resources dropped in that year.

These examples indicate that the public agencies do not themselves generate suffi-cient revenue to meet their own financial needs and cannot compensate for de-

Table 7-3. *Sources of Financing in Agricultural Public Agencies, 1976–83*
(million pesos)

Year	Total financing (1)	Budget allocation (2)	Own resources (3)	(2) ÷ (3)
1976	3,055.5	1,466.0	1,589.5	0.92
1977	4,321.4	1,987.3	2,334.1	0.85
1978	3,932.7	2,628.7	1,304.0	2.01
1979	5.123.7	3,528.5	1,595.2	2.21
1980	6,924.1	5,280.6	1,643.5	3.21
1981	8,834.5	6,253.3	2,581.2	2.42
1982	9,417.6	7,089.6	2,328.0	3.05
1983[a]	15,264.5	9,752.4	5,962.1	1.64

Note: ICA, INCORA, INDERENA, and HIMAT only; investment plus recurrent expenditures.
a. Preliminary estimate.
Sources: Ministry of Agriculture and World Bank estimates.

creased budget allocations. While they may be limited by the nature of their operations, the possibilities for generating revenue may not have been exhausted or
considered seriously enough by the agencies. In the course of time their growth has
imposed a strain on the national budget. Greater dependence on government transfers appears to be general throughout the public sector. These fiscal problems have
been compounded by the creation of new public agencies, which perform some of
the functions of the established institutions but which have not occasioned any
cutbacks of the latter.

The allocation of public expenditures in the agriculture sector by the main partic-
ipating agencies is shown in table SA-25. The four main public agencies ascribed to
the Ministry of Agriculture—ICA, INCORA, INDERENA, and HIMAT—received some 27
percent of the financing in 1981, including both budget allocations and own resources of these agencies. The autonomous regional corporations, which are concerned only in part with agriculture, received about 31 percent of the total allocations, while the rest of the entities—the Ministry of Agriculture itself and other
public enterprises that are involved in agriculture to varying degrees—received
about 42 percent. From 1970 through 1981 the ascribed entities maintained a
somewhat decreased share of the budget, while the rest of the entities decreased
their participation from 66 percent to 42 percent, the shortfall being explained by
the expansion of the new regional corporations.

So far, eleven autonomous regional corporations have been formed in response
to regional and local interests. Among their functions are the development of local
resources, land and water control, integrated agricultural services, technical assistance, power development, and conservation. The three corporations that at
present have agriculture-related projects of any significance are Cauca Valley Cor-

poration (cvc), Corpouraba, and Codechoco. cvc has irrigation projects and is involved in soil studies, property titling (under Ley 5ª), and an integrated agricultural aid program. The other two corporations also implement integrated agricultural development programs financed in part by contributions from the national budget and directly under Dutch technical assistance. The work of these regional corporations has duplicated to some extent the functions of INDERENA, established in 1968 to manage the development of natural resources in the country. In practice, it is difficult to reduce the budget or personnel or redefine the prescribed functions of bureaucracies once they have been established, and this problem may have caused some measure of parallel financing and duplication among the agencies.

Programs such as the Plan Nacional de Alimentación y Nutrición (PAN, the National Food and Nutrition Plan) and the Programa de Desarrollo Rural Integrado (DRI, the Integrated Rural Development Program) have attempted to coordinate the efforts of specialized government agencies by financing a concentration of their activities in selected areas, and these additional resources have helped to ease budget constraints of these agencies, ICA, INCORA, and INDERENA. This effect is not minimal, considering that in 1983, the budget of DRI and PAN was some Col$7,500 million, of which about 30 percent was for direct investments in agriculture, while that of the four principal public sector agencies was Col$15,265 million. This example highlights the difficulty of properly evaluating the public sector's role in agriculture in the face of the various types of cross-transfers among agencies in and out of the sector.

The Ministry of Agriculture directly executed only 0.5–0.7 percent of expenditures from investment and recurrent budget allocations during the period 1976–81. Specialized agencies and programs operate independent of the ministry. Thus, for instance, the regional corporations receive their investment funds by reallocation through the DNP; in 1982 the DRI and PAN programs received funds through the Ministry of Finance;[5] and the FFAP functions as an ascribed department of the Central Bank. Apart from these entities, there are the Servicio Nacional de Aprendizaje (SENA, the National Apprenticeship Service), which undertakes training, including that for agriculture; the Secretarías de Agricultura (agricultural secretariats at the departmental level); crop-specific private research and agricultural technology institutes; various producers' federations; and others.

The Budgetary Process and Problems

An important factor that limits the flexibility of budget allocation is the practice of earmarking tax receipts for functional areas such as transport, health, and education. The proportion of national government revenues that are earmarked increased gradually from 23.6 percent in 1974 to 29.0 percent in 1981.[6] In 1983, the level remained at 29 percent, which leaves the government discretionary control over only the remaining 71 percent. Of the discretionary 71 percent, the first claims are for recurrent expenditures and foreign debt service and only the balance could be considered for financing investment proposals submitted by individual ministries. In the budget only 23 percent of total resources was allocated to investment in 1983.

Attempts to free a larger portion of current income for discretionary allocation would require reduction in unnecessary earmarking and a continual review of necessary earmarking. According to 1983 estimates, about 16 percent of current revenues of the government are earmarked directly for various purposes. About 15 percent of the remaining 84 percent that is not thus earmarked—that is, 13 percent—forms the basis for the so-called Situado Fiscal (SF), which goes to departments for current expenditures in health and education. Together, the 16 percent and 13 percent make up about 29 percent, which is the total earmarked portion of current revenues.

Recipient departments should be able to take on more responsibility for raising their own funds, thereby releasing at least a part of the revenues now earmarked through the SF. The primary source of the SF has, until recently, been the Special Exchange Account (SEA). A measure was taken by the administration in 1983 (which became effective in 1984) to reduce earmarking by diverting most of SEA— an estimated Col\$50,000 million in 1983, or 16 percent of total national current income—for direct public investment; 75 percent of this amount went into the Public Investment Fund. Such a diversion correspondingly diminishes the base for calculating the SF. When applied to the 1983 budget estimates, it would have meant that 15 percent of Col\$50,000 million, or Col\$7,500 million, was the reduction in earmarking, implying a net effect of reducing total earmarked revenues as a proportion of current income from 29 percent to 26 percent. In 1984, however, contrary to expectations, the anticipated reserves of the SEA for investment were not realized because of declining international reserves.

The system of budgeting revenues and expenditures was described in the 1983 Economic Report of the World Bank.[10] By the National Budget Statute ("Normas orgánicas del presupuesto general de la nacion," 1973), the maximum allowable increase in forecast revenues above those of the preceding year is 10 percent and the maximum allowable decrease is 30 percent. This in principle limits the initial authorizations to similar levels, and projects must rely on additional authorizations during the year for continued implementation, although a variety of provisions make such additional authorizations a matter of routine.

The Ministry of Finance presents monthly estimates of recurrent and capital expenditures and quarterly estimates of maximum obligations of capital expenditures to the Treasury. These statements—"Acuerdo de ordenación de gastos y acuerdo de obligaciones"—are compared with the Treasury's estimate of expected revenues available for the next period. Here the accrual system of budgeting presents problems in that the carryover of unspent resources and the continual reestimation of accrued expenditure obligations causes much confusion about the size of the actual current surplus or deficit. The Treasury must be careful not to overcommit itself beyond expected liquidity levels in the next period. In the complex administrative process of rescheduling and counterbalancing the receipts and expenditures, trying to ensure that the allocations do reflect the original programming objectives and targets becomes a difficult task.

The timing of additional appropriations also causes problems. In the past, late appropriations or those that were not effected within the target period have contributed to underuse of capacity in the sectoral agencies, and financing has been out of phase with planned execution of targets. In some instances, funds that were meant for particular uses may have been used to stem other shortfalls in immediate requirements; this again has tended to blur the original targets.

Shifting the whole budgeting process to a cash basis rather than an accrual basis might reduce confusion about the actual size of current and projected government deficits and clarify the extent of the actual financing gap arising from a particular budget proposal. This issue has been of concern to government practitioners and warrants more detailed study of budget allocation procedures. It might be possible, in the interim, to implement a system whereby the Treasury would establish lines of credit that would guarantee the supply of funds to agencies for the next period while it replenished its resources from inflows, in effect creating a grace period during which the resources available for the next period but one would become more evident. In any case, a more sophisticated system of matching revenues and expenditures is called for, to relieve the uncertainty of funding projects and programs.

During the early 1960s, the national government adopted the practice of budget programming. The system worked well administratively and in the establishment of clear objectives. In time, however, the allocative process—for the agriculture sector as well as for the rest of the administration—has tended to develop "budget inertia," characterized by automatic increases of allocations to sustain established programs and agencies, often without sufficient reassessment of need, cost, or efficiency. Thus, for example, relatively new programs such as Cordoba II and Caqueta II have had to compete for residual funds and have therefore taken nearly ten years for their completion, even though they have been designated as priority programs. There is a need to review the budget allocation process to enable the execution of priority programs and the realization of declared objectives and to reestablish a coherence in budget programming. This need is apparent, not just at the sectoral level, but also at the national level, given the inflexibilities of allocations in the national budget as a whole.

The lack of proper program evaluation has made it impossible to establish relevant technical, social, and economic indicators by which to justify the desirability of increased resources for priority projects. Another problem has been the lack of standardization of what is included under "Investment expenditures" and "Recurrent expenditures." Salaries and wages, for example, may be classified under either category, depending on the agency. This makes it difficult to budget adequately for the payment of this large item. The tendency has been to divert funds rather haphazardly from investment or recurrent allocations to pay for this more immediate claim, producing, for instance, situations in which researchers lack equipment and inspectors lack funds for gasoline to fuel their vehicles.

Private Expenditures

A comparison of public and private investment trends is given in table 7-4. These data, based on national accounts figures, imply that public expenditures in the sector fell in real terms by some 2.2 percent a year during the period 1970–82. Private expenditures are estimated to have grown in real terms by about 4.0 percent a year and have compensated for shortfalls in public expenditures, causing the total to grow by about 3.2 percent a year. These are tentative measures, and considerable additional work would be useful to determine these trends with greater accuracy and establish the reasons for them.

In 1982 public expenditures—that is, current expenditures plus investment—in the sector made up less than 10 percent of total agricultural expenditures. Private expenditures were thus much larger in the sector, and the bulk of the differences in total expenditures between these two sources—that in, between public and private sources—arose on account of the far larger volume of current private expenditures. Roughly 90 percent of total public and private expenditures in agriculture is estimated to belong to the category of consumption expenditures and 10 percent to that of investment (fixed capital formation) during the period 1980–82.[7] According

Table 7-4. *Tentative Measures of Public and Private Expenditures in Agriculture, 1970–82*
(million 1975 pesos)

Year	Total	Public	Private	Percent public in total
1970	68,280	11,527	56,753	16.9
1971	70,761	10.915	59,689	15.6
1972	76,259	11,572	64,790	15.0
1973	86,257	12,741	73,714	14.5
1974	90,834	10,888	80,221	11.7
1975	87,929	7,124	80,805	8.1
1976	93,240	11,051	82,900	11.1
1977	109,192	11,922	98,165	10.1
1978	103,159	9,361	94,068	8.8
1979	100,214	9,017	91,434	8.8
1980	110,396	9,651	100,999	8.5
1981	93,873	9,054	84,996	9.5
1982	96,873	8,833	87,634	9.3

Note: Includes both current and investment expenditures.
Sources: Ministry of Agriculture, DANE, and World Bank estimates.

to DANE data, the private sector is estimated to have accounted for some 93 percent of consumption expenditures. These proportions were representative of the 1970s, and growth in agriculture has been sustained by a steady rate of replenishment of capital investment by the private and public sectors in approximately equal proportions, without any marked increase in infrastructural investments.

The private sector in Colombia appears to be well organized and, given appropriate encouragement, could be relied on to enhance government efforts to increase agricultural productivity. Agriculture has become increasingly commercialized, in part because of rapid outmigration of rural labor to the cities in search of jobs and amenities. Organizations of private producers undertake a wide range of activities in support of the production and marketing interests of their members. These activities range from investments in research, extension and training, and provision of credit, marketing, and processing facilities, to sales-promotion activities abroad and lobbying the government.

Major Organizations of Producers

Eleven of the bigger producer organizations were studied. The largest of these is FEDERACAFE, the federation of coffee producers, which represents almost all the 300,000 coffee producers in Colombia (see chapter 5). The other organizations are smaller in scale but nonetheless command impressive memberships. The Federación Nacional de Arroceros (FEDEARROZ, the federation of rice producers) represents almost all the rice producers in Colombia; the Federación Nacional de Cultivadores de Palma Africana (FEDEPALMA, the federation of oil palm growers) and the Asociación Colombiana de Productores de Flores (ASOCOLFLORES, the Colombian flower producers) represent about 85 percent of their growers; the Asociación Colombiana de Productores de Semillas (ACOSEMILLA, seeds) about 55 percent, and so on. Membership in such organizations as the Federación Colombiana de Productores de Papa (FEDEPAPA, the potato growers, 7 percent of the total) tend to be lower, because this is a crop cultivated largely by smallholders in conjunction with wheat, barley, and other highland crops and probably some livestock. Eighty percent of the members of FEDEPAPA are small farmers having perhaps total farm sizes of five to ten hectares, of which one hectare is in potatoes.

Seven of the eleven organizations have their own research programs, while the others rely on work being done by the ICA; seven undertake extension and training for their members on subjects ranging from accounting and business management to improved production techniques, through short courses, news broadcasts, field days, and organized tours to farms on which innovations are being tried. Credit is arranged by only the coffee and cotton producers' organizations, although the rice, potato, seed, and palm oil associations are active in the sale of inputs to members, usually at slightly more favorable prices than if they were procured elsewhere. Joint processing is organized by the cotton federation, and agroindustries to some extent by FEDERACAFE, which has an active and well-integrated program to promote the diversification of coffee farmers into other cash crops and to implement such downstream activities as agroprocessing, marketing, and retailing. FEDERACAFE also undertakes the provision of infrastructure far in excess of the normal purview of a producers' organization and in effect functions like a minigovernment among its coffee constituents, collecting coffee payments in kind; providing schools, nursery schools, hospitals, and roads; extending electrical power lines; and operating collecting centers, supermarkets, and banks.

With such different scales of activity, the numbers of staff employed and annual operating budgets of the various federations of producers vary tremendously. Sources of finance typically include membership dues; levies on production—on kilograms of paddy milled, for example, or grains, or seed sold; and taxes on imports such as wheat and corn; as well as grants from the Ministry of Agriculture, such as that given to the Federación Nacional de Cooperativas (FENALCO, the federation of cooperatives), to support training activities among its members. Apart from membership dues, taxes and levies in support of these private organizations are enabled by state legislation, yet another indication of successful lobbying by the federations of producers and the close collaboration that is possible between the government and an organized private sector in fostering agricultural development. That the government recognizes this function of the private sector is evident in the fact that the individual federations and their apex organization, the Sociedad de Agricultores de Colombia (SAC), are often entrusted with reviewing and even drafting agricultural legislation in the process known as concertation. With such institutions and processes in place, it would appear that with the exception of the small farmers, the highly commercialized private sector is poised to complement government policies in the agricultural sector, given sufficient incentives for investment.

Agricultural Borrowing

A significant gap in present knowledge concerns the extent and nature of agricultural borrowing, information on which would shed light on the trends and problems in agricultural expenditures. Most of the available information concerns institutional borrowing. Institutional lending for private agricultural investment is channeled almost entirely through Caja Agraria, commercial banks, and financial corporations.[8] In 1981 they accounted for a total of Col$75 billion in loans outstanding, provided by the agencies in the following proportions: Caja Agraria, 44 percent; commercial banks, 44 percent; and financial corporations, 12 percent. The relative importance of these institutions in agricultural lending remained essentially the same throughout the period 1977–81. As a percentage of their total portfolio of outstanding loans, agricultural loans assume varying degrees of importance; figures for 1981 show that 76 percent of the outstanding loans made by Caja Agraria were to this sector, while corresponding shares of commercial banks and financial corporations were 16 percent and 12 percent, respectively.

The most important single source of funds onlent for private investment in agriculture is a fund instituted especially for this purpose—the Fondo Financiero Agropecuario (FFAP). During the period 1977–82, funds provided by the FFAP typically made up about 37 percent of the total agricultural loan portfolio. The FFAP, enabled by legislation (Ley 5ª) in 1973, was an attempt to coordinate agricultural credit activities under one umbrella. Funds are raised through obligatory investments imposed by the Central Bank, which requires that all banks invest part of their reserves in the bonds and issues of the FFAP. FFAP funds are rediscounted by the Central Bank to banks for agricultural loans; these banks should apply a certain percentage of their own resources—say, 20–30 percent—to match the remaining rediscounted funds—say, 70–80 percent—from the FFAP. These rediscount margins—80 percent or so—as well as the interest rates to be charged on various categories of loan are determined from time to time by the Central Bank. In June 1983 interest rates on short-term loans—loans of up to one and a half years' duration—were 21 percent, and on medium- to long-term loans, interest rates varied from 15 percent (forestry), to 18 percent (smallholder cattle), 20 percent (larger cattle operations), 21 percent (cash crops such as cocoa, fruit, and African palm, construction of wells and farmhouses, and purchases of farmland).[9]

Recent Government Efforts

Recognizing the decline in public investment in agriculture, the present administration has been making a conspicuous attempt to increase allocations for 1984–86. Projections were available only for the four major public agencies of the sector, namely, the ICA, INCORA, INDERENA, and HIMAT. These agencies received proportional reductions in funds during the period 1970–83, a decrease of 2.5 percent annually, similar to that for the entire agricultural sector. For 1984–86, their projected allocations envisage a dramatic rate of growth, but it remains to be seen how much of this increase will be realized.

It has been suggested that priority to agriculture in the national budget could be augmented with better preparation of projects for domestic funding and for external funding, which would in turn require the government to make concomitant counterpart financing. A strong interest has been expressed in building up a pipeline of fundable projects and seeking such foreign participation that priority for budget allocations can also be assured. These moves are in line with the present administration's policy of emphasizing agricultural development as a vehicle of economic growth. They are consistent, too, with the function traditionally assumed by the public sector of investing in programs with high economic and social returns, which would generate the infrastructure and the climate for private investment and reduce the risks in connection with such investments.

Policy Conclusions

It is widely recognized that the private sector in Colombian agriculture is dynamic and responsive to incentives. Private investments have taken the lead in promoting agricultural growth, partly offsetting a decline in public sector investments during the last decade. The able stewardship of private organizations of producers is attested to in this book. The efforts of FEDERACAFE, FEDEARROZ, and ASOCAÑA in research and infrastructural development are examples. Recent declines in estimated private expenditure in real terms may have stemmed from, among other things, insecurity in the rural areas and declining incentives in the sector. Macroeconomic policies to reverse agricultural disincentives can be expected to stimulate agricultural investment.

The public sector has a critical function to perform in the provision of key infrastructural developments, such as rural roads and irrigation, and in supporting facilities that have more general application for a wider constituency than that of specialized producer or interest groups, which would indirectly support private initiatives. Since 1970, however, total public expenditures in agriculture, particularly long-term investments, are estimated to have decreased, both in real terms and as a proportion of total national budget allocations. The bulk of public expenditures has been in support of IDEMA's operations and for transfers and debt services, with investments in drainage and irrigation typically receiving 3–5 percent and research and extension 5–9 percent.

A general difficulty that affects other sectors as well concerns the growing dependence of public agencies on budgetary allocations and on transfers; there is need for public agencies to generate more revenues to meet their own financial requirements. The increase in the number of public agencies of various levels of government seems to have compounded the problem of transfers. A related issue is that of the inflexibility of budget allocations for investments, derived in part from the earmarking of revenues for a variety of current expenditures. In this respect, recent efforts to free more resources for investment should be noted, although their effect has yet to be fully assessed. In agriculture, the financial problems of Caja Agraria, the agricultural credit institution, and IDEMA have further constrained the availability of resources for investment.

Budgetary procedures appear to create considerable uncertainty regarding actual resources that will be available to the sector. The process spanning initial authorization, additional appropriations, and actual allocations is characterized by government practitioners as complex and cumbersome. Streamlining the procedures would seem to promise good returns, and a better system of matching revenues and expenditures may be necessary to relieve the uncertainty of project funding and reduce delays in execution.

Notes

1. Historic analyses of public expenditures in the Colombian context can be found in Victor J. Elias, *Government Expenditures on Agriculture in Latin America*, International Food Policy Research Institute Research Report no. 23 (Washington, D.C.: IFPRI, May 1981); and Marcelo Selowsky, *Who Benefits from Government Expenditure? A Case Study of Colombia* (New York: Oxford University Press, 1979).

2. Expenditures in agriculture are defined here as those, including investment and current expenditures from budget allocation and own resources, by the Ministry of Agriculture, its subsidiary agencies— the Instituto Colombiano Agropecuario (ICA), the Instituto Nacional de los Recursos Naturales (INDE-RENA), the Instituto Colombiano de la Reforma Agraria (INCORA), and the Instituto de Hidrología, Meteorología, y Adecuaciónes de Tierras (HIMAT)—and agricultural expenditures of autonomous regional corporations and other public enterprises.

3. In 1982, for example, government repayment to the Central Bank on behalf of Caja de Credito Agrario, Industrial, y Minero (Caja) and IDEMA for their past debts to the Central Bank were roughly Col$814 million and Col$577 million, respectively.

4. This pattern of increased relative dependence on government transfers appears to be general throughout the public sector. The principal increases have been in current transfers, both to decentralized agencies and to local government authorities.

5. As of October 1983, the DRI/PAN Program is managed by the Ministry of Agriculture but it still receives its funds through the Ministry of Finance.

6. World Bank data.

7. The predominance of current expenditures over investment expenditures is also demonstrated in Caja Agraria's allocations for agricultural sector loans, where only 5–9 percent of total lending for 1978 and subsequent years is envisaged for investment expenditures—machinery and equipment, agricultural land and infrastructure, houses and wells—while the rest, 91–95 percent, is for current expenditure for crop and livestock production, although the latter, in short-term loans, might really include capital expenditure as well.

8. INCORA and the Programa de Desarrollo Rural Integrado (DRI, the Integrated Rural Development Program) channel their loans through Caja Agraria. Most of the allocations from the National Coffee Fund under the diversification program of PRODESARROLLO are handled through Banco Cafetero, and some through Caja Agraria. Commercial finance companies are an additional source of agricultural loans, but in 1980 they had only Col$328 million in outstanding loans, or 0.6 percent of the total.

9. On some FFAP loans the larger farmers pay an additional 1 percent interest, which goes to the Fondo de Asistencia Tecnica a Pequeños Agricultores y Ganaderos, a fund that subsidizes extension services to the smaller farmers. The charges for technical assistance pertain only to extension services linked to loans for major field crops, flowers, sugarcane, livestock breeding, and the installation of machinery and wells, but not for coffee, reforestation, smallholder food crops, or milk production.

10. Published as World Bank, *Colombia*, pp. 77–82.

8

Agricultural Technology, Input Policy, and Marketing

THIS CHAPTER is devoted to the physical aspects of agricultural production, complementing the macroeconomic and pricing analysis in the first two parts, and extending the discussion of investment trends in chapter 7. In particular, input policies and problems will be examined, particularly constraints to a more rapid adoption of modern inputs. Government interventions in input pricing have been few compared to those in many other countries, although real possibilities of lowering production costs through government policy have been significant. Modest reductions in cost can be achieved through improvement of import policy and mechanisms, while more substantial long-term benefits can be obtained through investment in high-priority areas.

One set of factors reviewed at the outset that affect performance is technology and infrastructure, including research and extension, water development, and management of natural resources. Government investment in this area has lagged, and efforts to increase the size and efficiency of investment are in order. Important inputs that influence production trends are labor, fertilizer, machinery, and seeds. Achievement of a reduction in the cost of these inputs is a critical issue, while in the case of credit the current levels of subsidy in relation to market rates and their efficiency are issues worth examining. Agricultural marketing affects almost all crops, although the nature of marketing constraints is not well understood.

Trends and Problems in Input Adoption

In a recent study of Colombian agriculture during the last decade the positive association between rates of growth of agricultural production and the use of improved production inputs such as fertilizer, certified seeds, and machinery has been indicated.[1] As shown in table 8-1, the annual growth rate in the use of these inputs diminished significantly after the mid 1970s, particularly from 1978, during which time the expansion in agricultural production also showed a distinct downturn—an association worthy of further investigation. The 1975–81 slowdown in fertilizer affected noncoffee agriculture, since during this period the use of fertilizer in coffee growing increased above the sectoral average. These trends have given rise to recent policy measures to improve the supply of inputs and to reduce their real prices in order to encourage greater use of inputs and thereby boost agricultural yields and production.

There has been considerable variation in production performance and use of inputs among various agricultural activities (see tables SA-26–28). Value added in agricultural production as presented in table 8-1 is apportioned almost equally among coffee production, other agricultural production, and animal production, in shares that have remained broadly stable since 1970.[2] During the period 1970–82, the smallest expansion in output took place in animal production and the largest in coffee, other agricultural production falling in between. Within "other" production, rice, potatoes, and bananas grew at impressive rates. Important technological improvements have been made in these crops, as they have in coffee, and they are relatively input-intensive. On the other hand, domestic production of livestock, other food products such as yuca, and imported products such as wheat, corn, soya, and barley have not grown much, if at all. On the average these crops, most of which are produced by the small-farmer subsector, employ more traditional technologies than the export-oriented products, and they use relatively small amounts of modern inputs. It should be noted, however, that estimates of domestic products suffer from severe data limitations.

In itself, a slowdown in the rate of increase in the use of modern inputs may not necessarily be a cause for concern, since rates of use could taper off after the initial stages of rapid adoption. This pattern occurred in the case of rice in Colombia during the 1960s and coffee in the 1970s. For the sector as a whole, however, it cannot be said that the recent slowdown in use of inputs has followed high rates of adoption in earlier periods. According to World Bank estimates of fertilizer consumption per hectare of arable land, Colombia ranks about halfway among a group of countries and about 17 percent above the average for the middle-income countries. About 74 percent of the nitrogen consumed in Colombia in 1981 was concentrated on the production of coffee, rice, potatoes, and sugar.[3] Furthermore, while Colombia has achieved competitive levels of yield in crops such as coffee, rice, cotton, and sugarcane, considerable potential appears to remain for improvement of the yields of crops such as barley and corn (see table 8-2).

The slowdown in the adoption of modern inputs is at least partly attributed to the decline in incentives for noncoffee agricultural production. Furthermore, input costs, already believed to be high in Colombia, have outgrown output prices since 1970 (see table 8-3). Increases in the prices of labor, machinery, and diesel fuel have been especially pronounced. A general conclusion supported by various informal estimates of farm budgets, and one that deserves further study, is that agricultural producers have in recent years been facing a growing profit squeeze. For the long term, increases in productivity may have justified some of the increases in the prices

Table 8-1. Agricultural Production and Use of Inputs, 1970–82

Input or element of production	1970	1971	1975	1978	1981	1982	Annual growth rate 1970–82	1975–82	1978–82
Value added in agriculture (million 1975 pesos)[a]	86,488	88,059	108,490	123,624	136,285	134,483	3.8	3.1	2.2
Certified seed (thousand tons)	32,109	33,429	59,123	59,703	61,713	71,670	6.9	2.8	4.7
							1971–81	*1975–81*	*1978–81*
Fertilizers (thousand tons)	n.a.	479,014	565,754	759,449	661,147	n.a.	3.3	2.6	-4.5
Simple	n.a.	55,706	87,760	115,497	86,260	n.a.	4.5	-0.3	-9.3
Urea	n.a.	174,711	177,273	223,363	184,641	n.a.	0.6	0.7	-6.1
Compound	n.a.	248,597	300,721	420,587	390,570	n.a.	4.6	4.5	-2.4
Machinery									
Number of units	22,713	23,469	24,187	27,871	29,693	n.a.	2.5	3.5	2.1
Average horsepower	58.4	62.8	62.5	64.5	62.0	n.a.	—	—	—
Total horsepower (thousand)	1,327	1,474	1,514	1,798	1,841	n.a.	3.0	3.3	0.8

n.a. Not available.

— Not applicable.

a. DANE estimates of the combined value added in sectors 01, 02, 03, 08, and 12 (see tables SA-29 and SA-30), which, as noted in chapter 1, differ from data provided by the Central Bank.

Sources: Oficina de Planeamiento del Sector Agropecuario (OPSA), DNP, and World Bank estimates.

Table 8-2. *Comparison of Yields of Principal Crops, 1982*
(kilograms per hectare)

Crop	Colombia	South America	North and Central America	International average
Temporary				
Cereals	2,587	1,906	3,797	2,307
Rice	4,304	2,022	4,461	2,871
Wheat	1,605	1,610	2,382	2,009
Barley	1,667	1,108	2,836	2,068
Corn	1,401	1,942	5,994	3,465
Sorghum	2,611	2,966	3,534	1,447
Roots and other	11,330	11,194	18,828	11,619
Potatoes	12,500	11,198	27,070	14,421
Cassava	10,392	11,594	6,030	8,885
Beans, dry	652	535	891	558
Oilseed				
Soybeans	2,000	1,643	2,160	1,772
Sesame	579	570	551	286
Seed cotton	1,739	1,681	1,803	1,286
Permanent				
Coffee	773	573	573	499
Cocoa	575	483	398	332
Sugarcane	87,705	60,594	58,265	58,682
Tobacco	1,419	1,327	2,106	1,446

Note: The area compared is heterogeneous; this is only a rough comparison of yields.
Source: FAO, *Production Yearbook*, vol. 36 (1982).

Table 8-3. *Increases in the Prices of Agricultural Output and Inputs, 1970–82*
(annual percentage)

Output or input	1970–82	1970–75	1975–82	1978–82
Output price	20.8	18.6	22.3	21.5
Input price[a]				
Labor	26.3	22.6	29.0	26.3
Machinery	22.7	25.6	20.7	25.0
Diesel fuel	26.4	15.0	35.2	26.0
Fertilizer	24.3	37.0	16.0	19.5
Seed	18.5	19.1	18.1	16.5
Insecticide	19.1	22.0	17.0	19.8

a. In 1982, for rice, beans, potatoes, corn, sorghum, barley, sesame, and wheat, labor was estimated to constitute 26 percent of the cost of production, purchased inputs 49 percent (roughly consistent with the data in table 8-5), "others" 8 percent, and indirect costs 17 percent.
Sources: DANE, DNP, and OPSA data.

of inputs in relation to output prices, although more recent trends seem to give cause for concern.

Research, Technology, and Infrastructure

By and large, basic research in the past appears to have been adequate. Except for a few crops such as sorghum and cotton, the combined efforts of plant breeders and pathologists have generally both enhanced genetic yield potential and improved resistance to disease. The efforts of agronomic research and extension have varied significantly for various crops, but on the average, they have declined during the last decade. An important area of neglect has been in the adaptation of cultural practices to location-specific ecological and socioeconomic circumstances. This has been especially true with respect to crops such as soybeans, wheat, corn, and cotton, world market prices of which have also been declining. Cultural practices having to do with time of seeding, land preparation, the use of water and fertilizer, and pest control urgently need to be improved and propagated in order to restore profitability and competitiveness of crops in domestic and export markets.

A reason for the relative inactivity in the generation of new technologies has been the decrease in funding of the Instituto Colombiano Agropecuario (ICA, the Colombian Agricultural Institute). In addition, the institute has been burdened to a growing extent with regulatory functions that are not related to, and are sometimes at odds with, its research and extension objectives. These factors, as well as the loss of a number of first-rate scientists, have adversely affected the quality of ICA's research but are now being redressed through increased budgetary allocations for research. The efforts of privately supported crop research institutes for export crops such as sugarcane, coffee, and bananas have helped to make up some of this shortfall, but their programs may not be comprehensive enough, and they do not include other crops of national importance, such as food crops grown largely by traditional farmers.

Extension has also suffered from the fragmentation of the country's extension services and lack of policy orientation. There are some 2,000 private extensionists as well as numerous public or semipublic institutions responsible for extension, among other things, and these appear at times to overlap geographically and functionally. The record of the various extension services in Colombia is mixed and remains to be assessed. Use of certified seed is concentrated in commercial crops such as rice, cotton, and soya, with low participation in the case of others. Seed use per hectare increased only for rice and soya between 1971 and 1981. During the same period, total use of certified seeds in commercial crops increased at an annual rate of 7.9 percent, although since 1978 the rate has actually been declining. There were about fifty producers of certified seed, with a total production capacity of nearly 400,000 tons a year, in the early 1980s. During the 1970s the growth of this agroindustry permitted the country to stop its imports and become an exporter of seeds.

To turn now to infrastructure development, about 600,000 hectares, the equivalent of about 15 percent of the total cropped area, are estimated to have some sort of irrigation, drainage, or flood control available at present; 80 percent is under private schemes and the rest under government schemes. Another 120,000 hectares under government control is cultivable, but is not actually irrigated. The issue of irrigation and drainage development in Colombia concerns both the improvement of existing facilities and the provision of new ones by private agencies, with or without government support, and in some instances directly by public agencies. While private irrigation schemes—80 percent of which are located in the fertile Cauca Valley—are generally run efficiently and involve lower costs, most public irrigation districts are underused as a result of poor maintenance of infrastructure and poor land leveling. In response the government has embarked on a phased rehabilitation scheme beginning with eight districts, or 76,000 hectares, in the first phase of the project; seven other districts are to be included in a second phase.

On the provision of additional irrigation, care needs to be exercised in limiting investment to areas where water is indeed the constraint to higher yields and to obtaining two crops a year. For rice, yield levels are as high as can be reasonably expected. Yields for other large-scale field crops, such as sorghum, corn, and soybeans, on the other hand, are low, primarily as a result of the fact that farmers continue to follow traditional farming practices—that is, using little or no improved seed and agrochemicals. A lack of water has not always been a binding constraint in the adoption of new technologies. Under these circumstances, it would be essential to restrict investment of scarce public resources to places where it can be clearly shown that water is limiting increased production, or where a transition to high-value crops or more intensive cultivation has taken place and high returns are plausible.

On the other hand, public investment in agrohydraulic work for flood control and drainage could change areas that are now suitable only for extensive grazing into land that can be used for permanent crop farming. Such investment also seems cost-effective to the extent that it usually involves an outlay of only about 25 percent a hectare of that needed for irrigation. Various problems related to recovery of operation and maintenance costs in flood control and drainage districts are encountered, however, because a national tradition in the operation of this type of district has yet to evolve. In addition technical problems are encountered in the drainage of flat, low-lying tropical areas.

Investment in irrigation can be more easily justified where the marginal cost of completing projects already begun is low, as it is, for example, in the case of the World Bank's first irrigation rehabilitation project. A problem requiring particular attention is that of minimum district size. In the past, selection of public investments has been guided more by political criteria than by agricultural or engineering criteria, bringing about the establishment of such small districts that diseconomies of scale for operation and maintenance were the result.

Although the potential for expanding agricultural production on new land facilitated by some form of water control is substantial in Colombia, much of it remains

generally a more costly possibility than that of crop intensification on existing cultivated areas and in many instances probably also the opening of new rainfed frontier
land. Where new irrigation and water control schemes are warranted, the beneficiaries, the kind of agricultural development that is likely to take place, and the kind
of cost recovery charges that are feasible need to be identified and examined. It is
important to ensure that sound policies regarding water charges are adhered to.
Meanwhile, private investments in irrigation and drainage work should continue to
be supported when they are technically and economically justified, with credits and
appropriate incentives, and research should be developed with a view to bringing
about greater efficiency in the use of water through the development of improved
land-leveling techniques, and, more generally, through the use of cost-reducing alternatives, such as puddling for rice cultivation.

Renewable Natural Resources

Colombia is endowed with vast expanses of heterogeneous forests that have been
exploited at a growing rate in both tropical lowlands and cold highlands. During the
past twenty years, forest resources have been reduced by an estimated 10.5 million
hectares, corresponding to almost 20 percent of the approximately 55 million hectares of forest that existed in 1960. Deforestation, as a result of the establishment of
new settlers and the traditional replacement of the forest cover and other natural
vegetation with crops or pastures, has created serious problems of erosion and soil
conservation. The effects of this erosion include more frequent and more serious
flooding and reduced water flows during dry periods for hydropower generation
and for water supply systems. There is evidence that the siltation of reservoirs is
increasing. Protection and management of river basins and a rational use and management of tropical forests are critical to the preservation of Colombia's abundant
land and water resources and for ensuring a continuous supply of wood for domestic and export markets.

The government has been aware of these issues for many years. In 1969 it set up
the National Institute for Renewable Natural Resources and the Environment
(INDERENA), which subsequently established a natural resources code listing the recommendations and rules for managing the country's resources properly. But the
task is enormous, and INDERENA has been hampered by shortages of funds and
trained personnel. Nevertheless the initial steps, such as the identification of critical
areas for conservation and reforestation programs in the areas of influence of hydropower projects and the development of the Upper Magdalena Pilot Watershed
Management Project, are being taken.

A greater capacity to execute programs for the conservation and rational use of
renewable natural resources needs to be developed, and greater public awareness of
the problems will clearly be required. INDERENA's institutional capabilities for policy
implementation and project preparation need to be strengthened. In particular,

conservation education programs need to be stepped up. A program of research and baseline studies of critical areas is called for to enable INDERENA to evaluate policies and projects, funding for which might need to be sought externally.

The ad hoc approach to forestry development needs to be replaced by a more systematic policy. In particular, the execution of pilot projects, such as the Upper Magdalena Pilot Watershed Management Project, and the follow-up of larger-scale projects might be placed within the framework of a national forest and natural resources development program. The forestry components of various rural development projects, despite their small size, could be geared to addressing problems of properly harvesting, using, and managing the tropical rain forests of Colombia, designing and administering "forest colonization" projects, and developing and managing large-scale watershed management projects. Inexpensive small-scale reforestation activities could be stepped up, particularly under rural development and settlement projects such as the Integrated Rural Development Program (IRDP) and Caqueta. The potential for further large-scale industrial reforestation could also be investigated. Spontaneous settlement would be guided by the development of soil classification and of forest colonization projects, as opposed to traditional colonization, which is based entirely on agriculture, which is often inadequate for moist tropical zones. A research program analogous to the National Agricultural Research Plan could be developed on the basis of the National Forestry Research Plan (PLANIF) and implemented with external assistance, if it is needed.

Rural Labor and Income

Movements in the real wage show that between 1935 and 1964 the purchasing power of agricultural workers probably did not increase significantly, and its level was in fact 10 percent lower than that of unskilled construction workers.[4] In 1964 a far greater proportion of the poor were in the rural areas than at present. Some improvements in rural wages came about during the late 1960s, but it was only with the employment expansion of the 1970s that real agricultural wages began to rise significantly. Changes in survey methods between 1971 and 1976 may have overstated the true gains to some degree; nevertheless, between 1970 and 1976 real agricultural wages are estimated to have risen about 23 percent, and another 22 percent between 1976 and 1980. Consistent with the recent slowdown in growth of the agricultural sector, a small decline in real wages is reported to have occurred in 1981. Rapidly growing urban employment in the 1970s offered jobs to rural immigrants. At the same time, labor-intensive agricultural development was taking place in the coffee regions with the new plantings of the *caturra* variety, and cotton areas were competing for labor with clandestine drug plantations. Rapid expansion of exports had a strong salutary effect on labor demand and rural wages. These factors even led to seasonal and regional labor shortages, which in some instances also brought about increasing mechanization—the use of cotton harvesters in cotton areas, for example.

Enhanced demand for agricultural labor and slower growth in its availability provided much of the basis for the estimated growth in real wages—as an average for tropical and temperate regions in the country—for the second half of the 1970s. The rate of growth in the productivity of agricultural labor—value added per worker—during the period 1974–79 has been estimated at roughly 3.7 percent a year. Furthermore, beginning in 1973 real minimum wages also rose. Increases in the real agricultural wage during the 1970s directly or indirectly benefited most of the rural community, which includes the poorest segments of the Colombian population. Yet because agricultural and overall growth have slowed since 1978, real wages have probably stagnated according to some calculations on the basis of information from DANE. Nevertheless, as indicated in table 8-3, nominal wage increases in agriculture have outgrown increases in the prices of agricultural output, which has been noted by many observers as a main cause for a profit squeeze in the sector.

In view of the foregoing, wage policy presents difficult decisions. The increases in rural real wages during the 1970s reflected the favorable consequences for the distribution of income of rapid growth in Colombia. A problem facing economic management has been how to translate the slowdown in economic performance in the recent past into wage adjustments. As the economy attempts to catch up with the accumulated overvaluation in the nominal exchange rate, nominal wages ought not to adjust in line with movements in the exchange rate, since past changes in money wages have fully or more than fully accounted for inflation, whereas changes in the exchange rate have not. Wage negotiations for 1984 have caused a 28 percent increase in the minimum rural wage, well ahead of the expected inflation rate adjusted for increases in productivity.

Fertilizer Pricing

Aside from coffee, rice, potatoes, and sugar, which use fertilizer intensively, fertilizer use in Colombia remains only comparable to or below the average levels in Latin America, implying the scope for more intensive use of this input. More fertilizer application is particularly cost-effective for small-scale farmers growing subsistence crops such as corn, beans, and cassava. In the case of crops such as potatoes, net gains could be realized from a more balanced use of fertilizer than is now practiced. The use of fertilizer for these crops, for example, is estimated to be far from technically optimal levels, because commercially available generalized formulas are not always suitable to the large variety of ecoclimatic conditions found in Colombia or because of inadequate extension services. The increasing use of foliar analysis and more refined assessments of the need for fertilizer and the dissemination of this knowledge by the extension services could mean greater cost-effectiveness in the use of this input.

Fertilizer use has declined since 1978, and the DNP's analysis identifies several contributing factors: rising relative prices of agricultural inputs, declining profit margins, and overall stagnation in production and acreage. From an economic viewpoint a suboptimal use of the input has been caused by high farmgate prices for fertilizers—reaching more than twice the world market levels, except perhaps for coffee, for which the input price is less than that for others. These prices are to a small extent the result of taxes and tariffs and more significant, of port charges and high domestic transport costs (see table 8-4). Fertilizer import and price policies have been under active surveillance and state control, and intervention has been frequent because of pressures from one group or another. There has not been a concerted and deliberate policy, however, with clearly spelled-out objectives and definition of the desirable levels of subsidies and taxes to be borne by the various parties involved—the industry, the agricultural producers, COLPUERTOS (the Colombian Port Authority), the truckers, and the distributors; further analysis of these issues is clearly in order.

Credit Policy

Virtually all farmers receive institutional credit that is subsidized—in relation to free-market rates—directly or indirectly by the government. The volume of institutional credit for which the farmer is eligible usually represents more than 50 percent of the farmer's costs of production. Several intermediaries, including commercial banks, are involved in the distribution of credit. Two sources of funds, however, the FFAP (Agricultural Finance Fund) and the Caja Agraria (Agricultural Develop-

Table 8-4. *Illustrative Calculation of the Price of Urea, 1983*
(million pesos)

Stage	Price
F.o.b. (in bulk)	10,360.00
C.i.f.	12,225.00
Taxes and duties	1,036.00
Standard port charges	1,393.00
Storage, cost of delays, and other	455.00
Financial and administrative charges	2,726.00
Ex-port cost (in bulk)	17,835.00
Bagging cost	1,400,00
Ex-port cost (bagged)	19,235.00
Estimated cost and transport	3,000.00
Cost at retail	22,235.00

Source: World Bank calculation on the basis of data from the private fertilizer company ABOCOL.

ment Bank), account for about 70 percent of the institutional funds lent to agriculture. Caja lends its own funds and some of FFAP's. The remaining FFAP funds are lent by commercial banks and other banks, such as Banco Ganadero and Banco Cafetero. The term of the loan and the interest rate charged to the farmer depend on the lending institution, the crop being financed, and the assets of the farmer. The Caja Agraria, for example, charges lower interest rates to farmers whose levels of assets are low. There does not seem to be a government policy on the level of the interest subsidy. When market interest rates were falling, for example, the nominal interest rate for the largest line of credit, the FFAP, did not change. The Caja Agraria lowered its interest rates 5 to 7 percentage points in 1983 on loans for food crops. This move appears to have been prompted by a desire to stimulate food production, however, rather than by a desire to maintain a constant level of subsidy in the face of falling interest rates.

Most farmers eligible to receive the subsidized credit have been able to do so in the past. The subsidy does not cause some eligible farmers to be deprived of the credit, as often happens when a good is subsidized. The eligibility criteria include a title to the land, and the volume of credit is based on the crop and the area planted. In 1983, 5 percent of the FFAP funds that were committed to agricultural loans were not lent because of a lack of eligible farmers to demand the loans. The cause may have been bureaucratic delays in processing loans and in transferring lines of credit from one crop to another. In fact, there seems to be some diversion of money earmarked for agricultural credit into other activities. Therefore, the agricultural credit subsidy comes at the expense of the availability of credit in other sectors. The subsidy is not limited to specific crops and is available to small farmers.

In a study conducted jointly by the Inter-American Institute for Agricultural Sciences (IICA) and the Ministry of Agriculture, average rates of interest on agricultural loans were found to be between 45 percent and 60 percent of market interest rates during the period 1976–80.[5] The credit subsidy during this period was equal to 2.2 percent of agricultural GDP. In 1982 the weighted average effective interest rate on Caja Agraria loans to farmers was 31 percent, while FFAP funds were lent at 24 percent.[6] Market interest rates for unsubsidized loans in the formal sector were about 50 percent.[7] The benefit to farmers from government-subsidized loans may not simply be the difference between the government-subsidized rate and the market rate in the formal sector because of two other important considerations that work in opposite directions. On the one hand, government bureaucracies make the cost of transaction of government loans rather high for the farmer; on the other hand, most farmers have limited access to the formal market and would have to obtain credit in the informal sector, where interest rates are estimated to be 55 percent or higher. While data on loans given to farmers through the informal sector are not available, the proportion of loans made through the informal sector is thought to be low.

At first glance, the effect of the agricultural credit subsidy on the composition of agricultural output or on the choice of farming techniques does not seem to be distortionary, since credit is readily available for most purposes at roughly comparable interest rates. Some agricultural projects that may not be economically beneficial, however, will be undertaken because the private cost of borrowing is made less than the social cost by the subsidy. Insofar as these low-return projects are concentrated in a given subsector of agriculture, the composition of agricultural output will be affected. The subsidized credit in agriculture is also a source of distortion for other sectors, since part of the cheap and subsidized credit in agriculture comes at the expense of reduced availability of credit in other sectors. This increases the market interest rate in other sectors to a level above the cost to the economy in the absence of subsidies. Projects in other sectors that may be socially beneficial at the social cost of borrowing are therefore not undertaken because the private cost of borrowing is higher than the social cost. The lowering of the credit subsidy to agriculture is a delicate issue, because of assumptions concerning the effect of such a measure on production and distribution.

The effect of reducing the credit subsidy on agricultural production and farm incomes is likely to be modest. On the basis of an analysis of twelve major crops, including coffee, the interest costs of credit account for about 11 percent of the annual costs of production. Since the subsidized interest rate is about 55 percent of the market rate and the credit subsidy 45 percent, the subsidy accounts for about 9 percent of total production costs. Removing the subsidy would raise the production costs by less than 9 percent if, as expected, it led to lower market interest rates and farmers obtained credit from both sources. In comparison, fertilizer accounts for about 12.5 percent of annual production costs, while machinery rental accounts for about 14 percent (see table 8-5). It should be noted, however, that the measures in table 8-5 may understate the true credit costs and the difficulties faced by farmers in obtaining this input. Although the Caja figures are meant to be full interest costs, it is possible that the costs of noninstitutional credit are excluded. The calculation of the credit subsidy would still be adequate, however, since it affects only the institutional component. Much more needs to be known about agricultural credit and financing—both institutional and noninstitutional credit, the efficiency of existing arrangements, and their beneficiaries.

There has been an increasing number of field observations about the solvency and liquidity problems of farmers, and the effective cost of credit, including administrative and institutional costs—which are yet to be quantified—may be greater than the estimates mentioned here. The present comparisons nevertheless suggest that while the subsidy component of credit costs may not be insignificant, it may be an incentive for which other measures—depreciation of the exchange rate and reduction in costs of other inputs (by a reduction in tariffs or increased efficiency in transportation or ports)—can reasonably be expected to be substituted.

The financial situation of Caja Agraria, the largest bank in Colombia in geographical coverage (863 branch offices and 460 input and supply stores) and number of staff (14,500 employees), continues to be problematic. For equity and political reasons, Caja is required to provide a level of services far in excess of its resources

Table 8-5. *Input Costs as a Proportion of Total Costs of Production, 1982*
(percent)

Crop	Credit[a]	Fertilizer	Machinery rental	Pesticides[b]	Seeds
Wheat	6.89	11.68	24.01	4.28	11.23
Barley	6.62	10.63	26.57	6.24	7.58
Corn	8.03	6.10	11.37	0.59	4.70
Soybeans	7.58	10.99	14.34	8.58	9.56
Sorghum	7.41	20.24	14.46	6.49	2.57
Sesame	8.27	8.00	10.76	2.29	1.57
Beans	7.98	9.05	13.53	0.04	13.51
Coffee	13.85	13.76	18.76	2.19	1.30
Rice	7.84	10.99	10.01	9.07	13.74
Cotton	8.43	9.99	7.30	11.58	2.35
Potatoes	7.90	13.89	6.94	4.12	16.18
Yuca	13.54	5.58	10.19	1.97	4.84
Weighted average (with coffee)	10.93	11.86	13.73	4.33	6.02
Weighted average (without coffee)	8.82	10.49	10.08	5.88	9.45

Note: An arithmetic average of production with high-yielding and traditional varieties, except for coffee, which is a weighted average based on area planted.

a. Interest costs from farm budgets for semester B of 1982; weighted average for traditional and modern farms.

b. Includes pesticides, herbicides, fungicides, and insecticides.

Source: Caja Agraria.

and capabilities. This has caused net losses to the institution, since no compensatory financing is provided for these activities by the central government. On the income side, Caja cannot increase its lending interest rates—as a matter of fact, at the government's request it lowered its average lending rate in 1983—nor can it increase the proportion of its portfolio (fixed by law) invested in more productive lines of credit. On the cost side, Caja cannot easily reduce the number of branch offices, of which about 70 percent are operating at a loss, nor its input and supply stores, and it has not been able to keep its personnel costs under control by countervailing the demands of its very strong labor union.

In the past, Caja's financial problems have been managed through the use of special rediscount lines from the Central Bank, the paying of relatively low interest rates on savings deposits, and sporadic government contributions to replenish Caja's capital. At present, however, there is a consensus that these problems have to be dealt with in a more systematic manner, which requires structural and policy changes; on the institutional side, some of the required changes are Caja's responsibility, whereas others require government action to modify external factors that affect Caja's operations. Basically, the costs of the social function of Caja and the costs that arise from any inefficiencies need to be identified and quantified. The government, through specific periodic allocations suitably monitored, would assume responsibility for the social costs and would undertake to modify the external factors which are affecting Caja's operations negatively. On the other hand, Caja would assume responsibility for improving its operational efficiency.

Agricultural Marketing

Some improvements that have been made in wholesale marketing are evidenced by an estimated decline in the wholesale margin measured as a percentage of the producer price or the consumer price (see table 8-6). In some recent reviews these margins are considered large, implying the scope for improvements in marketing as those that were made under the programs of PRODESARROLLO and DRI/PAN. Retail margins seem to have increased during the 1970s.[8] These increases, however, might represent, at least in part, improvement in quality and greater shares of processing and packaging in the final products, in response to gradual increases in real income and perhaps lags in transferring consumer price increases to wholesale and producer

Table 8-6. *Average Marketing Margins for Selected Agricultural Commodities, 1970–80*
(percent of consumer price)

Commodity	1970–72	1973–75	1976–78	1979–80
Rice				
Wholesale	24.0	25.7	21.6	17.7
Retail	12.6	10.8	17.5	18.3
Corn				
Wholesale	12.6	11.0	8.6	8.0
Retail	14.2	16.4	13.7	20.9
Beans				
Wholesale	36.0	31.4	29.3	23.7
Retail	16.1	14.7	18.0	23.6
Potatoes				
Wholesale	29.5	22.9	23.8	21.4
Retail	23.6	20.0	31.2	31.1
Beef				
Wholesale	21.7	20.0	21.5	15.1
Retail	23.8	24.1	23.5	37.2
Milk				
Wholesale	30.0	35.1	45.4	28.3
Retail	3.9	4.3	4.2	7.1

Note: Average marketing margins are wholesale and retail margins as percentages of the retail price.
Sources: DNP and World Bank estimates made by German A. Rioseco.

levels. Inadequate improvements in marketing in the face of increasing demand for greater marketing might be another part of the explanation.

While the wholesale markets are working fairly efficiently, high margins seem to be based on the high cost of transport between markets, ranging from 3.3 cents to 6.0 cents a ton per kilometer. For fertilizers shipped from Barranquilla ports to Bogotá, the cost of transport is equivalent to an increase of approximately 25 percent over the ex-port price, and equivalent to $47 a metric ton, while the cost of freight from European ports to Barranquilla is $30 a metric ton. A comparable difference of 26 percent over the producer's price is observed in the costs of transport that affect rice exports. High costs of trucks and transport equipment on account of tariffs and import restrictions constitute a part of high transport costs. Estimated operating costs and taxes in January 1983, according to the Ministry of Public Works, were Col$30.5 a kilometer for a six-metric-ton truck and Col$45.0 a kilometer for an eighteen-metric-ton truck, taxes representing more than 15 percent of these costs. Also, freedom of entry into the trucking industry is limited in Colombia on two counts: first, the import of trucks (assembled or to be assembled in the country) requires prior approval of the Instituto del Transporte, and second, in order to operate, a trucker must be affiliated with a trucking company.

Seasonal and year-to-year price variability is also believed to be high, particularly for perishables, and these do not appear to have been reduced significantly through the years. Constraints involve the lack of adequate countrywide market and crop information and data, the lack of storage facilities and other needed infrastructure, and a shortage of marketing credit for investment in infrastructure and for recurrent expenditures related to purchases and costs of stock carryover.

In spite of the improvements, the overall adjustment of marketing may not have been fast enough to keep up with the requirements of rapid urbanization. Thus, wide fluctuations in price, relatively high marketing margins, and heavy losses, particularly in perishables, are attributed to deficiencies in marketing. Inadequate infrastructure in collection, storage, refrigeration, and processing and the lack of adequate crop-price and market information are serious problems. Given Colombia's fairly sophisticated and sizable entrepreneurial skills, any inadequacy in marketing—with the probable exception of the wholesale markets—needs to be examined in the light, first, of the existing legal and regulatory framework, and second, of the economic environment. Cases such as the slaughterhouses, which are usually small, inefficient units, operated by municipalities as sources of revenue and employment, need to be reviewed.

Among other factors, the pricing and marketing of agricultural products is affected by IDEMA's price support for staples, OPSA's price determination or negotiation for selected outputs, and the strong function of producer associations in many products. The marketing of fertilizer is dominated by Caja Agraria and FEDERACAFE, which together account for approximately 60 percent of the fertilizer trade, and among producer associations by FEDEARROZ and several associations of banana growers, which account for approximately 12 percent of total trade. Out of approximately forty-two enterprises that participate in the seed trade, Caja controls an average of 18 percent of the national sales. The balance of inputs, primarily pesticides, is handled largely by the private sector. Prices paid by producers for inputs, both locally produced and imported, are determined periodically by the Ministry of Agriculture.

The public function in marketing has been focused primarily on control, direct intervention, planning, and regulating. As already noted, IDEMA influences prices by purchasing at support prices, selling through the Bolsa Nacional Agropecuaria, S.A. (Bolsa), and wholesale and retail distribution centers, importing or granting licenses for imports, and exporting and maintaining regulatory stocks of a number of basic agricultural commodities—wheat, rice, corn, beans, sorghum, barley, soybeans, and sesame. Except when large imports are made by IDEMA, however, the government's market stabilization policies have had only a marginal effect because of IDEMA's limited resources. Aside from its credit role, Caja intervenes in the sale of farm inputs and supplies, handling about 40 percent of total trade through 440 outlets throughout the country.

In an attempt to improve marketing efficiency, the government has created and assisted in the creation of several mixed-economy companies. The Union of Agrarian Reform Cooperatives, Ltd. (CECORA) is concerned with the development of cooperatives, while the Enterprise for Marketing of Perishable Products (EMCOPER) is essentially responsible for building and operating cold-storage facilities in competition with the private sector. The Central Wholesale Market of Bogotá (CORABASTOS) and similar markets in Medellín and Cali were created to build and lease wholesale marketing facilities to private wholesalers; CORABASTOS also participates in day-to-day management of the public markets. The Bolsa, organized in 1979, is involved in commodity trading, processing, and the provision of market information. FEDERACAFE, although not a marketing institution, is implementing its crop diversification program in the coffee-producing areas, providing technical assistance to some forty multipurpose cooperatives and marketing certain products, most of them perishables. Also, important efforts for improving output marketing of small-scale farmers are being made in specific areas through the DRI/PAN programs.

Both Caja and IDEMA are blamed for being inefficient and incurring heavy losses. While these observations are largely true, by and large the underlying problems reflect not only the weaknesses of these two institutions but also extrainstitutional policy decisions regarding their operations. Caja and IDEMA are expected for reasons of equity and political considerations to provide a level of services that is either not in line with their resources and capabilities or most of the time causes net losses to the institutions without compensatory financing for these activities from the government.

Any measure to reduce the cost of inputs to agriculture—particularly to small-scale farms—other than through reducing the cost of operation of the ports, changes in taxes and tariffs, and transport and storage costs would need to be accompanied by substantial improvements in the efficiency of Caja's operations, particularly since it controls approximately 40 percent of trade, and, to some extent, determines the market price of inputs. Particular attention will need to be given to the possibility of completely separating the input supply function of Caja from the rest of its activities and to the need to improve its capacity to negotiate its freight needs with the trucking industry.

IDEMA's market-intervention activities could in principle generate sufficient revenues to make the institution self-financing, so it does not receive any budgetary or other kind of allocation to finance its recurrent expenditures. The institution is requested, however, to support producer prices and incomes through the purchase of agricultural commodities, mostly in marginal areas, and to maintain regulatory stocks and regulate consumer prices through direct market intervention. On the other hand, the only real source of income to IDEMA is that which is the result of price differentials on commodities imported by the institution. For several reasons, however, including the explicit policy of limiting government intervention in the market, the volume of imports and the size of the price differentials is largely insufficient as a source of income to IDEMA, causing a shortfall of operating funds.

Policy Conclusions

Research and extension suffered from relative neglect during the 1970s and current efforts to reverse this trend deserve full support. The decrease in funding for the ICA, the overburdening of the institute with regulatory functions, and the loss of first-rate scientists are problems to be overcome. Continuing efforts to upgrade research need to be quickly linked to extension, which has also suffered in the past from the fragmentation of the agricultural extension services in the country and inadequate funding and policy orientation.

Additional irrigation and drainage are of high priority in selected areas in which water is the constraint to higher yields and to the harvesting of two crops a year. In particular, public investment for flood control and drainage could be effective in converting pastures into land suitable for intensive cropping. Rehabilitation of irrigation is also justified in general by its cost-effectiveness. Expansion of agricultural production on new land with new irrigation facilities is generally a more costly option.

The rapid reduction of Colombia's rich forest resources, soil erosion and conservation problems, and increasing siltation of water reservoirs are serious policy concerns. A greater capacity to execute programs in the use of natural resources, which will clearly require greater public awareness of the problems, needs to be developed. INDERENA's institutional capabilities for policy execution need to be strengthened, and conservation education programs need to be stepped up. A program of research and baseline studies on critical areas is called for to enable INDERENA to evaluate policies and projects, funding for which might need to be sought externally. The ad hoc approach to forestry development needs to be replaced by a more systematic policy. In particular, the execution of pilot projects, such as the Upper Magdalena Pilot Watershed Management Project, and the follow-up to larger-scale projects should be placed within the framework of a national forest and natural resources development program.

The most significant element of estimated farm budgets is labor costs, which represent 40–50 percent of variable costs. Policy intervention consists principally of minimum wage legislation, arrived at through negotiations between the government and the agricultural unions. Negotiations for 1984 had produced a 28 percent increase in the minimum wage by midyear, outstripping the inflation rate adjusted for gains in productivity. Future wage negotiations need to be particularly cognizant of the sectoral and macroeconomic implications of excessive work increases.

High internal transport and port-handling costs, and to a lesser extent financial costs and import duties, have contributed to the high prices of urea in Colombia. Improvements in the functioning of COLPUERTOS would be vital to the achievement of long-term reduction in the prices of urea to farmers. Efforts to reduce internal transport costs might include measures to reduce high tariffs on agricultural equipment and transport vehicles, lower the unduly restrictive entry and low use of capacity in trucking, increase the transport of fertilizer in bulk, and expand the use of port facilities at Buenaventura on the Pacific, which is closer to important farm production centers such as those of the Cauca valley. In the matter of composite fertlilizers, more analysis is needed of the present level of protection and subsidy to the domestic industry, its efficiency, and its pricing policy. If the industry requires protection, ways and means of reducing the costs of its inputs should be explored before domestic output sales prices—that is, of the composite fertilizers—are raised.

Long-term improvements in wholesale marketing are evidenced by an estimated decline in the wholesale margin needed as a percentage of the producer price or the consumer price. These margins are nevertheless considered to be large by some recent reviewers, implying that there is scope for improvements in marketing, as has been the experience under the programs of PRODESARROLLO and DRI/PAN. Retail margins seem to have increased during the 1970s. These increases in margins, however, might in part represent improvement in quality and greater shares of processing and packaging in the final products in response to gradual increases in real income and perhaps to lags in transferring consumer price increases to wholesale and producer levels. Inadequate improvements in the face of growing customer demand for greater marketing services might be another part of the explanation. Proposals have recently been made for marketing projects intended to reduce marketing margins and to bring about institutional improvements; a clear conception of the way these efforts would contribute to agricultural development, however, is yet to emerge.

The estimated annual cost of institutional credit is about 11 percent of the production costs of twelve major crops, including coffee. The rates on institutional credit, while positive in real terms during 1983–84, are estimated to be as low as 55 percent of the market rate. (As noted earlier, a reason for "high" real market rates is the acceleration of the crawling peg.) The 45 percent credit subsidy implies a saving in credit cost to farmers of about 9 percent of their annual production costs. Removing the subsidy would increase production costs less than 9 percent if, as expected, it would lead to greater availability of credit, lower market interest rates, and the possibility that farmers could obtain credit from both sources. In comparison, fertilizer constitutes about 12.5 percent of production costs while machinery rental accounts for about 14 percent. While the subsidy component of the credit cost is not insignificant, other measures—an adequate exchange rate and a reduction in the costs of other inputs (by a further reduction in tariffs and greater efficiency in transport and port handling)—could eventually be substituted for it. The present estimates, however, may understate the full credit costs to the farmer, including nonfinancial costs of the institutional credit and the cost of noninstitutional credit. Additional sector work is proposed to analyze the sources of institutional and noninstitutional credit, the efficiency of existing arrangements and their beneficiaries, and the way the system can successfully cope once policy reforms in other areas have led to increased demand for inputs.

In the past, Caja Agraria's financial shortfalls have been managed through special rediscount lines from the Central Bank, the payment of relatively low interest rates on savings deposits, and periodic government contributions to replenish Caja's capital. A consensus is emerging, however, that these problems must be dealt with systematically through structural changes. The costs of the social function of Caja need to be identified and quantified separately from those that may arise from any inefficiencies. The government, through specific periodic allocations, suitably monitored, would need to assume responsibility for the social costs and try to reduce them. On the other hand, Caja should assume responsibility for improving its operational efficiency: Caja's credit and input functions might be split with a view to achieving greater financial accountability in each of these distinct areas.

Notes

1. DNP, "Diagnostico del sector agrario" (Bogotá, 1983, processed).

2. Value-added figures from DANE include a combined estimate for coffee (01), other agricultural products (02), and animal production (03), and separate values for processed coffee (08) and sugar manufacturing (12). These categories are as explained in chapter 1. In disaggregating (01), (02), and (03), approximations of gross output have been used, despite the obvious double counting that results. It should be noted that during the period 1970–81, the value added in the agricultural sector has consistently been equal to about 75 percent of gross output.

3. UNICO, *Feasibility Study Report for an Ammonia and Urea Project*, vol. 1 (Tokyo: UNICO International Corp., July 1984), table 4.

4. These and remaining estimates in this section are from Urrutia, *Winners and Losers in Colombia's Economic Growth of the 1970s*, and 1982 World Bank calculations using data from DANE.

5. A. Hernandez Gamarra and G. Jimenez Perdamo, "Consideraciones económicas y financieras sobre la viabilidad del seguro agrocredito en Colombia" Cuadro 4-3, Estudio de Consultoria para el Proyecto IICA-OPSA del Ministerio de Agricultura, September 1982.

6. The nominal interest rate on Caja loans was 26 percent, while FFAP loans were generally made at a nominal interest rate of 21 percent. Because of the Colombian system of deducting quarterly interest payments in advance, the effective interest rates turn out to be 24 percent and 31 percent. It must be noted, however, that some transactions are made at the nominal rate, although to what extent is not known.

7. See World Bank, *Colombia: The Investment Banking System and Related Issues in the Financial Sector* (Washington, D.C., 1985). Nominal rates were lower, and some transactions are expected to have been carried out at the lower rate.

8. A DNP study carried out in 1977, in which the marketing margins of twenty-four products are reviewed, indicates an average wholesale margin of 15.8 percent and a retail margin of 24.2 percent, for a weighted average of 36.2 percent. A similar study made in the United States by the Department of Commerce indicates a wholesale margin of 6.1 percent and retail margins of 21.4 percent for marketing chains and 18.9 percent for independent retailers; the average total margin was 24.3 percent.

9

Conclusion

THIS BOOK has been concerned with policies intended to bring about economic adjustment while at the same time sustaining development. In such a study Colombia has offered the opportunity for a joint treatment of macroeconomic and sectoral issues. While growth options in agriculture are central, the work has also provided a trade-related macroeconomic analysis that goes beyond the concerns of any particular sector. The study has been focused on the links between macroeconomic issues and agricultural prospects and has shown how these relations influence performance.

The first chapter showed how the dynamics of the principal export item, coffee, affect other agriculture and the rest of the economy and how macroeconomic policies—made partly because of coffee developments—affect agriculture. In many developing countries instability in the external and domestic sectors arises from wide price fluctuations in the world markets for a principal export commodity. Macroeconomic policy, particularly with respect to the exchange rate and import restrictions, poses policy dilemmas in such circumstances. Trade policies have a special significance for agriculture, which is a highly tradable sector, and restrictive trade measures can hurt this sector disproportionately; this factor gave rise to the further analysis of export and import policies in chapters 2 and 3.

In the five subsequent chapters developments were considered from the agricultural viewpoint, although macroeconomic effects are central to them. Thus, the agricultural incentives discussed in chapter 4 are derived as much from exchange-rate, import, fiscal, and monetary policies as from sector-specific interventions. Sectoral policies of price supports and credit subsidies are important, but their effects are smaller in Colombia than in some other countries. Issues of price stabilization are also related to overall import policies, even though the proposed measures, discussed in chapter 5, are sectoral. Coffee policy was considered in detail, also from the sectoral viewpoint, in chapter 6, while, as emphasized throughout the book, it is an area of considerable macroeconomic importance. Chapters 7 and 8 dealt with production policies in agriculture that should serve to complement economywide incentive and price policies.

Macroeconomic Policy, Performance, and Agriculture

While in this work the solid long-term performance of the Colombian economy has been noted, much of the policy discussion has concerned the more recent developments, which have been more difficult. The economy saw a slowing down of real growth rates and generation of employment during 1981–83, after the excellent record of the 1970s. By 1984, unemployment surveys in Colombia's four largest cities showed an unemployment rate of about 13.5 percent, almost twice the level registered at the end of 1981. The current account in the balance of payments and the fiscal balances also deteriorated during 1981–83, constraining the viability of growth-oriented policies. Significant improvements in the current account of the balance of payments were seen in 1984–85 with the initiation of adjustment policies. Both the public and the private sectors, however, continued to face significant difficulties in tapping the international capital markets. Consequently, the loss of net foreign exchange reserves, which was substantial—$1.8 billion—in 1983, continued in 1984. With a deepening of the adjustment measures, the reserves position can be expected to stabilize and improve, and present indications support this view.

The influence of external factors in the recent problems has been noted. Exports to Venezuela, for instance, one of Colombia's principal nontraditional trading partners, and to Ecuador, Mexico, Argentina, Brazil, Costa Rica, and Chile have declined significantly since 1982, following economic problems, major devaluations, and import restrictions in those countries. The external debt problems of other Latin American countries have also been a proximate cause of the pressure on the capital account of the balance of payments. The contribution of domestic developments to the recent difficulties has also been emphasized. The coffee boom of the second half of the 1970s, for example, set in motion an accelerated growth in the money supply and inflation despite the stabilization effort made by the authorities. In the absence of adequate adjustments in the crawling peg, these events led to a significant appreciation of the real exchange rate, reducing the incentives to produce noncoffee exportables. In addition, the fiscal deficit grew during the 1980s, contributing to a higher rate of growth of domestic credit and, thus, of domestic inflation than would have been likely to occur had measures to control the deficit been initiated more promptly.

In these circumstances, Colombia needs to adopt significant measures for adjustment with attention to creation of employment. If such measures are taken in a timely manner, the country will not need to sacrifice much growth or employment generation. An outward-looking strategy would be consistent with the need for further adjustment with growth and the creation of employment. Such is the present government's economic strategy. A program for fiscal, monetary, and exchange rate adjustments that would, among other things, improve the competitiveness of noncoffee tradables has been initiated, and politically difficult decisions to execute the policy package are being made; these policies for adjustment with growth and for employment generation need to be deepened and sustained. Colombia has a long record of responsible and careful economic management. Maintenance of the current efforts should once again provide the basis for continued and rapid development in the remainder of the 1980s.

The policies being put in place represent a critical phase of medium-term adjustment, in which stability would be achieved, permitting continuation of growth as the economy is redirected toward export promotion. Subsequently, policies would be concentrated on further strengthening of the incentives for external trade. In agriculture, medium-term policies would stimulate productivity and increase exports. Part of the macroeconomic adjustments are in place, as of this writing, and some positive results have already been obtained.

The 1985–86 macroeconomic policy package concerns further reductions in the expenditure-revenue gap of the public sector, including a review of public-sector investments and improvement of their effectiveness, postponement of large and long-gestating new projects, and maintenance of the prices of public utilities at appropriate levels; a slowdown in the expansion of credit to the government by the Central Bank; full correction of the overvaluation of the real exchange rate; liberalization of imports that are needed for exports; and a scaling down of external borrowing targets, reducing the demand for external funds. These policies are being complemented by measures to strengthen directly the financial and real sectors of the economy, with attention to generation of employment.

The authorities recognize that even with domestic policy adjustments, a resumption of external commercial bank financing—to, say, the 1981–82 levels—would be essential to the achievement of adjustment with growth. Projections of the balance of payments indicate the need for such a revival in commercial bank financing, to be followed by the prospect of significant expansion of resource-based exports—petroleum, coal, and nickel—and other nontraditional exports during the second half of the 1980s. In view of the government's adjustment efforts, the World Bank has augmented its policy and financial support to the country; an agreement could now be worked out with the commercial banks on the additional financing needed. The projection that is based on the combination of increased macroeconomic policy adjustments and capital inflows, with borrowing kept within prudent limits, envisages a revitalization of sectoral performance contributing to a more rapid economic growth with balance of payments stability and creation of employment.

The post-1975 agricultural expansion has been in good measure based on coffee, a product for which only a modest increase in demand in the world markets is projected for the 1980s. The principal macroeconomic constraints to more vigorous noncoffee expansion have comprised a high inflation rate, an overvalued exchange rate, and import restrictions, which impose a "tax" on a heavily tradable sector such as agriculture. The effects of macroeconomic policy may have been unintentional, but the net effect from the mid 1970s to 1983 on noncoffee agricultural tradables was negative. Through sectoral policies an attempt has been made to increase the incentives for the relatively small group of imported cereals through high levels of import protection and domestic price supports. In addition, credit subsidies to producers and storers, albeit moderate, have provided some sectoral incentives. At the same time, however, agricultural investments by the public sector are estimated to have declined significantly in real terms since the mid 1970s.

The adoption of a more neutral macroeconomic policy posture—as envisaged with the changes that are being made—would be essential, beginning with the elimination of overvaluation of the exchange rate, reduction of the fiscal deficit, rationalization of the investment program, liberation of imported inputs needed for exports, and strengthening of the financial sector. Depreciation of the real exchange rate began to take effect in a significant way in 1984, and further substantial progress was recorded in 1985. Such necessary macroeconomic adjustments can also produce difficulties at the financial and real sector levels which need to be addressed by policies in these areas. Once the principal macroeconomic disincentives were eliminated, special sectoral incentives such as price supports and credit subsidies would be less justified; in view of the efficiency losses of the latter, they could be phased out gradually. On the other hand, there is a case to be made for supporting high-priority investments for irrigation, input supply, research, extension, and marketing.

Coffee Policy and Noncoffee Production

Although coffee stocks may have contributed somewhat to strengthening Colombia's export share under the coffee agreements, the recent stock trends indicate significant costs to the coffee sector and the economy. At the end of 1984, Colombia was estimated to carry accumulated coffee stocks equal to some 122 percent of its exports. The Federation of Coffee Growers is committed to a containment of coffee incentives and is pursuing a mix of policies not only to match production with demand, but also to sustain the long-term yield and health of the *caturra* variety. An effort is being made to hold the coffee price guaranteed to producers and to eliminate fertilizer subsidies to coffee growers. At the same time, the federation has embarked upon a program to provide income support through direct production and marketing incentives to other products in the coffee zones.

The domestic producer prices of coffee increased at a rate lower than that of the consumer price increase during 1980–83. A source of the recent pressure on the producer price, however, has been the significant increase in the rate of the crawling peg, which, together with some increase in the external coffee price, produced a large increase in the peso value of the export surrender price during 1984. Considering that the exchange rate is expected to continue to depreciate rapidly, a continued resolve might be essential to hold the domestic producer price.

Even if the producer price should be maintained in real terms, production might only be stabilized, despite the increases in production costs and the recent outbreak of *roya*. Unless there is a dramatic increase in demand for Colombian coffee, given the ICA, some decline in production may be needed during the second half of the decade. Several issues need to be analyzed further. Given the life cycle of existing trees, what incentive structure would be needed to bring about the needed adjustment in production? Also to be evaluated are the possible mixes of coffee disincentives and diversification incentives: how much incentive might be allocated for stumping coffee trees? What additional efforts would be required for diversification?

Sectoral Incentives

One of the sectoral incentives reviewed was the price support offered by IDEMA for rice, corn, sorghum, soya, wheat, barley, and sesame, all of which except rice are also imported. The domestic support price of these commodities exceeded the f.o.b. import price—unadjusted for special circumstances such as export subsidies abroad—by 50–100 percent during 1983, although the rapid depreciation of the peso in 1984–85 may have reduced this difference subsequently. Despite the fact that IDEMA has a virtual monopoly on imports and makes a profit on the sale of its imports, the agency has run a deficit on the whole on account of its price support operations. Apart from the fiscal issue, there is also the efficacy question of providing special incentives for crops, such as wheat, in which Colombia does not appear to have a comparative advantage. Technical analysis so far has pointed to potential net gains from phasing out the high protection for some products. Several issues need to be examined in greater detail. What would be the time path for phasing out these output subsidies? How would it be linked to liberalization in the importation of the same commodities? Would the approach produce undesirable income distribution effects, and if so how could they be offset? How can some of the price instability concerns be better addressed through selective use of futures markets?

The high price of inputs, particularly of fertilizer, is one of the most often mentioned sectoral disincentives. A suboptimal use of fertilizer in most noncoffee commodities has been the result of high farmgate prices for fertilizers—reaching a level twice the world market levels, except perhaps for coffee, for which the input price is still less than that for others. These prices are to some extent caused by taxes and tariffs and, more significant, by high port charges and high domestic transport costs. Policies to reduce port and internal transport costs would therefore be highly beneficial to the sector. Fertilizer import and price policies themselves have been under government control, but interventions have frequently been the results of pressures from one group or another. There has not been a concerted price policy with clearly spelled out objectives and definitions of the desirable levels of subsidies and taxes to be borne by the various parties involved. Further analysis of these issues is clearly in order.

While subsidized credit has provided some special agricultural incentives, the present system has several inadequacies. During the past decade growth in agricultural credit was erratic, and the average annual increase in outstanding loans was below the growth in agricultural output. At the same time an increasing share of agricultural credit has come to depend on the Central Bank's rediscounts, while the resources mobilized by commercial banks and agricultural banks—Caja Agraria, Banco Cafetero, Banco Ganadero—have declined. Furthermore, the existing system favors short-term investments over long-term, larger farmers over smaller, and agricultural primary production over processing and marketing credit. Finally, the administrative costs of handling agricultural credit seem to be high, especially in the case of Caja Agraria, the main agricultural bank.

Related work by the World Bank on the financial sector issues has suggested policy directions for agricultural credit. Issues to be translated into concrete policy recommendations concern interest rates, term transformation, and levels of subsidies. On interest rate policies, the existing forced investment requirements that are applicable to resources of financial institutions need to be lowered gradually in order to reduce the segmentation between the free and subsidized credit markets. Concerning term transformation, introduction of a floating interest rate might be considered, linking lending rates to an index representing the average cost of raising deposit resources. Turning to levels of subsidy, the Central Bank's rediscounting of funds might replace the current fixed interest rate system by a floating rate system. Furthermore, the proportion of the loans refinanced by the official financial funds needs to be reduced in time, and the financial intermediary should be expected to contribute a larger share from deposit resources mobilized from savers in financing term loans.

While the greater part of agriculture-related investments is made by the private sector, it has been shown that public sector investment is significant in selected areas such as infrastructure development, including rural roads (Ministry of Transportation), storage (IDEMA), rural electrification, irrigation, and land development (HIMAT, INCORA), research and extension (primarily ICA), provision of credit (the Central Bank through the Agricultural Fund and Caja Agraria), and watershed management (INDERENA and Department Development Corporations). During the past decade, public expenditures in the sector have decreased steadily and significantly. In 1984 a part of the agricultural investments of the public sector was to be financed out of a Public Investment Fund, which depended on the decreasing income of the Special Exchange Account; consequently there were serious imbalances between investment expenditures and recurrent expenditures that are difficult to reduce.

In this study a comprehensive review of the public and private sources and use of funds for agriculture has been called for, with a view to ensuring that agricultural investments are in line with the expected contribution of the sector to growth, exports, and employment. The results of the review would be used to devise programs to support the availability of funds for high-priority agricultural investment in commercial and traditional agriculture, improve the financial discipline of agricultural line agencies and their budgetary monitoring and control capabilities, and carry out annual reviews of the investment program and recurrent expenditures, relating performance and expenditures to the agricultural objectives.

APPENDIXES

A

The Interaction of Coffee, Money, and Inflation in Colombia

Sebastian Edwards

IN THIS APPENDIX a simple model of the effects of changes in the price of coffee on the competitiveness of the rest of the economy is presented. In order to simplify the exposition, a model will first be derived in which the monetary effects of changes in the price of coffee are assumed away; this assumption will be relaxed later by introducing a money market. The model will then be tested, using annual data for Colombia. It will trace quite closely the behavior of the price level and of the relative producer prices of noncoffee traded goods in Colombia, which is central to the analysis presented in chapter 1.

Changes in the Price of Coffee and Competitiveness

Consider a small open economy with a fixed exchange rate that produces three goods: coffee, C, other tradables, T, and nontradables, N.[1] Assume further, for the sake of simplicity, that the exchange rate is equal to 1; this assumption will be relaxed later. The excess demand for nontradables is assumed to depend on prices and income.

Consider first the case in which this excess demand is not affected by the relative price of coffee. As a first approximation, this can be justified by assuming that domestic residents do not consume coffee—or consume negligible amounts in relation to the amount exported—and that factors used in the production of coffee are sector-specific, in both the short run and the long run. These assumptions will be relaxed subsequently. In equilibrium the excess demand for nontradable goods will be equal to zero, and under these assumptions it can be written as:

$$(A.1) \qquad N = N(q_T, \ Y) = 0,$$
$$\qquad\qquad\qquad (+) \ (+)$$

where q_T is the domestic price of tradables in relation to the price of nontradable goods—that is, $q_T = P_T/P_N$—and Y is real income in terms of nontradables. The signs in parentheses below the arguments of the function refer to the assumed signs of the partial derivatives. The positive sign of q_T stems from the assumption of gross substitutability between nontradable goods and tradable goods. Equilibrium in the nontradable sector requires that the excess demand for this type of good is equal to zero, both in the short run and in the long run. In this model it is possible to think of q_T as the real exchange rate. The reason for this is that in a country that produces a major commodity export good—that is, coffee in Colombia, or oil in Indonesia—the appropriate measure of the real exchange rate will be the relative price of tradables other than the commodity export to the price of nontradables.[2]

In (A.1) Y is expressed in terms of nontradable goods and is given by

$$(A.2) \qquad\qquad Y = H_N^S + q_T H_T^S + q_C \overline{C},$$

where H_N^S, H_T^S, and $q_C \overline{C}$ are supplies of nontradables, tradables, and coffee, respectively, and q_C is the relative price of coffee in terms of nontradable goods. The supply of coffee is held fixed in order to simplify the analysis. If it is further assumed that real income, Y, equals expenditure E, equation (A.1) for nontradable goods equilibrium implies that the external sector is also in equilibrium.

Maintaining the assumption of gross substitutability, we can depict the equilibrium situation in the nontradables market in figure A-1, which has been adapted from Dornbusch.[3] The NN schedule describes the combination of q_T and q_C that is compatible with equilibria in the nontradable goods market. The slope of this curve is given by:

$$(A.3) \qquad\qquad \frac{dq_T}{dq_C} = \frac{-(\partial N/\partial Y)\overline{C}}{[(\partial N/\partial q_T) + (\partial N/\partial Y)H_T^S]} < 0.$$

The ray OT, on the other hand, measures the price of other tradable goods in relation to the price of coffee, P_T/P_C. The initial equilibrium position is given by A, with equilibrium relative prices being equal to q_T^0 and q_C^0, respectively.

Assume now that there is an exogenous increase in the price of coffee. What will be the effect on the relative price and degree of competitiveness of other tradables? The OT ray will then rotate clockwise toward OT' as in figure A-2. If the (nominal) price of nontradables were constant, the new equilibrium would be given by B, with a constant relative price of noncoffee tradables with respect to nontradables. As long as the slope of the NN is negative, however, at B there will be excess demand for nontradables that will require an increase of the relative price of these goods, with respect to the prices both of coffee and of other tradables. The final equilibrium will then be attained at C.

As a consequence of the increase in the price of coffee, there has been a decrease of the relative price of noncoffee tradables, both with respect to coffee—that is, P_T/P_C—and with respect to nontradables—that is, from q_T^0 to q_T^1. This reduction in the relative price of other tradables, of course, will encourage resources to move out of the other tradables sector into the other sectors of the economy. This phenome-

Figure A-1. *The Prices of Coffee and Other Tradables in Relation to the Prices of Nontradables*

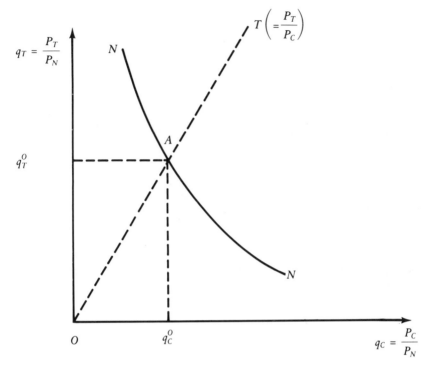

Source: Adapted from Rudiger Dornbusch, "Tariffs and Non-traded Goods," *Journal of International Economics*, vol. 4 (May 1974), pp. 177–85.

non is similar to what occurred in oil-exporting countries as a consequence of the increase in the price of oil in the 1970s and has been labeled the Dutch disease or the deindustrialization effect.[4]

In figure A-2 the degree of loss of competitiveness of the noncoffee tradables sector—that is, the degree of decline of q_T (= P_T/P_N)—depends on the slope of the NN curve. At one extreme, if the NN curve is a vertical line the negative effect on q_T of an exogenous increase in the price of coffee will be maximum. On the other hand, if *all* the additional income generated by the higher price of coffee is spent on tradables, with none of it being spent on nontradables, the NN curve is a horizontal line, and there will be no effects on q_T of an increase in the price of coffee. The final effect of a higher-priced coffee on the real exchange rate will depend in a crucial way on the proportion of the higher income generated by the coffee boom that is spent on nontradables.

Figure A-2. *The Effect of an Increase in the Price of Coffee on the Prices of Other Tradables*

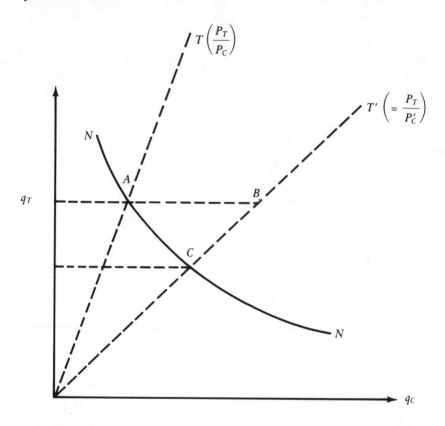

Consider now the more general case, in which coffee is also consumed domestically, but in which factors used in its production are still sector-specific. Then, the excess demand for nontradables will be given by:

$$(A.4) \qquad N = N(q_T, \ q_C, \ Y) = 0,$$
$$\qquad\qquad\qquad (+) \quad (?) \quad (+)$$

where the sign of $\partial N/\partial q_C$ will be positive if coffee and nontradables are substitutes, negative if they are complements.

The slope of the NN curve will now be equal to:

$$(A.5) \qquad \frac{dq_T}{dq_C} = - \frac{(\partial N/\partial q_C) + (\partial N/\partial Y)\bar{C}}{(\partial N/\partial Y)H_T^S + (\partial N/\partial q_T)}.$$

This expression can be either positive or negative, depending on the sign of $\partial N/\partial q_C$. If coffee and nontradables are complements ($\partial N/\partial q_C < 0$), it is possible that the numerator of equation (A.5) will be negative and the slope of the NN curve will be positive. (Notice that $\partial N/\partial q_C < 0$ is a necessary—but not sufficient—condition for NN to be positively sloped. The sufficient condition is that $\partial N/\partial q_C + (\partial N/\partial Y)\bar{C} < 0$.) In this case an increase in the price of coffee will cause an increase in the relative prices of other tradables and thus in resources that move from the nontradable goods sector into the other tradables sector.

If coffee and nontradables are substitutes, however—which is the more plausible assumption, given the level of aggregation considered in this model—the NN curve will be negatively sloped and the analysis presented in figures A-1 and A-2, which indicates that a higher price of coffee will reduce the degree of competitiveness of other tradables, will still hold. In the rest of this section it will be assumed, unless otherwise indicated, that the three goods involved are substitutes in consumption, so that equation (A.5) is negative and the NN curve is negatively sloped, as in figure A-1.

The preceding analysis shows that under a set of plausible assumptions, increases in the price of coffee will generate an equilibrium reduction in the relative prices of other tradables—in relation to both coffee and nontradables. This movement of relative prices will reduce the level of competitiveness of this sector, noncoffee tradables, with resources tending to move out of it. To the extent that this is an equilibrium result, no particular policy measures should be taken to avoid it.[5] If the change in the price of coffee is only temporary, however, and the capital market presents some imperfections, there is an argument for implementing policies that will help firms in the noncoffee tradables sector to "survive" this short-run squeeze in their profitability. The more interesting aspect of the model presented here, however, is that it shows that even in the absence of money and inflation, increases in the price of coffee will tend to reduce the degree of profitability of other tradable goods.

Coffee, Money, Inflation, and Competitiveness

The preceding analysis has been focused on the long-run effect of an exogenous increase in the price of coffee on the real exchange rate and competitiveness of the rest of the tradables industries. The analysis, however, has excluded dynamic aspects. In this section some dynamic considerations will be introduced into the model. To accomplish this two things will be done: first Harberger will be followed in the explicit introduction of a slowly clearing monetary sector, and second, a crawling peg system will be considered.[6]

In order to organize the discussion it will first be assumed that the exchange rate is fixed. Later, the exchange rate assumption will be changed. Under these circumstances, an increase in the price of coffee, in addition to its real effects, will affect both the supply of and the demand for money. It will increase the supply of money by producing a balance of payments surplus, which the Central Bank will monetize. (It is assumed that the capital account is exogenous and subject to controls.) The demand for money will increase as well, as a result of the increase in income brought about by the higher price of coffee. Theoretically, the overall result may be either a short-run excess flow or supply of money or an excess demand for it. By Walras's law these situations, respectively, imply an excess demand for goods—both tradables and nontradables—and an excess supply of goods. In the former situation, the excess demand for nontradable goods caused by this short-run monetary disequilibrium will create inflationary pressures that will reinforce the effect caused by the real factors discussed earlier—the increase in income caused by the increase in coffee prices. The result of this process will be that the real exchange rate, q_T, will decrease in the short run by a greater amount than would be caused by real factors alone. In this case, the nominal price of nontradable goods will tend to overshoot its new long-run equilibrium, and the loss of competitiveness of the non-coffee tradables sector—measured by the decrease of q_T—will be greater in the short run than in the long run. If, on the other hand, there is an excess demand for money, q_T will decrease in the short run by less than real factors alone would indicate. In either situation—excess supply of money or excess demand for money—as the monetary equilibrium is slowly restored through balance of payments surpluses or deficits (under the fixed-rate assumption), q_T will move to its new long-run equilibrium value as determined by the real factors in the model discussed in the preceding section.

   This discussion can be formalized. The excess flow supply for money in nominal terms, M^E, is given by:

$$(A.6) \qquad\qquad M^E = \Delta M^S - \Delta M^D,$$

where ΔM^S is the change in the nominal supply of money, and ΔM^D is the flow demand for money in nominal terms. Assuming that the demand for money equation M^D (in nominal terms) depends on the usual arguments—real income, the interest rate, i, and the price level—we can write M^D as:

$$(A.7) \qquad\qquad M^D = PL(\ i\ ,\ Y\ ),$$
$$(-)\ (+)$$

where P is the price level given by:

$$(A.8) \qquad\qquad P = p_T^\alpha p_N^{1-\alpha},$$

and where the domestic price of the noncoffee tradable goods is given by

$$(A.9) \qquad\qquad P_T = eP_T^*,$$

where e is the exchange rate and P_T^* the international price of noncoffee tradables. Notice that in the definition of the price level, P, in order to simplify the exposition the price of coffee has not been included.

   It is further assumed that M^E is equal to zero only in the long run. In particular, an increase of ΔM^S will cause a short-run excess flow supply of money, which, under the assumption of fixed rates, will be slowly eliminated through the balance of payments. It is further assumed that an excess flow supply of money will be reflected in an excess demand for nontradables and an excess demand for noncoffee tradables. Then, equation (A.1) must be modified to incorporate the assumption that in the short run, an excess flow supply of money is translated in part into an excess demand for nontradables.

(A.10)
$$N = N(q_T, M^E, Y).$$
$$(+) \ (+) \ (+)$$

In terms of figure A-1 an increase in M^E will produce a downward shift of schedule *NN*. The model is completed by specifying the balance of payments and money supply equations.

The balance of payments is defined as:

(A.11)
$$B = \Delta R = P_c \bar{C} - P_T E_T + CF,$$

where E_T stands for excess demand for traditional tradables; $\bar{C}$ is the amount of coffee exported; CF refers to capital flows, which are assumed to be exogenous; and ΔR is the change in international reserves. It is also assumed that $\partial B / \partial P_C > 0$; that is, an increase of the price of coffee will bring about an improvement in the balance of payments.[7]

The supply of money, on the other hand, is given by

(A.12)
$$M^S = M^S_{-1} + \Delta R + \Delta D,$$

where M^S_{-1} is the supply of money in the preceding period, ΔR is the change in international reserves—that is, the balance of payments—and is given by equation (A.11), and ΔD is the increase in domestic credit. From (A.12), of course, $\Delta M^S = \Delta R + \Delta D$. This means that ΔM^S could be considered high-powered money.

From (A.11) and (A.12) it is easy to see that to the extent that an increase in the price of coffee will produce a balance of payments surplus, $\Delta M^S > 0$.[8] Further, assuming that this positive value of ΔM^S produces a short-run excess flow supply for money, M^E will increase, and there will be an excess demand for nontradable goods (see equation [A.10]). In terms of the diagrammatical analysis, this case is captured by figure A-3.[9] The exogenous increase in the price of coffee simultaneously causes a downward shift of the *NN* curve to $N'N'$—as a consequence of the excess supply of money—and a rotation of the *OT* ratio to OT'. The *NN* curve will shift downward, since if there is an excess supply of money at the old relative prices for nontradables, there will be an excess demand for these goods. The new short-run equilibrium will be attained at *S*.

Final equilibrium will be obtained, as before, at *C*. The dynamics are characterized by shifts of the $N'N'$ curve to the right towards the *NN* curve. The speed of this adjustment will depend on how fast the excess flow supply of money is eliminated. As can be seen, in this case relative price of noncoffee tradables will undershoot its final equilibrium level. This means that the loss of competitiveness of the

Figure A-3. *The Effects of an Increase in the Price of Coffee on the Money Supply and Equilibrium*

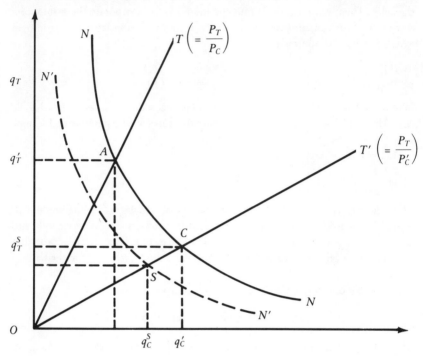

noncoffee tradables sector, as measured by the decline of q_T, will be greater in the short run than in the long run.

For the sake of simplicity, a fixed exchange rate has been assumed in the analysis presented up to this point. If, however, a crawling peg system is allowed, the results presented will not be altered in any significant way. Specifically, equation (A.10) on the nontradables market equilibrium condition remains unchanged. Now, however, it will be seen that in the steady state, assuming that P_C^* and P_T^* do not change, the following expression will hold (from [A.8] and [A.9]):

(A.13) $\hat{e} = P_N = P,$

where (ˆ) refers to percentage change. From (A.13), it can be seen that the real exchange rate—defined as $s = eP_T^*/P_N$—will be constant. As was discussed, as a consequence of an increase in the price of coffee there will be pressures—stemming from both the income effect and the inflationary effect—for P to increase. If the monetary authorities do not alter the rate of devaluation of the crawl, the following will be the result:

(A.14) $\hat{e} < P < P_N.$

In other words, the real exchange rate will decline with the consequent loss of competitiveness in the noncoffee tradables sector. Notice that the foregoing discussion can be considered a special case, where $\hat{e} = 0$. Of course, the monetary authority has the option of accelerating the rate of crawl so that this real appreciation can be avoided, at least in part. This, however, was not what happened in Colombia during the last coffee bonanza. In fact, as discussed in chapter 1, the authority slowed the rate of devaluation of the crawling peg. This reaction of the government seems to be consistent with empirical evidence on the determinants of crawling peg rules.[10]

Empirical Results

It has been argued that an increase in the price of coffee would tend to produce a balance of payments surplus, an increase in the quantity of money, and inflation, which, if not matched by an equivalent devaluation, would generate a real appreciation of the domestic currency, squeezing the profitability out of the noncoffee tradable goods sector. These aspects will be analyzed empirically in this appendix, using annual data for the period 1952–80. Specifically, whether higher (lower) prices of coffee have caused higher (lower) rates of growth of high-powered money in Colombia will be investigated. The relation between the growth of high-powered money and inflation will also be analyzed.

The model tested in this section is given in semireduced form by equations (A.15) and (A.16), where, as before, (^) refers to a percentage change.[11]

$$(A.15) \qquad \hat{M}_t = \alpha_0 + \sum_{i-1}^{3} \alpha_i \hat{M}_{t-1} + \gamma_1 DEH_t + \gamma_2 \hat{P}_{c_t} - u_t$$

$$(A.16) \qquad \hat{P}_t = \alpha_0 - \delta_i \hat{M}_t + \delta_2 \hat{y}_t + \delta_3 \widehat{PX}_t + \delta_4 DUM_t + \epsilon_t$$

where: P = price level (consumer price index)
  M = high-powered money
  DEH = ratio of fiscal deficit (in nominal pesos) to high-powered money
  P_c = nominal price of coffee, in pesos
  y = real income
  PX = "world" price of tradables expressed in pesos
  DUM = dummy variable that takes a value of zero between 1952 and 1966 and 1 from 1967 onward.

Equation (A.15) postulates that the rate of growth of high-powered money depends on its past rates of growth (up to three periods), on the magnitude of the fiscal deficit, and on the rate of increase of the price of coffee. Variable DEH —which measures the fiscal deficit in relation to high-powered money—is included, since the fiscal deficit in Colombia is financed in part by the creation of money.[12]

From an empirical point of view the deficit included in (A.15) has to be calculated excluding from government revenues those generated by the revaluation of reserves through the Special Exchange Account. On the other hand, the inclusion of P_c in (A.15) captures the hypothesis that changes in the price of coffee will bring about the accumulation of international reserves and a higher rate of change of high-powered money. In the estimation of (A.15), it is expected that $\gamma_1 > 0$ and $\gamma_2 > 0$.

Equation (A.16), on the other hand, is a traditional open-economy inflation equation.[13] This expression relates the rate of inflation, $\hat{P}$, to the rate of growth of high-powered money, the rate of growth of income, and the rate of change of external prices. This equation responds to the notion that the price level is of the following form:

$$P = P_T^{\alpha} P_N^{(1-\alpha)},$$

(see equation [A.22]), with the prices of nontradables, P_N, responding to monetary pressures (and the rate of devaluation), and the prices of tradables, P_T, being affected by external prices (world inflation *plus* the rate of devaluation). In theory the change in interest rates should also be included in equation (A.16); lack of the appropriate data, however, made this impossible. In equation (A.16) it is expected that $\delta_1 > 0$, $\delta_2 < 0$, $\delta_3 > 0$, and $\delta_4 > 0$.

The estimation of (A.15) and (A.16) for 1952–80 by ordinary least squares (OLS) yielded the following results, where t-statistics are in parentheses, D.W. refers to the Durbin-Watson statistic, and R^2 is the coefficient of correlation. The results for (A.15) are:

(A.17) $\quad \hat{M}_t = -0.005 + 0.636\,\hat{M}_{t-1} - 0.128\,\hat{M}_{t-2} + 0.139\,\hat{M}_{t-3}$
$\qquad\qquad\ \ (-0.164)\quad (3.608)\qquad\quad (-0.720)\qquad\quad (2.276)$

$\qquad\qquad + 0.219\,DEH_t + 0.072\,\hat{P}_{c_t}.$
$\qquad\qquad\ \ (3.325)\qquad\quad (1.997)$

$$R^2 = 0.741$$
$$D.W. = 2.232$$

The estimation of (A.16) for 1952–80, using OLS, yielded:

(A.18) $\quad \hat{P} = 0.033 + 0.458\,\hat{M}_t - 0.747\,\hat{y}_t + 0.200\,\widehat{PX}_t + 0.022\,DUM_t.$
$\qquad\qquad\ (0.605)\quad (2.933)\quad\ (0.764)\quad\ (1.871)\qquad\ (0.804)$

$$R^2 = 0.562$$
$$D.W. = 1.854$$

The fit of the equations is quite satisfactory as measured by the R^2. More important, the coefficients of all relevant parameters have the expected signs and are significant at conventional levels. From equation (A.17) it can be seen that the rate of growth of high-powered money in Colombia can be well explained by lagged rates of growth of M, by the fiscal deficit, and by changes in the price of coffee. These results show that, with other things given, an increase (decrease) in the price of coffee would cause higher (lower) rates of growth of high-powered money. The estimated coefficient is highly significant at conventional levels.

Equation (A.18), on the other hand, presents the results obtained for the inflation equation. All coefficients have the expected signs, with those corresponding to M_t and PX_t being significant at the conventional levels. The coefficient of M_t indicates that, holding other things constant, an increase of 10 percent in high-powered money will generate a rise in the rate of inflation of approximately 5 percent. This coefficient is lower than the hypothesized unitary value for closed economies. It is perfectly consistent with the case of a semiopen economy, however, in which it can be postulated that an increase in the quantity of money will be reflected in part in prices and in part in a loss of international reserves, a change in the exchange rate, or both. The coefficient of PX_t suggests that if money is held constant an increase of 10 percent in the rate of growth of the peso price of tradables—generated by a higher rate of world inflation or a faster rate of devaluation—will produce an increase of only 2 percent in the rate of inflation. This result, which may seem somewhat surprising, is consistent with the findings by Hanson, who, using different data and a slightly shorter period, found a significant coefficient of 0.25.[14] This result should be taken with caution, however, in the analysis of policy alternatives. In particular, it should be emphasized that a faster rate of devaluation will be translated into 0.2 percent higher rate of inflation only if all other variables are held constant. If, for example, this is not the case, and both the rate of devaluation and the rate of growth of high-powered money are increased 10 percent, the rate of inflation will tend to increase approximately 7 percent.

In order to analyze whether the results obtained from the estimation of equation (A.15) are sensitive to the specifications, an alternative equation was run.[15] In this case $\hat{P}_c$ was replaced with P_c—the logarithm of the price of coffee in domestic currency. The following result was obtained:

(A.19) $\hat{M}_t = -0.146 + 0.498\,\hat{M}_{t-1} - 0.637\,\hat{M}_{t-2} + 0.063\,\hat{M}_{t-3}$
$\qquad\qquad (-2.967)\quad (3.608)\qquad\quad (-4.640)\qquad\quad (1.005)$

$\qquad\qquad +\ 0.190\,DEH_t + 0.053\,\hat{P}_{c_t}.$
$\qquad\qquad\quad (2.423)\qquad\quad (5.281)$

$$R^2 = 0.827$$
$$\text{D.W.} = 1.429$$

In order to test whether this result is sensitive to the period, alternative periods were also used; the results are presented in table A-1.

The results for the rate of growth of high-powered money and inflation equations reported above were obtained using OLS. The reason for using OLS is that this

Table A-1. *Equations for the Rate of Growth of High-Powered Money in Different Periods*

$$\hat{M}_t = \alpha_0 + \sum_{i=1}^{3} \alpha_i \hat{M}_{t-i} + \gamma_1 DEH_t + \gamma_2 \hat{P}_{c_t} + u_t$$

	Period	Equation (A.15) 1952–70	Equation (A.16) 1952–75	Equation (A.17) 1952–77	Equation (A.18) 1952–73
α_0		−0.272	−0.131	−0.110	−0.182
		(−2.096)	(−1.798)	(−2.034)	(−2.063)
α_1		0.405	0.433	0.428	0.448
		(2.018)	(2.443)	(2.599)	(2.446)
α_2		−0.722	−0.684	−0.665	−0.712
		(−4.041)	(−4.541)	(−4.730)	(−4.511)
α_3		0.061	0.047	0.044	0.050
		(0.804)	(0.682)	(0.666)	(0.706)
γ_1		0.200	0.210	0.200	0.209
		(1.978)	(2.296)	(2.427)	(2.220)
γ_2		0.079	0.054	0.050	0.063
		(3.283)	(3.921)	(5.006)	(3.853)
D.W.		1.878	1.727	1.725	1.850
R^2		0.723	0.635	0.738	0.637
L		35.02	45.09	49.60	41.20

Note: The values in parentheses refer to t-statistics; D.W. is the Durbin-Watson statistic; R^2 is the coefficient of correlation; and L is the log of the likelihood function.

system (equations [A.15] and [A.16]) is block recursive, with growth of money, M, entering the inflation equation, but with the rate of inflation *not* entering the rate of high-powered money equation. There is a possibility, however, that equation (A.15) is still subject to simultaneity bias, since P_c is increased in pesos, and changes in M_t may affect the exchange rate. For this reason equation (A.15) was also estimated using two stages of least squares. The results obtained were:

(A.20) $\hat{M}_t = -0.006 + 0.634 \hat{M}_{t-1} - 0.124 \hat{M}_{t-2} + 0.140 \hat{M}_{t-3}$
                    (−0.117)   (3.596)   (−0.691)   (2.293)

          $+ 0.222 DEH_t + 0.079 \hat{P}_{c_t}.$
             (3.354)   (2.023)

$$\text{SEE} = 0.037$$
$$\text{D.W.} = 2.238$$

As can be seen, the estimation technique does not affect the main finding: changes in coffee prices have affected the behavior of the creation of money in Colombia.

Conclusion

In this appendix the relation between coffee and inflation in the Colombian economy was analyzed, and a Dutch-disease type of model was tested. As set out in chapter 1, it is shown that changes in the price of coffee will generally tend to cause a higher rate of inflation and a lower real exchange rate. Specifically, the empirical analysis tested the link between the price of coffee, the fiscal deficit, and the rate of growth of high-powered money and also the relation between money and inflation in Colombia. The results confirm some of the main characteristics of the Dutch-disease type of model. In particular, these results indicate that, with other things given, a higher (lower) price of coffee will cause a higher (lower) rate of inflation and a lower (higher) real exchange rate, in the absence of commensurate adjustments in the exchange rate.

Notes

1. This model is based in part on Sebastian Edwards and Masanao Aoki, "Oil Export Boom and Dutch-Disease: A Dynamic Analysis," *Resources and Energy*, vol. 5 (September 1983); and on Sebastian Edwards, "Coffee, Money, and Inflation in Colombia," *World Development*, vol. 12 (November/December 1984).

2. On this point see, for example, Arnold C. Harberger, "Dutch Disease: How Much Sickness, How Much Boon," *Resources and Energy*, vol. 5 (March 1983), pp. 1–20.

3. Rudiger Dornbusch, "Tariffs and Non-traded Goods," *Journal of International Economics* (May 1974).

4. W. Max Corden and J. Peter Neary, "Booming Sector and De-Industrialization in a Small Open Economy," *Economic Journal*, vol. 92 (December 1982), pp. 825–48.

5. If externalities are present in the traded goods sector and the accumulation of foreign assets must be restricted, however, intervention may be called for; see Sweder van Wijnbergen, "Dutch Disease: A Disease after All?" *Economic Journal*, vol. 94, no. 373 (1984), pp. 41–55. There could also be income distribution considerations for intervention.

6. Harberger, "Dutch Disease"; see also Sebastian Edwards, "Commodity Export Prices and the Real Exchange Rate in Developing Countries: Coffee in Colombia," in *Macroeconomic Adjustment and Real Exchange Rates in Developing Countries*, National Bureau of Economic Research Conference Volume, ed. Sebastian Edwards and Liaquat Ahamed (forthcoming).

7. The effect of a coffee price increase on the balance of payments is $dB/dP_C = \bar{C} - P_T dE_T/dP_C$, where $dE_T/dP_C \lesseqgtr 0$. A sufficient condition for the coffee price increase to produce a $dB > 0$ is $dE_T \leq 0$.

8. Actually $dM^S/dP_C = C - P_T dE_T/dP_C$, and if, as assumed, $(dE_T/dP_C)/dP_C < 0$, $dM^S/dP_C > 0$.

9. For an alternative diagrammatical definition of the monetary effects of a commodity export boom, see Peter Neary, "Real and Monetary Aspects of the Dutch Disease," in *Structural Adjustment in Developed Open Economies*, ed. K. Jungenfeld and D. S. Hague (London: Macmillan, 1984).

10. For an analysis of the relation between coffee prices and the rate of devaluation of the crawling peg in Colombia, see Edwards, "Commodity Export Prices."

11. For a fuller discussion, see Sebastian Edwards, "Coffee, Money, and Inflation in Colombia," *World Development*, vol. 12 (November/December 1984). Some of the results presented here are drawn from that article.

12. J. A. Ocampo and Guillermo Perry, "La reforma fiscal, 1982–1983," *Coyuntura económica*, vol. 13, no. 1 (March 1983), pp. 215–64; Sebastian Edwards, "The Short-Run Relation between Inflation and Growth in Latin America: Comment," *American Economic Review*, vol. 74 (June 1983), pp. 477–88.

13. Harberger, "Dutch Disease"; James Hanson, "Short-Run Macroeconomic Development and Policy in Colombia" (Washington, D.C.: World Bank, Industry Department, 1982, processed).

14. Hanson, "Short-Run Macroeconomic Development."

15. Estimation of (A.15) using OLS may cause a simultaneity bias, since P_C is in pesos and therefore depends on the world price of coffee and the exchange rate, and changes in M_t can affect the exchange rate. We find, however, that the exchange rate is econometrically exogenous to M_t, and the problem is thus avoided.

B

The Exchange Rate and Noncoffee Exports

Sebastian Edwards

IN A NUMBER of studies the determinants of noncoffee exports in Colombia have been investigated econometrically.[1] The results obtained have generally supported the hypothesis that both the real exchange rate—or the domestic relative price of noncoffee exports—and the level of world economic activity have been important in determining the volume of noncoffee, or minor, exports. As can be seen from table B-1, these studies have generated a wide range of values for the relevant elasticities. The elasticities presented in this table, however, have been obtained using different methods and different specifications of the noncoffee exports function, and in that sense, the results are not directly comparable and should be interpreted as providing only approximate orders of magnitude. One of the purposes of the results presented in this appendix is to narrow the range in the previous estimates by providing our own recent results.

A central purpose of this appendix is to provide policy support in the area of exchange rate management. Much confusion has surrounded the issue of whether noncoffee exports respond to changes in the real exchange rate. This appendix shows that, while there is little doubt that world economic growth and quantitative restrictions abroad seriously affect Colombia's exports, the level of the real exchange rate also provides the crucial edge.

A Simple Model to Determine Colombia's Noncoffee Exports

In general the quantity of a good exported depends on relative prices and levels of economic activity in the rest of the world and in the country under consideration. It would be expected that the quantity exported depends positively on the domestic relative price of exports and on the level of economic activity in the rest of the world. On the other hand, exports may vary negatively with the level of activity in the domestic economy, if a higher domestic level of activity increases the domestic demand for exportable goods and reduces the exportable surplus of that good. With

Table B-1. *Estimated Elasticities of the Functions of Noncoffee Exports from Colombia*

Study	Dependent variable	Price elasticity	Income elasticity	Period
Teigero and Elan[a] (1973)	Value of minor exports, excluding gold and bananas	1.34		1948–71 (annual)
Teigero and Elan (1973)	Value of manufactured exports	5.43		1966–71 (quarterly)
Díaz-Alejandro[b] (1976)	Change in value of minor exports	0.81–0.87		1955–72 (annual)
Díaz-Alejandro (1976)	Change in value of minor exports, except coffee, bananas, sugar, and tobacco	0.59		1955–70 (annual)
Díaz-Alejandro (1976)	Annual changes in value of minor exports	0.68–1.04		1955–72 (and sub-periods; quarterly)
Cardona[c] (1976)	Real minor exports	1.36		1967–76
Carrizosa[d] (1979)	Noncoffee real exports	0.57	5.34	1960–76 (annual)
Echavarría[e] (1980)	Minor real exports, excluding gold	0.90	0.91	1960–67 (annual)
Echavarría (1980)	Minor real exports, excluding gold and diamonds	0.94	1.12	1960–67 (annual)

a. J. D. Teigero and R. A. Elan, "El crecimiento de las exportaciones menores y el sistema de fomento de exportaciones en Colombia" (Bogotá: FEDESARROLLO, July 1973, processed).

b. C. F. Díaz-Alejandro, *Foreign Trade Regimes and Economic Development: Colombia* (New York: Columbia University Press for the National Bureau of Economic Research, 1976).

c. Marta E. Cardona, "El crecimiento de las exportaciones menores y el sistema del fomento de exportaciones en Colombia," *Revista de planeación y desarrollo*, vol. 9, no. 2 (April–September 1977).

d. Mauricio Carrizosa, "El futuro de la balanza comercial," *La economía colombiana en la decada de los ochenta* (Bogotá: FEDESARROLLO, 1981).

e. Juan José Echavarría, "La evolución de las exportaciones colombianas y sus determinantes: Un analisis empirico," *Ensayos sobre política económica*, no. 2 (September 1982), pp. 257–94.

these premises, if it is further assumed that the long-run export function has a double-log form, the following reduced form for export behavior can be postulated:[2]

(B.1) $$\log X_t = a_0 + a_1 \log PX_t + a_2 \log YW_t + a_3 \log Y_t + u_t,$$

where X_t = long-run volume of exports
PX_t = domestic relative price of exports
YW_t = world real level of economic activity
Y_t = domestic real level of economic activity.

It is expected that $a_1 > 0$, $a_2 > 0$, and $a_3 < 0$. Since PX_t is the domestic relative price of exports, it will depend on their world price in foreign currency, on the effective exchange rate, and on the peso prices of other goods:

(B.2) $$PX_t = E_t \cdot PXW_t / P_t,$$

where PXW_t = world price of exports (in dollar terms)
  E = effective nominal exchange rate—that is, it incorporates the role of export subsidies
  P_t = peso prices of other goods.

Since E_t in (B.2) is the effective nominal exchange rate it will be given by

(B.3) $$E_t = e_t(1 + s_t),$$

where e_t is the nominal exchange rate and s_t is the average export subsidy. From (B.3), (B.2), and (B.1) it can be seen that an increase of s_t, with other things given, will cause a higher relative price of exports and thus a higher quantity exported.

In the case of Colombia's noncoffee exports, subsidies have been quite important since 1967.[3] Since that year, the exports incentives system in Colombia has been based on three major tools—Plan Vallejo, PROEXPO credit, and CAT/CERT.[4] Recently, both the implicit subsidy in PROEXPO credit and the CAT/CERT rates have been increased in an effort to compensate in part for the overvaluation of the peso.

It is generally accepted that the quantity of any particular good actually exported does not adjust instantaneously to changes in its determinants.[5] For that reason, the reduced-form equations usually used to describe the behavior of actual exports (X_t) include lagged coefficients of its determinants.

(B.4) $$\log X_t = \alpha_0 + \sum_{i=0}^{k} \beta_i \log PX_t i + \sum_{i=0}^{k} \gamma_i \log YW_t i + \sum_{i=0}^{k} \delta_i \log Y_{t-i} + \omega_t.$$

Under this formulation, β_0, γ_0, and δ_0 can be interpreted as short-run elasticities, while the sums of the β_is, γ_is, and δ_is are long-run elasticities. In the next section results obtained from the estimation of equations of the type of (B.4), using Colombian quarterly data for 1970–81, will be presented.

Estimation of the Model

The first problem faced in the estimation of equation (B.4) is that of finding the appropriate data. The dependent variable is X_t, the quantity, or volume, of noncoffee exports. Export data, however, are generally available in the form of an index of the value of exports VX_t. For this reason, X_t was defined as:[6]

(B.5) $$X_t = \frac{VX_t}{PNC_t},$$

where PNC_t is the price index of noncoffee exports. A problem with (B.5), however, is that there are no directly available data for PNC_t. This index was therefore constructed using data on the total export price index PXT_t and on a coffee exports price index PC_t, which are available from IFS. Assuming that PXT_t has a Cobb-Douglas form $PXT_t = PC_t^\alpha PNC^{1-\alpha}$, PNC_t can be computed as:

(B.6) $$PNC_t = \exp(1 - \alpha)^{-1}[\log PXT_t - \alpha \log PC_t].$$

In the actual computation of PNC_t, both PNT_t and PC_t were obtained from IFS. With respect to α it was considered to be variable—that is, α_t varies for each t—and in each period it was taken to be equal to that period's ratio of the value of coffee exports to total exports. The relative price variable, PX, was constructed as the effective nominal rate of the peso to the U.S. dollar times the U.S. WPI, divided by the Colombian CPI. In that sense, PX can be interpreted as being a measure of the real exchange rate. The rest of the world level of activity, YW, was proxied by the U.S. real GNP, which was taken from IFS. The domestic real level of activity, on the other hand, was defined as domestic real GNP, using data from Montes and Candelo, which were supplemented for the recent years by the DNP.

Equation (B.4) was estimated using polynomial distributed lags—that is, Almon

Table B-2. *Noncoffee Exports Function: Almon Lags, Quarterly Data, 1971–81*
(third-degree polynomial, no end constraints)

Lag (i)	Constant	$\log REX_{t-i}$	$\log YW_{t-i}$	$\log y_{t-i}$
0	−123.063	1.331	2.676	−0.115
	(−2.584)	(2.503)	(1.977)	(−0.118)
1		0.690	2.236	−0.661
		(2.774)	(2.765)	(−1.283)
2		0.217	1.794	−0.981
		(1.240)	(2.260)	(−2.380)
3		−0.088	1.349	−1.075
		(−0.378)	(1.494)	(−2.198)
4		−0.227	0.902	−0.943
		(−0.920)	(1.064)	(−1.949)
5		−0.197	0.452	−0.585
		(−1.157)	(−0.816)	(−1.792)
Sum of lagged coefficients		1.725	9.409	−4.360
D.W.	1.552			
R^2	0.329			
SEE	0.180			

Note: Numbers in parentheses are t-statistics; SEE is the standard error of estimate, D.W. is the Durbin-Watson statistic.

lags.[7] A problem usually faced when Almon lags are used is that it is not possible to know a priori the appropriate order of the polynomial or the constraints to be imposed on its form. For this reason, and in order to check for the robustness of the empirical results, alternative combinations of the polynomial degree and the constraints were tried.[8] The length of the lag structure—that is, the value of k in equation (B.4)—was varied between four and twelve quarters, and the "best" results, which are those reported here, were obtained when a six-quarters lag structure was used.

Tables B-2, B-3, B-4, and B-5 contain the results obtained from the estimation of the reduced form for noncoffee exports for Colombia under alternative formulation of the polynomial structure. As can be seen, the results are quite satisfactory. Even though the R^2s are rather low, all the coefficients have the expected signs, and many of them are significant at the conventional levels. The sum of lagged coefficients, moreover, was always significant for the relative price, REX, and world real income, YW, variables. They, however, were never significant for the domestic real income variable, Y.

These results, then, indicate that a strong level of economic activity in the rest of the world, more specifically in the industrial countries, is crucial in order for Colombia's noncoffee exports to grow. From a policy perspective, however, the most important finding from these estimations is the significant effect of the real exchange rate on the behavior of noncoffee exports.

Table B-3. *Noncoffee Exports Function: Almon Lags, Quarterly Data, 1971–81*
(fourth-degree polynomial, no end constraints)

Lag (i)	Constant	log REX_{t-i}	log YW_{t-i}	log y_{t-i}
0	−85.278	1.848	0.379	−0.133
	(−1.492)	(2.136)	(0.162)	(−0.133)
1		0.459	3.433	−0.846
		(0.973)	(2.930)	(−0.931)
2		−0.221	3.331	−0.942
		(−0.360)	(2.409)	(−1.102)
3		−0.398	1.505	−0.663
		(−1.076)	(1.612)	(−1.067)
4		−0.282	−0.614	−0.252
		(−0.867)	(−0.460)	(−0.368)
5		−0.080	−1.592	0.049
		(−0.182)	(−1.044)	(−.072)
Sum of lagged coefficients		1.327	6.442	−2.786
D.W.	1.605			
R^2	0.380			
SEE	0.180			

Note: Numbers in parentheses are *t*-statistics.

Table B-4. *Noncoffee Exports Function: Almon Lags, Quarterly Data, 1971–81*
(third-degree polynomial, far end constraint)

Lag (i)	Constant	log REX_{t-i}	log YW_{t-i}	log y_{t-i}
0	−116.482	0.793	2.143	−0.528
	(−2.382)	(2.507)	(2.479)	(−0.734)
1		0.903	2.782	−0.827
		(2.608)	(2.735)	(−1.025)
2		0.580	2.391	−0.928
		(2.546)	(2.765)	(−1.656)
3		0.076	1.444	−0.865
		(0.389)	(1.653)	(−1.927)
4		−0.356	0.413	−0.668
		(−1.174)	(0.401)	(−1.037)
5		−0.465	−0.226	−0.369
		(−1.611)	(−0.258)	(−0.603)
Sum of lagged coefficients		1.530	8.949	−4.184
D.W.	1.581			
R^2	0.315			
SEE	0.181			

Note: Numbers in parentheses are *t*-statistics.

Table B-5. *Noncoffee Exports Function: Almon Lags, Quarterly Data, 1971–81*
(fourth-degree polynomial, far end constraint)

Lag (i)	Constant	log REX_{t-i}	log YW_{t-i}	log y_{t-i}
0	−68.529	2.647	1.706	−0.401
	(−1.154)	(2.466)	(0.632)	(−0.383)
1		0.079	1.815	−1.235
		(0.095)	(0.835)	(−1.216)
2		−0.805	2.325	−0.572
		(−1.048)	(1.398)	(−0.596)
3		−0.660	2.249	0.452
		(−0.931)	(1.413)	(0.464)
4		−0.144	0.602	0.702
		(−0.179)	(0.280)	(0.729)
5		0.088	−3.604	−0.958
		(0.010)	(−1.225)	(−0.876)
Sum of lagged coefficients		1.206	5.093	−2.012
D.W.	1.736			
R^2	0.426			
SEE	0.182			

Note: Numbers in parentheses are *t*-statistics.

Notes

1. See, for example, Fernando Montes, "Principales determinantes del comportamiento de la cuenta coriente durante la década," in *Ensayos sobre política económica*, vol. 2 (September 1982), pp. 187–255, and José Antonio Ocampo, "En defense de la continuidad del régimen," in *Coyuntura económica*, vol. 13, no. 1 (March 1983), pp. 198–214.

2. This equation can also be regarded as a reduced form for the volume of noncoffee exports.

3. See C. F. Díaz-Alejandro, *Foreign Trade Regimes and Economic Development* (New York: Columbia University Press for the National Bureau of Economic Research, 1976).

4. The original scheme, CAT, was revised recently as CERT to provide greater flexibility in the incentive.

5. John F. Wilson and Wendy E. Takas, "Differential Responses to Price and Exchange Rates Influences in the Foreign Trade of Selected Industrial Countries," *Review of Economics and Statistics*, vol. 61, no. 2 (May 1979), pp. 267–79; and Morris Goldstein and Mohsin Khan, "Income and Price Effects in Foreign Trade" (Washington, D.C.: International Monetary Fund, 1983, processed).

6. Edward Leamer and Richard Stern, *Quantitative International Economics* (Boston: Allyn and Bacon, 1970); and Gabriel Montes and Ricardo Candelo, "El crecimiento industrial y la generación de empleo in Colombia," *Revista de planeación y desarrollo*, vol. 12, nos. 1 and 2 (January–June, 1981).

7. See Goldstein and Khan, "Income and Price Effects," for a discussion on lagged representation in international trade empirical analyses.

8. Gabriel Montes and Ricardo Candelo, "El enfoque monetario de la balanza de pagos: El caso de Colombia, 1968–1980," *Revista de planeación y desarrollo*, vol. 14, no. 2 (May–August 1982), pp. 11–40.

C

The Rate of Devaluation and the Nominal Interest Rate

Sebastian Edwards

COLOMBIA'S IS a semiopen economy with a growing, but still partially repressed, capital market.[1] This appendix derives a model for interest rate determination in a small semiopen economy, and tests it empirically, using quarterly data for the period 1968–82. The model addresses the relation between the rate of devaluation and the nominal interest rate, which is central to the devaluation issue discussed in chapter 2; the model is also helpful in determining the effect of changes in monetary policy on the rate of interest.

Interest Rate, Rate of Devaluation, and Money

In a fully open economy, where economic agents are risk neutral and foreign and domestic bonds are perfect substitutes, the internal and external interest rates are rigidly linked through the interest parity condition:[2]

$$(C.1) \qquad\qquad i_t = i_t^w + D_t^e$$

where i_t = domestic nominal interest rate

i_t^w = foreign (world) nominal interest rate, on instruments that have the same maturity as the domestic papers

D_t^e = expected rate of devaluation of the domestic currency between period t and the period corresponding to the maturity of the corresponding financial instruments. The subscript t indicates that this expectation is formed in period t.

If in the economy in question there are no impediments to capital movements, equation (C.1) will tend to hold in both the short run and the long run. The available empirical evidence suggests that a slightly revised version of equation (C.1)—which replaces D^e by the forward premium, incorporates transaction costs, and considers foreign interest rates—holds closely for the case of industrial countries.[3]

In the case of semiopen or closed economies, however, expression (C.1) does not seem to hold. The recent experience of the Southern Cone countries—Argentina, Chile, and Uruguay—and of Colombia suggests that in semi-industrialized, semiopen economies the divergencies from (C.1) can be substantial.[4]

Equation (C.1) can be modified in several ways, in order to incorporate the features of a semiopen economy. In particular, it is possible to write an expression that indicates that the domestic interest rate tends to equate the world rate of interest plus the rate of devaluation and a risk premium in the long run, but that it can differ from it in the short run. First define i_t as

$$(C.2) \qquad\qquad i_t^* = i_t^w + D_t^e + \beta_t,$$

where β_t is a risk-premium term.[5] Equation (C.1) can then be replaced by the following expression:

$$(C.3) \qquad\qquad \Delta i_t = \theta(i_t^* - i_{t-1}),$$

where $0 < \theta < 1$. This equation states that movements of the domestic nominal interest rate will respond to discrepancies between i_t and the domestic rate in the preceding period. According to (C.3), in the long run the domestic interest rate will be equal to the foreign rate plus the expected devaluation and the risk premium. In the short run, however, these two rates, i_t and i_t, can differ. The coefficient θ is a measure of the speed at which discrepancies between i_t and i_{t-1} will tend to be corrected. For example, if it only takes one period for these interest-rate differentials to disappear, θ would be equal to 1.0.

In a semiopen economy, where capital movements are subject to a number of controls, domestic monetary policy could also have some effect on the short-run behavior of the interest rate.[6] Specifically, it can be postulated that disequilibria in the money market will have an effect on interest-rate movements, with situations of excess liquidity—an excess supply of money—driving the interest rate down— that is, a liquidity effect—and with excess demands for money causing an increase in the domestic interest rate. This possible effect can be captured by the following expression:

$$(C.4) \qquad\qquad \Delta i_t = \theta(i_t^* - i_{t-1}) - \lambda(\log m_t - \log m_{t-1}^d),$$

where m_t is the real quantity of money in t, and where m_{t-1}^d is the quantity of money demanded in period $t - 1$. This equation explicitly allows for internal monetary disequilibria to affect interest rate movements. The parameter λ measures the importance of these disequilibria, and the negative sign reflects the hypothesis that an excess supply (demand) for real money will generate a decline (increase) in the interest rate. An alternative way to write the monetary disequilibrium term would include the contemporaneous value of both the quantity of money and the quantity demanded. In this case the interest-rate equation can be rewritten as

$$(C.5) \qquad\qquad \Delta i_t = \theta(i_t^* - i_{t-1}) - \lambda(\log m_t - \log m_t^d).$$

Estimation

In this section results obtained from the estimation of reduced forms for equations (C.3) through (C.5) for Colombia, using quarterly data for the period 1968–82, are presented. In order to simplify the analysis it is assumed that D_t is equal to the actual annualized rate of devaluation in quarter t. This is a plausible assumption, since during the period under consideration Colombia followed a crawling peg exchange-rate policy, where the rate of the crawl was altered fairly slowly.[7] On the other hand, regarding the risk premium (β_t) it was assumed that it can be represented as a constant plus a random element.

Regarding the demand for money function, it was assumed that it has a conventional Cagan form:

(C.6) $$\log m_t^d = b_0 + b_1 \log y_t - b_2 i_t$$

for y_t = real income.

Estimation of Equation (C.3)

Equation (C.3) can be rewritten in the following form (where ϵ_t is an error term with the usual characteristics):

(C.7) $$i_t = \alpha_0 + \alpha_1 i_t^* + \alpha_2 i_{t-1} + \epsilon_t.$$

Notice that since $\alpha_1 = \theta$ and $\alpha_2 = 1 - \theta$, θ is overidentified. Equation (C.7), however, was run without imposing the constraint $\alpha_1 = 1 - \alpha_2$. The result obtained was the following, where the values in parentheses are t-statistics.[8]

(C.8) $$i_t = \underset{(0.484)}{0.011} + \underset{(1.671)}{0.321\, i_t^*} + \underset{(7.261)}{0.765\, i_{t-1}}$$

$$R^2 = 0.768$$
$$\text{D.W.} = 2.422$$

The coefficients of i_t and i_{t-1} are significant at the conventional levels. As can be seen, the direct estimate of θ is 0.321, indicating that approximately a third of the discrepancy between i_t and i_{t-1} is eliminated in one quarter. This means that after one year an interest rate differential of 10 percentage points would be reduced to 2.1 percentage points. This coefficient can also be interpreted as a measure of the effects of an increase on the rate of devaluation or the interest rate.

The indirect estimation of θ—as 1 minus the coefficient of i_{t-1}—gives a value of 0.235, suggesting a slightly slower speed at which discrepancies between i_t and i_{t-1} will be eliminated.

Estimation of Equation (C.4)

Combining (C.6) and (C.4), and adding an error term w_t, the following reduced form of equation (C.4) can be written:

(C.9) $i_t = \gamma_0 + \gamma_1 i_t^* + \gamma_2 i_{t-1} + \gamma_3 \log m_t + \gamma_4 \log y_{t-1} + w_t,$

where it is expected that $\gamma_1 > 0, \gamma_2 > 0, \gamma_3 < 0$, and $\gamma_4 > 0$. The expressions for the γs in terms of the structural equations (C.4) and (C.6) parameters are

$$\gamma_1 = \theta$$
$$\gamma_2 = 1 - \theta + \lambda b_2$$
$$\gamma_3 = -\lambda$$
$$\gamma_4 = \lambda b_1.$$

The estimation of (C.9) using OLS yielded the following result for the period 1968:3–1982:4 (*t*-statistics in parentheses):

(C.10) $i_t = -0.489 + 0.404\, i_t^* + 0.383\, i_{t-1}$
             $\quad\;\;(-1.990)\quad (2.337)\qquad (2.847)$

$R^2 = 0.815$

             $\quad\;\; -0.275\, \log m_t + 0.379\, \log y_{t-1}$
             $\quad\;\;(-1.963)\qquad\qquad (3.539)$

$D.W. = 2.211$
$N = 58$

This result is quite satisfactory, with all the coefficients significant at conventional levels and having the expected signs. The estimated structure coefficients computed from (C.10) turn out to be the following:

$$\hat{\theta} = 0.404$$
$$\hat{\lambda} = 0.275$$
$$\hat{a}_1 = 1.378$$
$$\hat{a}_2 = 0.775.$$

As can be seen, the estimated parameters for the demand for money in Colombia are within the plausible range of values.[9] Also, these results indicate that after one quarter, 40 percent of a unitary uncovered interest-rate differential will have been corrected. After one year, 87 percent of this discrepancy will have been corrected.

The coefficient of i_t, θ, can also be used to simulate the effect of an increase in the rate of devaluation on the interest rate. Assume that the initial—in period 0— domestic interest rate is 40 percent and that the rate of devaluation is 22 percent a year. Assume now that in period 1 the rate of devaluation is increased to 32 percent, and maintained at this higher level, with all the rest of the relevant variables remaining constant. The evolution of the domestic interest rate under this case, using the estimated parameters from equation (C.10), is given in table C-1:[10] after six quarters the domestic rate of interest has practically reached its new equilibrium.

Equation (C.10) also provides some information regarding the effect of the quantity of money on interest-rate behavior—specifically, this estimate provides a semielasticity of the interest rates with respect to real money of -0.275. The corresponding elasticity, of course, will be variable and will depend on the level of the interest rate. In table C-2 the corresponding elasticities for some initial values of the nominal interest rate are given.

From table C-2 it can be seen that for the case of a nominal interest rate of 40 percent the corresponding elasticity will be -0.688, indicating that, with other things given, an increase of 10 percent in the real quantity of money will reduce the nominal interest rate by 6.9 percent. According to our model, however, in order to reduce the interest rate it is necessary to increase the real quantity of money, requir-

Table C-1. *Simulation of the Effect of a Higher Rate of Devaluation of the Crawling Peg on the Domestic Interest Rate*
(percent)

Quarter	Nominal domestic interest rate (i)	Rate of devaluation
0	40.0	22
1	44.0	32
2	46.5	32
3	47.9	32
4	48.7	32
5	49.2	32
6	49.5	32
7	49.7	32
8	49.8	32

Source: See text.

Table C-2. *Elasticity of the Interest Rate with Respect to Real Money*

Interest rate (percent)	Interest rate elasticity with respect to real money
30	-0.917
35	-0.786
40	-0.688
45	-0.611
50	-0.550

Source: See text.

ing that an increase in the rate of growth of nominal money not be matched by higher equiproportional inflation.

In order to investigate the level of significance of the structural coefficients from the demand for money, equation (C.9) was estimated, using a nonlinear least squares procedure that imposes the respective restrictions across coefficients. The following results were obtained: a_1 had an estimated value of 1.380, with a t-statistic of 1.963, and a_2 was estimated to be 0.773, with a t-statistic of 1.368.

Estimation of Equation (C.5)

The reduced form of equation (C.5), with an error term, v_t, added, has the following form:

(C.11) $$i_t = \delta_0 + \delta_1 i_t^* + \delta_2 i_{t-1} + \delta_3 \log m_t + \delta_4 \log y_t + v_t.$$

This expression differs from (C.10) in that log y now enters contemporaneously. The interpretation of the δs in terms of the structural parameters, however, is quite different.

$$\delta_1 = \frac{\theta}{1 + \lambda a_2} \qquad\qquad \delta_3 = \frac{-\lambda}{1 + \lambda a_2}$$

$$\delta_2 = \frac{1 - \theta}{1 + \lambda a_2} \qquad\qquad \delta_4 = \frac{\lambda a_1}{1 + \lambda a_2}$$

In this case it is expected, as before, that $\delta_1 > 0$, $\delta_2 > 0$, $\delta_3 < 0$, and $\delta_4 > 0$. The estimation of (C.11), using OLS for the period 1968:3 to 1982:4, generated the following result, where the numbers in parentheses are the t-statistics:

(C.12)

$$i_t = -0.434 + 0.402\ i_t^* + 0.363\ i_{t-1} - 0.389\ \log m_t + 0.171\ \log y_t$$
$$\quad\ (-1.832)\quad (2.405)\qquad (2.845)\qquad\ (-2.536)\qquad\qquad (4.171)$$

$$R^2 = 0.840$$
$$\text{D.W.} = 2.112$$
$$N = 58$$

As can be seen, once again all the coefficients have the expected signs, and now their level of significance is even higher than before. The computed structural parameters are

$$\hat{\theta} = 0.525$$

$$\hat{\lambda} = 0.298$$

$$\hat{a}_1 = 1.175$$

$$\hat{a}_2 = 0.785.$$

As can be seen, these numbers are quite similar to those obtained from the estimation of equation (C.10). Now, however, the speed at which discrepancies between i_t and i_{t-1} are eliminated is faster. Actually, these results indicate that, with other things given, in one quarter more than half of a unitary interest-rate differential will be corrected. An increase in the rate of devaluation of the crawling peg of 10 percentage points—that is, from 22 percent to 32 percent—will produce, in the first quarter, an increase in the domestic interest rate of 5.3 percentage points. After two quarters the increase would have been 7.7 percentage points and after one year 9.5 percentage points.

Regarding the estimated coefficient of log m_t (−0.298), it indicates that with a nominal interest rate of 35 percent, the elasticity of the interest rate with respect to the real quantity of money will be equal to −0.851. This means that, with other things given, an increase of 10 percent in the real quantity of money will tend in the short run to reduce the interest rate to 26.5 percent.

Forecasting the Interest Rate

In order to compare further the relative merits of the three interest rate models tested [equations (C.3) through (C.5)], their forecasting properties are analyzed by reestimating the models for a shorter period, 1968:3–1980:4, and by using the estimated coefficients to make out-of-sample estimates for the seven quarters 1981:1 to 1982:4. Table C-3 presents the actual values of the interest for this period, and the forecast values obtained from each equation. Table C-4, on the other hand, presents a number of statistics that measure the degree of accuracy of these forecasts. As can be seen in table C-3, for many of the quarters involved the interest

Table C-3. *Actual and Out-of-Sample Forecast Values of the Interest Rate in Colombia, 1981:2–1982:4*
(percent)

Year and quarter	Actual	Equation (C.3) forecast	Equation (C.4) forecast	Equation (C.5) forecast
1981:1	36.7	—	—	—
1981:2	60.9	35.4	40.1	40.6
1981:3	48.6	54.5	48.4	50.0
1981:4	63.7	45.1	43.7	43.8
1982:1	65.7	56.3	45.4	46.2
1982:2	49.5	57.7	48.7	50.0
1982:3	53.8	45.0	44.4	45.7
1982:4	57.2	49.0	44.8	44.9

— Not applicable.
Source: See text.

Table C-4. *Summary Statistics for Comparison of Actual and Predicted Interest-Rate Series: Out-of-Sample Forecasts, 1981:2–1982:4*

Statistic	Equation (C.3)	Equation (C.4)	Equation (C.5)
Correlation coefficient between actual and predicted	0.604	0.671	0.656
Root mean square error	0.183	0.188	0.186
Mean absolute error	0.152	0.151	0.148
Mean error	0.116	0.151	0.144
Theil's U-statistic	0.180	0.193	0.189
Fraction of error caused by bias	0.404	0.641	0.601
Fraction of error caused by different variation	0.225	0.109	0.124
Fraction of error caused by different covariation	0.371	0.250	0.276

Source: See text.

rates forecast are quite different from the actual values. It is important to consider that this is an out-of-sample experiment, however, and that during the period through which the forecast was done interest rates were particularly volatile.[11]

In order to have a more systematic evaluation of the statistical quality of these forecasts, table C-4 provides some summary statistics from the comparison of actual and forecast values, which indicate that these forecasts are quite satisfactory. The coefficients of correlation between actual and predicted series are fairly high, with the mean errors and Theil's inequality coefficient being on the low side. From these results, however, it is not straightforward to determine which equation provides better forecasts. While some statistics—root mean square error, mean-error, and Theil's inequality coefficient—suggest that equation (C.3), which excludes monetary considerations, does a better job of forecasting the interest rate, other statistics—mean absolute error, and the correlation coefficient—point toward equations (C.4) and (C.5), respectively, as providing better forecasts.

Conclusion

For this analysis it was recognized that Colombia's is a semiopen economy and that, as a consequence, open-economy models and closed-economy models are inappropriate. Three alternative formulations for the determination of the interest rate in a semiopen economy were developed and tested, using quarterly data for the period 1968–82. The results obtained were remarkably good and indicated that the domestic (nominal) interest rate will tend to converge slowly through time toward the world interest rate plus expected devaluation. The estimates indicate that in one quarter, between a third and half of a unitary discrepancy between the domestic rate and the world rate plus the expected rate of devaluation will be corrected. In six quarters an acceleration of the rate of devaluation of the crawling peg will be almost completely translated into an equivalent increase in the domestic rate of interest. An excess supply of real money will exercise significant negative pressures on the nominal interest rate—that is, there will be a liquidity effect. Finally, out-of-sample forecasts were presented, using the three alternative formulations. The results showed that despite being out of sample, the forecasts were quite satisfactory.

Notes

1. On the behavior of the Colombian capital market see World Bank, *Colombia: Economic Development and Policy under Changing Conditions* (Washington, D.C., 1984), chapter 5, and Juan Carlos Jaramillo, "El proceso de liberación del mercado financiero colombiano," in *Ensayos sobre política económica*, no. 1 (March 1982), pp. 7–19.

2. This expression abstracts from consideration of taxation.

3. See Jacob A. Frenkel and Richard M. Levich, "Covered Interest Arbitrage: Unexploited Profits?" *Journal of Political Economy*, vol. 83, no. 2 (April 1975), pp. 325–38; and "Transaction Costs and Interest Arbitrage: Tranquil versus Turbulent Periods," *Journal of Political Economy*, vol. 85, no. 6 (December 1977), pp. 1209–26.

4. See Sebastian Edwards, "Stabilization with Liberalization: An Evaluation of the Years of Chile's Experiment with Free Market Policies, 1973–83," *Economic Development and Cultural Change*, vol. 33 (January 1985).

5. On the existence of a risk premium in interest arbitrage equations see, for example, Lars Peter Hansen and Robert J. Hodrick, "Forward Exchange Rates as Optimal Predictors of Future Spot Rates: An Economic Analysis," *Journal of Political Economy*, vol. 88, no. 5 (October 1980), pp. 829–53.

6. On controls of capital movement in Colombia, see recent issues of International Monetary Fund, *Annual Report on Exchange Arrangements and Exchange Restrictions* (Washington, D.C.).

7. In order to check the extent to which past rates of devaluation predicted the actual rate of devaluation, a regression of the following form, using quarterly data, was run:

$$D_t = a_1 D_{t-1} + a_2 D_{t-2} + u_t.$$

For 1968–82 the following result, which indicates that the assumption $D_t = D_t$ is a fairly good one, was obtained (*t*-statistics in parentheses):

$$D_t = \quad 0.928 \ D_{t-1} \ + \ 0.001 \ D_{t-2}$$
$$(15.318) \qquad\quad (0.010)$$

$$\text{D.W.} = 2.2$$

8. All the data were obtained from Gabriel Montes and Ricardo Candelo, "El enfoque monetario de la balanza de pagos," *Revista de planeación y desarrollo*, vol. 14, no. 2 (May–August 1982), pp. 11–40; the DNP; and the International Monetary Fund.

9. Montes and Candelo, in "El enfoque monetario," estimated that for the period 1968–80 the elasticity of the demand for money with respect to real income was 0.955 and that the interest-rate elasticity of the demand for money was −0.20.

10. In obtaining these results it was, in fact, assumed that the monetary authorities manipulate the supply of money in such a way that the money disequilibrium (log m_t − log m_{t-1}) remains constant.

11. Unfortunately, out-of-sample forecasts are not usually made. In most studies, the forecasts usually reported are those made within the sample, which do not have much value.

D

The Stability and Predictability of Prices, Producers' Income, and Profitability

John Nash

IN THIS APPENDIX the way indexes were constructed for several crops to measure the stability and predictability of several economic variables during the period 1970–81 (see chapter 5) will be described. The crops are barley, beans, coffee, corn, cotton, potatoes, rice, sugar, and wheat. The variables are the international price, the domestic producer price, the domestic consumer price, producers' income, the profit per ton, and the profit per hectare planted—or, for some crops, gross income per hectare. All variables are in real terms of the 1975 peso adjusted by the implicit price deflator of the gross internal product. The methods by which they were computed and the method of computing the indexes will be described; then the results will be presented (table D-1) and discussed.

Data Sources

The international price for each product in each year is the implicit import-export price, that is, it is the total value in pesos of the imports or exports of the product divided by the quantity imported or exported. The prices were provided by the Sociedad de Agricultores de Colombia. For rice, two years of missing data were constructed by taking the preceding year's price and adjusting it in such a way that the price moved by the same percentage as did rice prices on world markets. (This information was taken from *International Financial Statistics*.) The implicit export price for sugar was for processed sugar. Since it was necessary to make this comparable to producer prices for sugarcane, the export price of sugar each year was adjusted by the overall average percentage markup from cane to processed sugar to give some indication of the way sugarcane prices would have moved had they been governed by movements in international prices. The implicit international price of beans is not available.

Producer prices were taken from a DNP working paper, a Banco de la Republica source, and, for coffee, a FEDERACAFE publication, "Boletin de información estatistica sobre el cafe," no. 48. Consumer prices were taken from a DNP-UEA working paper of February 28, 1983, "Series de precios del sector agropecuario: 1950–1982." Consumer prices of barley, coffee, and cotton were not available. Output was taken from table 7-1 of the statistical appendix to *Colombia: Economic Development and Policy under Changing Conditions*, by José B. Sokol and others (Washington, D. C.: World Bank, 1984). Yield per hectare was taken from a DNP document, "Indicatores fisicas nacionales del sector agropecuario, 1950–1981." For corn, cotton, rice, and wheat, real production costs (per ton) were taken from table 4-11 of "Aspects of Agricultural Development in Colombia," by Jorge García-García (Bogotá, April 1983, processed), a paper prepared for this book. Producer income at domestic prices was computed by multiplying the producer price by output. Likewise, producer income at international prices was computed by multiplying the international price by output. For the four crops for which production costs per ton were available, the profit per ton at domestic and international prices was computed by subtracting the cost from the appropriate price each year.

The gross income per hectare at domestic and international prices was computed by multiplying the appropriate price by the yield (in tons per hectare) each year. The profit per hectare at domestic and international prices was computed by multiplying the profit per ton by the yield.

Method of Calculation of the Indexes

After the series were computed for each crop, two indexes were calculated for each of the following series for each crop: international price, producer price, consumer price, profit per ton at domestic prices, profit per ton at international prices, producer income, and profit per hectare or, for crops for which production cost was not available, gross income per hectare.

Index 1 is an index of variability or instability. It is simply the standard error of a linear least-squares regression of the series, using time as the independent variable (to remove any secular trend). For the price series and the profit per ton series, the standard error was divided by the mean price in order to transform it into percentage terms and make the indexes comparable across crops. After all, an average $1,000 yearly change in the price of coffee, with a price of around $89,000 a ton, would indicate much less instability than the same average change in the price of barley, with a price of around $17,000 a ton; to be comparable, the indexes should be in percentage terms. For the same reason, the indexes for the series of producer income were computed by dividing the standard error by the respective means. This was not done for the series profit per hectare and gross income per hectare. The reason is that the indexes from these series were designed to measure the insta-

Table D-1. *Indexes of Instability and Unpredictability*

Economic variable and crop	Index 1	Index 2
1. *International price*		
Barley	0.223	0.252
Coffee	0.347	0.371
Corn	0.218	0.286
Cotton	0.163	0.227
Potatoes	0.261	0.377
Rice	0.277	0.388
Sugar	0.692	0.658
Wheat	0.382	0.339
2. *Producer price*		
Barley	0.146	0.221
Beans	0.143	0.240
Coffee	0.219	0.286
Corn	0.118	0.277
Cotton	0.167	0.259
Potatoes	0.204	0.342
Rice	0.092	0.305
Sugar	0.081	0.229
Wheat	0.165	0.251
3. *Ratio, 1:2*		
Barley	1.53	1.14
Coffee	1.59	1.30
Corn	1.85	1.03
Cotton	0.97	0.88
Potatoes	1.28	1.10
Rice	3.01	1.27
Sugar	8.55	2.87
Wheat	2.32	1.35
4. *Consumer price*		
Beans	0.103	0.238
Corn	0.119	0.261
Potatoes	0.144	0.308
Rice	0.084	0.252
Sugar	0.221	0.399
Wheat	0.161	0.258
5. *Producer income at international prices*		
Barley	0.341	0.409
Coffee	0.407	0.415
Corn	0.172	0.315
Cotton	0.265	0.316
Potatoes	0.302	0.465
Rice	0.393	0.485
Sugar	0.712	0.701
Wheat	0.423	0.500

(*Table continues on the following page.*)

Table D-1 *(continued)*

Economic variable and crop	Index 1	Index 2
6. *Producer income at domestic prices*		
Barley	0.286	0.386
Beans	0.277	0.218
Coffee	0.262	0.295
Corn	0.085	0.237
Cotton	0.294	0.366
Potatoes	0.179	0.332
Rice	0.163	0.239
Sugar	0.066	0.210
Wheat	0.290	0.478
7. *Ratio, 5:6*		
Barley	1.19	1.06
Coffee	1.56	1.41
Corn	2.03	1.33
Cotton	0.90	0.86
Potatoes	1.68	1.40
Rice	2.42	2.03
Sugar	10.79	3.34
Wheat	1.46	1.05
8. *Profit per ton at international prices*		
Corn	0.397	0.396
Cotton	0.221	0.252
Rice	0.319	0.391
Wheat	0.444	0.395
9. *Profit per ton at domestic prices*		
Beans	0.162	0.193
Corn	0.225	0.225
Cotton	0.228	0.308
Rice	0.159	0.168
Wheat	0.192	0.181
10. *Ratio, 8:9*		
Corn	1.77	1.76
Cotton	0.97	0.82
Rice	2.01	2.33
Wheat	2.32	2.18
11. *Gross income per hectare at international prices*		
Barley	1245.0	2115.2
Coffee	11240.0	12451.8
Potatoes	11970.0	19675.7
Sugar	1726.0	1636.1
12. *Gross income per hectare at domestic prices*		
Barley	1012.0	2003.9
Coffee	3065.0	4066.4

Table D-1 (continued)

Economic variable and crop	Index 1	Index 2
Potatoes	6663.0	11223.4
Sugar	224.6	587.1
13. Ratio, 11:12		
Barley	1.23	1.06
Coffee	3.67	3.06
Potatoes	1.80	1.75
Sugar	7.68	2.79
14. Profit per hectare at international prices		
Corn	1601.0	1597.1
Cotton	12410.0	14494.2
Rice	2442.0	2993.0
Wheat	1857.0	1670.8
15. Profit per hectare at domestic prices		
Beans	1503.0	1853.2
Corn	1221.0	1243.0
Cotton	9778.0	13214.7
Rice	2599.0	2706.5
Wheat	1056.0	996.7
16. Ratio, 14:15		
Corn	1.31	1.28
Cotton	1.27	1.10
Rice	0.94	1.11
Wheat	1.76	1.68

Sources: See text.

bility of return on investment, the investment being in a hectare of land. The return on investment is the profit (or gross income) divided by the cost of the investment (the implicit rental value of the land). Since the implicit rental value of the land itself is not dependent on the crop planted, it would be the same for each crop. Dividing each crop's standard error by the same number would not change the ordering of the indexes so there is really no reason to do so.

Index 2 is designed to measure uncertainty or unpredictability. It is important to draw the distinction between instability and unpredictability, since it is conceptually possible that a variable—price, for example—would be quite unstable but perfectly predictable. If so, the instability would create no risk, in the sense of uncertainty, though it might create other problems, such as destabilization of macroeconomic variables. Thus, both indexes are potentially important, each for analyzing a different kind of issue.

Index 2 was computed as follows. After each series was de-trended by a linear regression against time, the residuals were taken and fitted to a first-order autoregressive process of the form $X_t = \lambda X_{t-1} + \epsilon_t$, where ϵ_t is "white noise." Index 2 is the standard error of this regression, divided where appropriate by the mean in order to transform it to percentage terms. This index represents the average absolute size of the prediction error involved in predicting one year's value of the variable from the preceding year's value. It is thus a measure of the degree to which each series is unpredictable.

The results are reported in table D-1. That domestic prices are in general more stable than international can be seen in the table, where the ratio of international price instability to domestic price instability can be seen to be greater than unity for most crops. For potatoes, a crop with relatively little intervention, the ratio is rather low, providing some evidence that the government's intervention programs may be a factor in stabilizing price. This cannot be said about some of the other variables, however. In table D-1, for example, the variability of producer income for potatoes at international prices is larger in relation to variability at domestic prices than is this ratio for several other crops. It is not clear, therefore, that government stabilization programs have stabilized incomes.

E

The Welfare Cost of Price Stabilization

John Nash

IN THIS APPENDIX the origin of the efficiency cost estimates of price stabilization, which are presented in table 5-2, will be explained. To illustrate the methodology, the explanation will be phrased in terms of a simple model of an export good whose price in the world market assumes only two values, P_1 or P_2 ($P_1 \geq P_2$), each with probability of 0.5, and whose domestic producer price is stabilized at the mean value, $\bar{P}$, by means of a tax-subsidy scheme devised so that the average protection is 0; that is, when the world price is P_1 there is a tax of $P_1 - \bar{P}$ on the export; when world price is P_2, there is a subsidy of $\bar{P} - P_2$. The results can easily be extended to an import good, a good with multiple possible prices, and a good with a rate of protection which differs from 0, either positively or negatively. In the explanation a linear supply schedule is assumed. To derive the formula exactly, this must be true, at least locally.

Consider figure E-1. With a price stabilization scheme, since producers always receive price $\bar{P}$, they always produce quantity Q. When the world price is P_1, the government receives area A in export taxes; when the world price is P_2, the government gives subsidies equal to $C + D$. When the world price is P_1, exporters forgo a producer surplus increase of $A + B$ by selling only quantity Q at a price $\bar{P}$. But area A is not a welfare loss to the country because it goes to the government in taxes. The welfare loss from maintaining the producer price at $\bar{P}$ is area B. Area B is a triangle whose area is $\frac{1}{2} (P_1 - \bar{P}) (Q_1 - Q)$. The quantity $Q_1 - Q$ can be expressed as $dQ/dP (P_1 - \bar{P})$, so area $B = \frac{1}{2} (P_1 - \bar{P})^2 (dQ/dP) E$, where E is the export supply elasticity. By the same kind of logic, the welfare loss to the economy from maintaining an internal price of $\bar{P}$ when the world price is P_2 is area D, which is $\frac{1}{2} (P_2 - \bar{P})^2 (Q/\bar{P}) E$. So, the average yearly loss is $\frac{1}{2} E(Q/\bar{P})$ var (P), where var (P) is the variance of the world price. By definition, the variance is the average of $(P_1 - \bar{P})^2$ and $(P_2 - \bar{P})^2$.

Also, by similar logic, the welfare loss from stabilization of the price of an imported good can be shown to be $\frac{1}{2} |N| (Q/\bar{P})$ var (P), where $|N|$ is the absolute value of import demand elasticity.

Figure E-1. *The Effect of Price Stabilization*

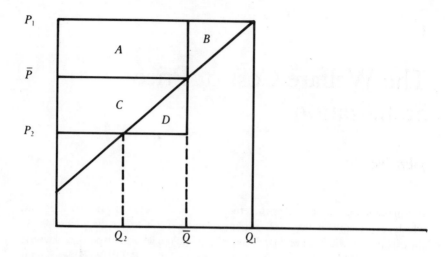

To give some idea of the magnitude of such welfare losses, the values of Q, P, var (P) and $\frac{1}{2}$ $E(Q/P)$ var (P) or $\frac{1}{2}$ $|N|(Q/P)$ var (P) are reported in table E-1 for a small sample of crops. The import and export elasticities are computed from estimates of domestic elasticities of demand and short-run supply and are thus the elasticities that would prevail in a market with no governmental interference in free trade. The estimates of domestic elasticities were taken from the results of the background study for an article on nutrition in Colombia.[1]

Table E-1. *Annual Welfare Losses from Price Stabilization*
(1975 pesos)

Crop	Q (MT)	P ($/MT)	var(P)	N	$\frac{1}{2}$$|N|$(Q/P)var(P)	E	$\frac{1}{2}E(Q/P)$var P
Import crops							
Wheat	364,167	3,471	1,642,000	−0.69	59,434,446	—	—
Corn	57,125	3,072	541,900	−12.08	60,864,084	—	—
Barley	50,125	3,898	710,200	−0.19	867,595	—	—
Export crops							
Rice	22,467	7,660	4,093,000	—	—	38.60	231,694,311
Cotton	50,317	32,961	26,950,000	—	—	5.28	108,611,811
Potatoes	6,708	4,571	2,299,000	—	—	74.87	126,298,630

— Not applicable.
Note: Q, quantity; P, price; N, absolute value of import demand elasticity; E, export supply elasticity.
Source: Author's estimates.

Note

1. Per Pinstrup-Andersen, Norha Ruiz de Londoño, and Edward Hoover, "The Impact of Increasing Food Supply on Human Nutrition: Implications for Commodity Priorities in Agricultural Research and Policy," *American Journal of Agricultural Economics*, vol. 58 (May 1976), pp. 131–42.

F

The Organization and Management of the Coffee Economy

John Nash

FOR MORE THAN FIFTY years the National Federation of Coffee Growers (hereafter referred to as the federation or FEDERACAFE), a private nonprofit association of coffee producers that engages in commercial activities, has been the main body charged by the government with administering coffee policy.[1] The federation is responsible for the management of the National Coffee Fund (NCF), for the provision of technical assistance to the industry, for the control of domestic and export marketing, and for advice on the setting of certain rates of taxation and prices which affect the industry. The relationship between the government and the federation has been controlled since 1928 by a series of contracts that set out the duties to be delegated to the latter and the remuneration that it will receive in return for its services. The most recent of these covers the ten-year period that began December 31, 1978.

Although the federation is allowed considerable freedom of action in running the coffee industry, the government can control its operations in a number of ways. First, the budget of the federation is subject to the approval of the government and, in addition, under the present contract, the federation submits to the government quarterly financial projections. Second, the appointment of the general manager of the federation is subject to the approval of the president. Third, whenever it sees fit the government can convene an extraordinary meeting of the National Congress of Coffee Growers, the supreme authority of the federation. Ministers can present the views of the government to the Congress, although they have no power to vote, and certain major decisions of the Congress are subject to the approval of the president. Finally, under the present contract the government and the representatives of coffee growers have equal representation on the important National Committee of Coffee Growers, which executes the decisions of the Congress. In addition to this control of the federation, the government determines the rate of taxes in the country, including those specific to the coffee industry, and has a majority in the committee that determines the price at which the federation purchases coffee from growers.

Apart from administering the NCF and supervising the marketing of the crop, the main activities of the federation are carried out by the departmental committees. In addition to the taxes set aside for specific campaigns, the committees obtain income from their own assets, from various government departments, and from the local community. The activities of the committees are diverse, ranging from the provision of extension services and technical education to improvement of the infrastructure in coffee-growing areas and the provision of social services. The committees, therefore, benefit the community at large as well as growers of coffee and, to the extent that the resources of the committees are drawn from taxation of the coffee sector, their activities bring about a redistribution of income from this sector to the rest of the economy.

The NCF was originally established, in 1940, to finance the surplus stocks expected to accumulate as a result of the international export quota arrangement introduced in that year. Throughout the life of the fund its administration has been delegated to the federation. With the passage of time the functions of the fund have increased in scope so that it has become the main instrument for regulating the supply and the price of coffee. It has also become an important investor in activities related to the production of and trade in coffee.

Coffee Marketing and Export

Usually coffee is partially processed on the farm, then sold in the form of dried "parchment." The dried parchment is brought to the nearest village or town, where it is sold either at one of the 500 purchasing points of the federation or to commercial buyers, such as exporters and dealers, who subsequently sell to the federation or to private exporters. The parchment is then bulked and transported to the nearest depot or mill of the federation or the exporter concerned, as the case may be.

The federation guarantees to purchase parchment coffee delivered to its agents at the same price throughout the country, provided that the parchment is of federation type—that is, of quality higher than a given standard. This price, hereafter referred to as the minimum price, is established by a committee that includes the ministers of agriculture and finance and the general manager of the federation.

Coffee is exported both by the federation and by private traders. The latter export not only coffee purchased from growers and private dealers but also coffee sold to them from the stocks of the federation. The price at which the federation sells for this purpose is set in terms of an ex-dock New York price, expressed in cents per pound, and is varied frequently. The volume of coffee exported by the federation and by private exporters is compared in table F-1 for crop years since 1969/70.

All proceeds from the export of coffee must be surrendered to the Central Bank within twenty days of registration for export. After deduction of the ad valorem tax, the bank in the past exchanged these proceeds for currency exchange certifi-

Table F-1. *Exports of Coffee by the National Federation of Coffee Growers and by Private Exporters*
(sixty-kilogram bags)

Crop year	Federation	Private exporters	Total[a]	Proportion by federation (percent)
1969/70	2,963,781	3,910,284	6,874,065	43
1970/71	2,478,130	3,852,543	6,330,673	39
1971/72	2,302,435	4,184,517	6,486,952	35
1972/73	2,589,297	3,665,266	6,254,563	41
1973/74	3,226,002	4,181,856	7,407,858	44
1974/75	3,027,621	4,514,498	7,542,119	40
1975/76	1,489,127	5,533,834	7,022,961	21
1976/77	1,742,338	3,549,892	5,292,230	30
1977/78	4,811,162	2,747,072	7,558,234	64
1978/79	8,838,438	2,592,775	11,431,213	77
1979/80	11,357,071	182,814	11,539,885	98
1980/81	6,106,128	2,924,491	9,030,619	67
1981/82	5,241,000	3,749,000	8,990,000	58
1982/83	5,110,000	4,064,000	9,174,000	56

a. Official registered exports only.
Source: FEDERACAFE.

cates, which could be converted to pesos immediately at a discount of between 6 and 15 percent or after 120 days at their full face value; recently this discount was eliminated.

To ensure that the amount of foreign exchange corresponding to the actual earnings from exports enters the country, a minimum surrender price is set by the Monetary Board of the Central Bank for coffee and certain other commodities. For green coffee the minimum surrender price, the *reintegro cafetero*, represents the amount of foreign exchange per seventy-kilogram bag that exporters are required to surrender to the bank. As the international price varies, the amount of the *reintegro* is adjusted so that the *reintegro* payments to the bank are equal to the foreign exchange earnings from the export of coffee. In practice there has tended to be a time lag between changes in the international price and in the *reintegro*. In rising markets the result has tended to be *reintegros* below the unit values of foreign exchange earnings, thereby allowing exporters to accumulate holdings of foreign currency and increase their margins by virtue of the fact that the export tax is based on the *reintegro*. When coffee prices fall, the *reintegro* price tends to be higher than the unit value of export earnings, and exporters have had to purchase foreign exchange on the free market in order to be able to make the full payment of the *reintegro* to the bank. Changes in the *reintegro* price, expressed in U.S. cents per pound, and the ico indicator price for Colombian Mild Arabicas ruling on the day of the change are given for the period since 1975 in table F-2.

Table F-2. *Prices and Effective Dates of Coffee Reintegro and the ICO Indicator Price for Colombian Mild Arabicas, 1975–83*

| Effective date | Reintegro | | ICO indicator price for mild Arabicas (U.S. cents per pound) |
	U.S. dollars per seventy-kilogram bag	U.S. cents per pound	
1975			
July 22	117.00	75.82	
1976			
January 15	130.00	84.24	102.50
February 20	143.00	92.66	107.50
April 1	153.50	99.47	118.50
April 7	170.00	110.16	123.25
April 12	193.00	125.06	136.00
May 7	207.00	134.14	147.75
May 18	231.00	149.69	156.50
May 27	245.00	158.76	168.00
June 8	259.25	167.99	185.00
November 29	284.65	184.45	195.00
December 28	307.60	199.32	223.00
1977			
February 11	331.00	214.49	236.00
February 17	354.00	229.39	249.50
February 24	376.50	243.97	275.00
February 28	423.00	274.10	304.00
March 9	440.00	285.12	309.00
March 23	457.00	296.13	325.00
April 14	477.00	309.09	334.00
May 26	466.50	302.29	290.00
June 16	415.00	268.92	229.50
July 12	376.50	243.97	241.00
July 16	361.00	233.93	245.00
August 18	313.75	203.31	202.00
1978			
April 8	290.00	187.92	193.00
June 16	275.00	178.20	191.50
July 17	259.00	167.83	229.50
1979			
January 24	243.00	157.46	160.00
January 31	217.00	140.62	148.00
February 22	188.40	122.08	129.00
April 19	202.00	130.89	142.00
May 5	216.00	139.97	155.00
June 5	251.00	162.65	186.00

(Table continues on the following page.)

Table F-2 *(continued)*

| Effective date | Reintegro | | ICO indicator price for mild Arabicas (U.S. cents per pound) |
	U.S. dollars per seventy-kilogram bag	U.S. cents per pound	
1980			
May 9	287.32	186.18	205.00
October 3	201.00	130.52	151.00
December 10	181.95	118.15	130.00
1981			
April 24	186.55	121.14	141.00
May 6	201.90	131.10	157.00
December 14	206.50	134.09	153.00
1982			
March 13	217.25	141.07	158.00
May 24	206.50	134.09	146.00
1983			
February 19	191.00	123.77	n.a.
October 15	195.50	126.68	n.a.
November 30	204.50	132.52	n.a.

n.a. Not available.

Source: FEDERACAFE.

Export Taxes and Contributions

Sales of coffee by growers are subject to indirect taxes and contributions. Before receiving permission to export, an exporter of coffee must provide evidence of payment of the first three of these taxes.

The Retention Quota

Private exporters must contribute to the NCF without compensation an amount of parchment related to the *excelso* to be exported. The parchment must be delivered to a warehouse of Almacafe, a wholly-owned subsidiary of the federation. Exports by the federation are made on behalf of the fund, and the tax on these exports is an internal transaction within the fund.

While its original purpose, in 1958, was to accumulate in public hands the coffee withheld from the market under a retention agreement among Latin American producers, the retention tax has come to be used as a device to manipulate domestic prices and to shield domestic producers from the full effects of changes in world prices. In periods when the world price was high, the retention tax was increased to keep domestic prices relatively low, as in 1976, when the tax was at 85 percent; conversely, in periods of low world prices, the retention tax was reduced to prevent domestic prices from falling too much (see table F-3).

The Pasilla and Ripio Tax

Before a license is issued for the export of a consignment of green coffee, an exporter must provide the federation with evidence of sale of an amount of low-grade *pasilla* and *ripio* parchment equivalent to 6 percent of the volume of the consignment. For the delivery, which must comprise eleven parts *pasilla* to one part *ripio* and be made to a warehouse of Almacafe, the exporter receives a payment of six pesos per 62.5-kilogram bag of hulled coffee. This rate of payment has been unchanged since 1941 and now represents only a fraction of a percentage point of the value of the coffee. The *pasilla* and *ripio* tax is designed to remove low-grade coffee from the export market and provide the federation with stocks for sale to the domestic market.

The Ad Valorem Tax

A tax equal to 6.5 percent of the *reintegro* price is currently payable to the Central Bank in foreign exchange by all exporters of coffee, including the federation. Out of this, an amount equal to 3.2 percent of total export value is paid by the bank to the NCF, and another 0.8 percent of total export value is paid to the departmental committees to be used for projects in the coffee zone. The remainder is paid into the Special Exchange Account of the Treasury and represents an important contribution to the national revenues; it averaged about 7.5 percent of total government revenues during the period 1974–81. In the third quarter of 1983 the so-called *reintegro anticipado* was introduced in an effort to induce early surrender of coffee revenues to the Central Bank. The measure provided exporters with a forward exchange rate of up to sixty days for future coffee sales.

The ad valorem tax was established in 1967 at the rate of 26 percent as part of the tax reforms that accompanied the abolition of the special rate of exchange for coffee. The rate of the tax was reduced in steps of 0.25 percent a month until it reached the rate of 20 percent in December 1968, at which level it was held until the end of 1974. The rate was then cut by 1 percentage point each year from 1975 to 1978, when it had fallen to 16 percent. Changes in the rate since 1978 are shown in table F-3. The loss in revenue from these reductions was borne entirely by the Treasury. Of the portion of the tax received by the NCF, a fifth passes directly to the campaign for economic and social progress administered by the departmental committees of the federation.

Table F-3. *Coffee Price and Tax Variables*

Effective date	Reintegro minimo (U.S. dollars per seventy-kilogram bag)	Ad valorem tax (percent)[a]	Retention quota (percent)
1978			
January 1	313.75	16	80
April 8	290.00	16	80
June 17	275.00	16	80
July 12	259.00	16	80
1979			
January 25	243.00	16	80
February 1	217.00	16	80
February 22	188.40	16	80
February 27	188.40	16	45
April 19	202.00	16	45
May 5	216.00	16	55
June 5	251.00	16	58
1980			
May 9	287.32	16	62
October 3	201.00	16	25
December 9	201.00	4	25
December 10	181.95	4	25
December 11	181.95	4	15
1981			
April 24	186.55	20	20
September 1	186.55	12	20
September 18	186.55	12	25
November 6	201.90	12	30
December 14	206.50	12	35
1982			
March 13	217.25	12	39
May 24	206.50	12	35
October 1	206.50	9	40
1983			
February 19	191.00	9	40
September 10	191.00	6.5	45
October 15	195.50	6.5	50
November 30	204.50	6.5	50
December 12	204.50	6.5	58
1984			
February 1	204.50	6.5	62
March 22	206.00	6.5	66

a. The ad valorem tax is divided between the government and the coffee sector. The National Coffee Fund has always received 3.2 percent, the departmental committees 0.8 percent, and the government the remainder. Of the 6.5 percent tax, the government now receives 2.5 percent.

Source: FEDERACAFE, División de Investigaciones Económicas.

The Discount on Currency Exchange Certificates

When surrendering the proceeds of coffee sales in dollars to the Central Bank, the exporter receives a certificate, which in the past—from May 1977 through October 1980—could be redeemed at face value in 120 days or sold immediately at a discount. This system acted as an indirect tax on coffee exports. As noted earlier, the discount has now been eliminated.

Table F-4 contains a brief summary of the evolution of the various taxes on coffee since 1950. As can be seen, the retention tax has been gaining in importance in recent years and now provides almost 70 percent of total tax revenues.

The Tax System and the Producers' Price

By using the various taxes and prices, the government is able to determine the price received by growers, to influence production, and to determine whether growers sell to the federation or to private exporters, as discussed in chapter 6.

An exporter pays to the Central Bank the foreign exchange received from the sale of coffee, and the bank pays the equivalent in pesos, converted at the current official rate of exchange less the value of the ad valorem tax based on the *reintegro* price. This amount is paid in the form of currency exchange certificates, which the exporter values at less than their face value. From this must be deducted the cost of internal transport, grading, and warehousing, and the minimum acceptable amount of profit. The balance is available for payment for the volume of parchment necessary for the export order and for the payment of the retention tax. Division of the balance by this volume—including retention and the amount needed to convert pergamino into excelso—gives the maximum price per unit of parchment that the exporter is prepared to pay. In practice an exporter will take other factors into account when determining this price, such as the small payment received for deliveries of *pasilla*.

By setting the minimum price of the federation higher than the price that some, or all, exporters can offer, or by increasing taxes, thereby forcing the exporter's price below that of the federation, the government can induce growers to sell to the federation and can reduce or eliminate sales to private exporters. Conversely, by setting the federation price below the price which private exporters can pay, the government can reduce or eliminate sales to the federation. In table F-5 the prices paid by the federation and by exporters are given for each month since January 1975. A grower might be expected to sell coffee to the buyer that offers the higher price. The higher of the prices can therefore reasonably be considered the market price to growers in each month.

Table F-4. *The Value of Taxes Levied on the Coffee Sector and the Value of Coffee Production, Selected Years 1950–82*
(million pesos)

Year	Ad valorem tax	Exchange differential and exchange discount	General export tax	Pasilla and ripio tax	Retention quota	Total taxes and contributions	Value of production	Total taxes and contributions as a percentage of the value of production
1950	...	...	1.0	0.9	...	1.9	1,070.1	0.2
1955	...	14.6	1.3	1.2	...	17.1	1,825.4	0.9
1960	324.0	94.4	1.3	1.3	212.5	633.5	2,573.8	24.6
1965	...	613.7	1.2	1.4	242.6	858.9	4,304.0	20.0
1969	1,563.2	...	1.4	1.4	1,275.2	2,841.2	8,342.1	34.0
1971	1,392.9	...	1.4	1.4	1,260.1	2,655.8	7,894.5	33.6
1972	1,807.3	...	1.4	1.4	1,630.8	3,441.9	10,922.8	31.5
1973	2,683.9	...	...	1.4	2,424.8	5,110.1	14,497.5	35.2
1974	2,744.0	...	...	1.5	3,319.0	6,004.5	17,229.9	35.2
1975	3,402.5	...	...	1.8	3,587.5	6,991.8	20,397.8	34.3
1976	6,156.0	...	...	1.0	10,071.0	16,228.0	39,251.3	41.3
1977	8,964.0	2,550.0	...	4.0	20,545.0	32,063.0	65,928.0	48.6
1978	10,878.3	5,397.0	...	9.6	29,707.2	45,992.1	77,099.0	59.6
1979	12,342.0	5,036.0	...	4.0	29,846.0	47,228.0	78,764.0	60.0
1980	15,025.0	4,068.0	...	4.0	31,116.0	50,213.0	99,683.0	50.4
1981	11,468.0	n.a.	...	4.0	9,597.0	21,069.0[a]	102,000.0	20.7
1982	10,607.0	n.a.	...	5.0	23,531.0	34,143.0[a]	120,000.0	28.0

n.a. Not available.

... Zero or negligible.

a. Excluding exchange discount.

Sources: FEDERACAFE; ICO, *Coffee in Colombia 1979/80* (London, September 1980).

Table F-5. *Prices Paid to Growers by the Federation and by Private Exporters, 1975–83*
(pesos per 125 kilograms of federation-type pergamino)

Year	Month	Federation[a]	Private exporters[a]
1975	Average	2,730	2,934
	January	2,500	2,596
	February	2,500	2,492
	March	2,500	2,406
	April	2,435	2,256
	May	2,350	2,500
	June	2,350	2,561
	July	2,560	2,833
	August	3,000	4,143
	September	3,000	3,551
	October	3,065	3,442
	November	3,250	3,496
	December	3,250	3,500
1976	Average	5,533	5,828
	January	3,496	4,131
	February	3,845	4,528
	March	4,120	4,430
	April	4,495	5,356
	May	4,495	6,115
	June	6,079	6,669
	July	6,560	6,221
	August	6,560	6,283
	September	6,560	6,271
	October	6,560	6,225
	November	6,619	6,479
	December	7,000	7,200
1977	Average	7,179	6,946
	January	7,000	7,445
	February	7,000	7,371
	March	7,000	7,541
	April	7,000	7,291
	May	7,048	6,589
	June	7,300	6,524
	July	7,300	6,560
	August	7,300	6,828
	September	7,300	6,869
	October	7,300	6,645
	November	7,300	6,839
	December	7,300	6,849

(Table continues on the following page.)

Table F-5 *(continued)*

Year	Month	Federation[a]	Private exporters[a]
1978	Average	7,300	6,946
	January	7,300	7,008
	February	7,300	7,001
	March	7,300	6,921
	April	7,300	6,991
	May	7,300	6,923
	June	7,300	6,938
	July	7,300	6,905
	August	7,300	7,009
	September	7,300	7,073
	October	7,300	6,960
	November	7,300	6,849
	December	7,300	6,773
1979	Average	7,270	7,179
	January	7,300	6,920
	February	7,236	6,860
	March	6,400	6,150
	April	6,400	6,363
	May	6,574	6,578
	June	6,946	6,955
	July	7,143	7,110
	August	7,340	7,276
	September	7,714	7,759
	October	7,900	7,919
	November	8,066	8,076
	December	8,216	8,185
1980	Average	8,663	8,528
	January	8,300	8,305
	February	8,300	8,333
	March	8,356	8,450
	April	8,733	8,761
	May	8,733	8,763
	June	8,733	8,484
	July	8,733	8,313
	August	8,733	8,345
	September	8,733	8,318
	October	8,733	8,665
	November	8,733	8,675
	December	9,140	8,898
1981	Average	9,453	9,271
	January	9,200	8,893

Table F-5 *(continued)*

Year	Month	Federation[a]	Private exporters[a]
	February	9,200	8,861
	March	9,200	9,036
	April	9,200	9,100
	May	9,200	9,000
	June	9,200	8,893
	July	9,200	9,156
	August	9,200	9,380
	September	9,460	9,310
	October	9,800	9,673
	November	10,241	9,956
	December	10,330	10,000
1982	Average	11,171	11,003
	January	10,330	10,166
	February	10,330	10,214
	March	10,795	10,619
	April	11,050	10,868
	May	11,050	10,770
	June	11,050	10,930
	July	11,050	10,913
	August	11,050	10,891
	September	11,050	10,923
	October	12,100	11,839
	November	12,100	11,963
	December	12,100	11,935
1983	Average	13,075	n.a.
	January	12,100	12,095
	February	12,100	12,156
	March	12,100	12,102
	April	12,800	12,460
	May	12,800	12,363
	June	12,800	12,563
	July	12,800	12,543
	August	12,800	12,615
	September	13,900	13,151
	October	14,150	n.a.
	November	14,150	n.a.
	December	14,400	n.a.
1984	March	14,800	n.a.

n.a. Not available.

a. Often the higher price paid by the federation than that paid by private exporters is explained by differences in quality.

Source: FEDERACAFE.

Table F-6. *Proceeds of the Taxes on Coffee and Their Distribution,
as Percentage of the Total, 1974–82*

Year	Total taxes and levies (million pesos)	National coffee fund share	Share of the departmental committees of FEDERACAFE	National government share
1974	6,064	62.9	1.8	35.3
1975	6,992	58.5	2.1	38.4
1976	16,228	68.8	1.7	29.5
1977	32,063	69.3	1.3	29.4
1978	45,992	69.0	1.0	30.0
1979	47,228	68.0	2.0	30.0
1980	50,213	68.0	2.0	30.0
1981[a]	21,069	59.0	3.0	38.0
1982[a]	34,143	83.9	2.3	13.8

a. Excluding the exchange discount.
Source: FEDERACAFE.

The Recipients of Coffee Taxes

Of the total taxes and levies on the export of coffee, in recent years more than two-thirds have gone to the National Coffee Fund, which obtains its revenues entirely from taxes on coffee. The whole of the retention tax is received by the fund, and the share received by the fund from all forms of taxation on coffee has tended to increase as this tax has gained in importance in relation to the ad valorem tax, which, apart from the tax implicit in the system of currency exchange certificates, is the only indirect tax on the coffee sector received by the government.[2] Total proceeds and their distribution are shown in table F-6.

Notes

1. Much of this appendix, which supports the analysis presented in chapter 6, is drawn from a publication of the International Coffee Organization (ICO), *Coffee in Colombia, 1979/80* (London, September 1980).
2. Note, however, that the value of the retention tax does not accrue to the federation or the National Coffee Fund until the coffee has been sold. The bags of coffee received as retention tax but never sold are of no value. The figures in table F-6 were computed on the assumption that the coffee delivered to the federation as retention tax should be valued at its market value. To the extent that this coffee has a true value less than its market value these figures are an overestimate of the total taxes and the shares of the NCF and the departmental committees. The government, on the other hand, receives its taxes in cash.

STATISTICAL APPENDIX

Table SA-1. *Gross Domestic Product, by Type of Expenditure, at Current Market Prices, 1971–84*
(million pesos)

Economic variable	1971	1972	1973	1974	1975	1976
Gross domestic product at market prices	155,886	189,614	243,160	322,384	405,108	532,270
Gross domestic consumption	131,819	155,877	195,780	258,766	332,095	422,031
Private consumption	114,724	137,733	172,769	230,558	295,919	378,349
Government consumption	17,095	18,144	23,011	28,208	36,176	43,682
Gross domestic investment	30,266	34,371	44,425	69,170	68,838	93,481
Gross fixed investment	27,302	30,486	38,416	52,843	62,129	84,571
Change in stocks	2,964	3,885	6,009	16,327	6,709	8,910
Exports of goods and nonfactor services	19,414	26,392	36,614	48,453	66,961	97,317
Imports of goods and nonfactor services	25,613	27,026	33,659	54,005	62,786	80,559
Net factor income from abroad	– 3,508	– 4,286	– 5,082	– 5,030	– 8,134	– 10,859
Gross national product at market prices	152,378	185,328	238,078	317,354	396,974	521,411

Note: Exports and imports of goods and nonfactor services and net factor income are balance of payments figures of the Central Bank, converted to Colombian pesos by World Bank staff members, which differ from DANE's figures of national accounts. The exchange rates used in the conversion in this table are the official average rates. Private consumption is a residual item in the account.

Table SA-2. *Gross Domestic Product, by Type of Expenditure, at Constant Market Prices, 1970–83*
(million 1975 pesos)

Economic variable	1970	1971	1972	1973	1974	1975
Gross domestic product at market prices	307,496	325,825	350,813	374,398	395,910	405,108
Gross domestic consumption	254,373	275,958	292,327	309,224	322,415	332,095
Private consumption	227,063	241,484	259,481	273,033	287,055	295,919
Government consumption	27,310	34,474	32,846	36,191	35,360	36,176
Gross domestic investment	63,148	65,844	64,244	70,073	83,967	68,838
Gross fixed investment	53,201	55,786	54,687	59,443	64,604	62,129
Change in stocks	9,947	10,058	9,557	10,630	19,363	6,709
Exports of goods and nonfactor services	47,961	50,036	56,514	58,489	57,889	66,961
Imports of goods and nonfactor services	57,986	66,013	62,272	63,388	68,361	62,786
Net factor income from abroad	– 11,258	– 10,143	– 10,308	– 9,473	– 6,784	– 8,134
Gross national product at market prices	296,238	315,682	340,505	364,925	389,126	396,974

Note: Net factor income is a balance of payments figure deflated by members of the World Bank staff using the manufacturing unit value index (MUV). Private consumption is a residual item in the account.

1977	1978	1979	1980	1981	1982	1983	1984[a]
716,029	909,487	1,188,817	1,579,130	1,982,773	2,497,298	3,036,661	3,691,586
556,712	719,187	942,437	1,265,852	1,650,133	2,110,924	2,587,532	3,050,201
501,496	641,367	831,715	1,106,481	1,443,259	1,838,158	2,235,983	2,626,197
55,216	77,820	110,722	159,371	206,874	272,766	351,549	424,004
134,270	166,293	215,782	301,117	408,927	511,625	588,238	698,932
104,041	139,897	183,325	264,894	350,048	436,091	512,780	653,405
30,229	26,396	32,457	36,223	58,879	75,534	75,458	45,507
126,670	157,925	198,226	275,166	254,909	306,719	319,383	457,757
101,623	133,918	167,628	263,005	331,196	431,970	458,492	515,304
− 10,004	− 11,768	− 10,852	− 14,893	− 30,733	− 70,510	− 96,682	151,578
706,025	897,719	1,177,965	1,564,237	1,952,040	2,426,788	2,939,979	3,540,008

a. Preliminary estimate.
Sources: DANE, Central Bank, and World Bank estimates.

1976	1977	1978	1979	1980	1981	1982	1983
424,263	441,906	479,335	505,119	525,765	537,736	542,836	548,055
351,946	367,505	398,487	413,144	439,649	454,808	467,448	476,078
314,398	328,177	355,555	364,892	385,285	398,421	408,442	414,975
37,548	39,328	42,932	48,252	54,364	56,387	59,006	61,103
75,245	87,468	93,516	93,220	103,358	117,037	123,279	117,858
68,039	68,518	74,923	77,775	88,021	93,539	96,307	95,715
7,206	18,950	18,593	15,445	15,337	23,498	26,972	22,143
66,519	62,154	77,452	88,061	90,727	80,770	82,496	72,226
69,447	75,221	90,120	89,306	107,966	114,879	130,386	118,107
− 9,503	− 7,638	− 7,189	− 5,477	− 6,245	− 11,770	− 23,399	− 27,219
414,760	434,268	472,146	499,642	519,520	525,966	519,437	520,836

Sources: DANE, Central Bank, and World Bank estimates.

Table SA-3. *Gross Domestic Product at Factor Cost, by Sector, at Current Prices, 1970–83*

(million pesos)

Sector	1970	1971	1972	1973	1974	1975
Gross domestic product at factor cost	122,874	144,591	176,534	226,583	300,100	373,425
Agriculture[b]	33,515	36,863	46,033	58,961	78,952	97,337
Mining	2,920	3,534	4,544	6,234	6,022	7,407
Manufacturing	21,278	25,052	32,220	44,427	60,523	73,184
Construction	4,953	5,994	7,168	9,960	12,436	12,604
Electricity, gas, and water	1,413	1,685	1,922	2,619	3,104	3,968
Transport and communication	11,701	14,040	16,826	19,375	24,499	34,865
Trade	16,171	19,217	22,941	30,432	43,557	52,442
Banking, finance, rent, and insurance	17,775	21,899	25,140	31,010	41,062	54,613
Public administration and defense[c]	9,641	12,216	14,644	17,603	22,418	28,281
Other branches[d]	6,957	8,361	9,902	11,990	15,508	19,964
Less: imputed banking charges	3,450	4,270	4,806	6,028	7,981	11,240

a. Preliminary estimate.
b. Includes fishing, hunting, and forestry.
c. Equals government services.

Table SA-4. *Gross Domestic Product at Factor Cost, by Sector, at Constant Prices, 1970–83*

(million 1975 pesos)

Sector	1970	1971	1972	1973	1974	1975
Gross domestic product at factor cost	280,605	297,892	323,354	348,611	365,334	373,425
Agriculture[b]	78,379	78,958	85,182	87,096	91,883	97,337
Mining	9,218	8,408	8,911	9,617	7,146	7,407
Manufacturing	50,253	55,019	62,410	69,951	73,137	73,184
Construction	10,012	10,317	10,962	13,256	13,980	12,604
Electricity, gas, and water	2,271	2,588	2,934	3,489	3,684	3,968
Transport and communication	24,210	25,977	28,675	32,039	34,622	34,865
Trade	37,382	40,939	44,022	48,081	51,563	52,442
Banking, finance, rent, and insurance	42,506	46,130	47,215	49,718	52,648	54,613
Public administration and defense[c]	21,223	23,829	26,108	27,559	28,146	28,281
Other branches[d]	13,736	15,110	16,271	17,506	18,846	19,964
Less: imputed banking charges	8,585	9,383	9,336	9,701	10,321	11,240

a. Preliminary estimate.
b. Includes fishing, hunting, and forestry.
c. Equals government services.

1976	1977	1978	1979	1980	1981	1982	1983[a]
482,578	641,046	810,477	1,065,871	1,420,746	1,815,356	2,282,769	2,785,098
126,061	179,567	209,951	255,905	305,286	381,281	468,770	568,262
10,410	10,617	12,055	17,347	35,764	48,270	63,739	87,047
93,430	115,505	138,741	180,424	267,910	327,768	406,736	483,523
18,366	26,241	35,431	47,989	71,147	98,374	124,829	149,384
6,144	8,229	11,413	16,305	20,802	34,040	48,849	67,426
46,078	61,621	77,332	107,666	143,716	176,267	213,835	252,215
66,594	89,457	119,677	157,301	204,058	262,363	332,926	395,993
69,433	88,063	118,182	163,435	210,969	276,822	352,472	417,968
35,243	45,235	63,051	85,277	120,494	160,715	210,900	272,229
24,972	34,068	47,102	63,193	80,789	108,063	138,470	174,627
14,153	17,557	22,458	28,971	40,189	58,607	78,757	83,576

d. Composed of house rentals and personal services.
Source: DANE.

1976	1977	1978	1979	1980	1981	1982	1983[a]
390,285	404,169	429,225	447,501	472,113	485,591	488,249	494,238
99,952	103,107	111,549	117,058	119,144	123,017	120,841	122,911
6,795	5,852	5,463	5,548	6,594	6,941	7,055	7,966
76,547	75,527	76,338	76,610	86,361	85,296	83,084	83,575
14,008	15,093	14,634	14,722	16,833	18,190	19,047	20,045
4,158	4,163	4,377	4,891	5,232	5,511	5,652	5,865
37,216	40,622	45,699	48,681	49,863	52,631	54,872	54,147
55,048	56,979	61,214	63,543	64,804	65,873	67,144	65,743
56,440	59,345	64,198	67,296	71,643	75,741	78,158	80,381
30,647	32,737	34,594	36,857	40,515	42,835	43,891	45,624
20,935	22,209	23,759	24,857	25,219	26,199	26,896	27,497
11,461	11,465	12,600	12,562	14,095	16,643	18,391	19,516

d. Composed of house rentals and personal services.
Source: DANE.

Table SA-5. *Gross Domestic Product at Market Prices, Agriculture and Total, 1970–83*
(thousand pesos)

	Current pesos			1975 pesos		
Year	Agriculture[a]	Noncoffee agriculture[b]	Entire economy	Agriculture[a]	Noncoffee agriculture[b]	Entire economy
1970	36,194	28,216	132,768	86,488	68,056	307,496
1971	39,595	32,092	155,886	88,059	69,931	325,825
1972	49,439	39,692	189,614	93,772	74,709	350,813
1973	65,203	50,752	243,160	96,022	76,599	374,398
1974	84,386	69,585	322,384	100,944	81,131	395,910
1975	108,490	86,703	405,108	108,490	86,703	405,108
1976	147,300	106,444	532,270	108,805	88,589	424,263
1977	211,216	146,487	716,029	109,904	90,142	441,906
1978	240,133	170,801	909,487	123,624	97,579	479,335
1979	285,523	211,026	1,188,817	132,306	101,635	505,119
1980	362,075	261,746	1,579,130	135,499	103,989	525,765
1981	407,649	323,896	1,982,773	136,285	106,095	537,736
1982	503,897	401,423	2,497,298	134,591	103,405	542,856
1983[c]	612,239	n.a.	3,036,661	137,445	n.a.	548,055

n.a. Not available.

a. Consists of pergamino coffee (01), other agricultural products (02), animal products (03), processed coffee (08), and sugar manufacturing (12).

b. Consists of other agricultural products (02), animal products (03), and sugar manufacturing (12).

c. Preliminary estimate.

Sources: DANE, *Cuentas nacionales de Colombia, 1970–1982* (Bogotá, August 1984), and information not yet published for 1982 and 1983.

Table SA-6. Exports (f.o.b.) and Imports (c.i.f.), 1970–83

(million current pesos)

	Exports (f.o.b.)						Imports (c.i.f.)			
Year	Agriculture^a	Processed coffee (08)	Sugar (12)	Broad agriculture^b	Rest of the economy	Total	Agriculture^a	Sugar (12)	Rest of the economy	Total
1970	2,095	8,749	1,472	12,316	5,303	17,619	769	10	18,545	19,324
1971	2,118	8,279	336	10,733	7,921	18,654	1,324	...	23,644	24,968
1972	2,781	10,646	672	14,099	11,034	25,133	1,223	...	23,044	24,267
1973	3,103	15,165	783	19,051	17,239	36,290	2,365	...	28,429	30,794
1974	4,694	16,703	1,927	23,324	23,551	46,875	3,560	...	46,830	50,390
1975	7,809	23,622	2,883	34,314	29,763	64,077	2,574	...	54,188	56,762
1976	8,650	42,329	993	51,972	38,760	90,732	3,639	...	70,320	73,959
1977	11,229	60,751	106	72,086	48,677	120,763	4,084	22	90,401	94,507
1978	13,132	79,060	1,049	93,241	57,970	151,211	4,618	317	120,561	125,496
1979	14,241	88,762	2,445	105,448	75,448	180,896	5,968	...	153,870	159,838
1980	19,918	116,793	9,273	145,984	110,119	256,103	13,370	1	232,926	246,297
1981	25,618	85,773	4,705	116,096	118,887	234,983	12,130	2	293,575	305,707
1982	26,421	109,330	3,799	139,706	132,820	272,526	18,677	2	360,684	379,368
1983^c	30,456	131,087	6,180	167,723	155,276	322,999	21,846	2	381,358	403,206

... Zero or negligible.

Note: Exports and imports for the economy as a whole comprise both goods and nonfactor services. These data differ slightly from the national accounts statistics of the Central Bank.

a. Consists of pergamino coffee (01), other agricultural products (02), and animal products (03).

b. Consists of 01, 02, 03, processed coffee (08), and sugar (12).

c. Preliminary estimate.

Sources: DANE, Cuentas nacionales de Colombia, 1970–1982 (Bogotá, August 1984), tables 21.1 and 22.1, and information not yet published for 1982 and 1983.

Table SA-7. Exports (f.o.b.) and Imports (c.i.f.), 1970–83
(million 1975 pesos)

	Exports (f.o.b.)						Imports (c.i.f.)			
Year	Agriculture	Processed coffee (08)	Sugar (12)	Broad agriculture	Rest of the economy	Total	Agriculture	Sugar (12)	Rest of the economy	Total
1970	5,981	18,153	1,565	25,699	20,335	46,034	2,870	...	50,702	53,572
1971	5,162	18,651	1,685	25,498	22,639	48,137	4,318	...	60,045	64,363
1972	5,342	18,835	1,992	26,169	27,689	53,858	3,522	...	52,383	55,905
1973	4,554	19,253	1,779	25,586	32,341	57,927	4,087	...	53,889	57,976
1974	5,348	19,931	1,843	27,122	28,869	55,991	3,764	...	60,009	63,773
1975	7,809	23,622	2,883	34,314	29,763	64,077	2,574	...	54,188	56,762
1976	7,690	20,431	1,436	29,557	32,476	62,033	3,547	...	60,215	63,762
1977	8,114	15,921	291	24,326	34,916	59,242	3,177	70	66,732	69,979
1978	8,942	27,473	2,141	38,556	35,597	74,153	4,529	1,009	78,940	84,478
1979	7,283	33,991	3,041	44,315	36,032	80,347	3,871	...	81,268	85,139
1980	8,381	34,753	3,591	46,725	37,725	84,450	6,111	...	94,994	101,105
1981	8,714	29,018	2,196	39,928	34,529	74,457	4,990	1	101,064	106,055
1982	7,116	28,416	3,825	39,357	33,940	73,297	7,004	1	107,500	114,505
1983[a]	6,682	29,524	3,716	39,922	33,115	73,037	6,787	1	97,078	103,866

... Zero or negligible.

Note: Exports and imports for the economy as a whole comprise both goods and services. For definitions of agriculture and broad agriculture, see notes to table SA-7.

a. Preliminary estimate.

Sources: DANE, Cuentas nacionales de Colombia, 1970–1982 (Bogotá, August 1984), tables 21.2 and 22.2, and information not yet published for 1982 and 1983.

Table SA-8. *Commodity Exports, 1970–83*
(million U.S. dollars)

Item	1970	1971	1972	1973	1974	1975	1976	1977	1978	1979	1980	1981	1982	1983
Major export														
Green coffee	467.0	400.0	430.0	598.0	622.0	672.0	967.2	1,497.9	1,979.0	2,005.0	2,361.0	1,423.3	1,561.5	1,506.2
Minor exports														
Agrobased products	101.4	105.2	155.0	166.5	225.9	327.4	267.5	353.8	339.3	381.1	643.0	589.6	506.8	420.3
Cotton	34.6	29.7	51.2	38.1	48.6	76.1	59.4	164.0	72.5	52.0	159.3	148.4	66.5	22.5
Cattle and beef	21.8	28.2	37.7	43.4	36.0	56.8	52.1	45.0	46.5	37.2	27.3	54.1	46.1	30.5
Sugar	14.0	15.7	28.4	30.2	68.6	95.1	24.1	2.2	19.5	49.6	165.0	76.9	54.7	68.9
Bananas	18.1	14.7	13.7	15.4	25.4	31.6	40.9	45.6	76.0	84.8	94.0	122.4	131.1	147.7
Tobacco	7.2	9.2	9.9	15.0	18.9	12.8	25.5	19.2	27.5	24.2	25.7	19.6	21.7	22.9
Flowers	1.0	1.8	3.1	8.4	16.0	19.3	21.6	32.6	53.4	79.2	99.4	108.6	111.5	120.6
Rice	0.0	0.0	0.7	3.4	0.5	22.9	21.4	19.9	4.6	8.8	16.6	9.5	32.6	2.8
Cheese	...	0.2	1.4	3.3	0.4	1.2	2.8	6.8	16.1	17.1	20.4	16.7	10.0	0.2
Fish	4.7	5.7	8.9	9.3	11.5	11.6	19.7	18.5	23.2	28.2	35.3	33.4	32.6	4.2
Manufactured products	83.3	118.4	168.5	256.4	479.3	414.1	448.0	469.7	620.5	695.4	889.4	984.7	969.8	951.6
Food products[a]	11.1	11.7	15.7	8.1	11.9	19.3	16.1	30.5	31.3	34.0	54.3	94.1	67.9	152.0
Footwear, clothing, and textiles[b]	18.7	26.7	42.6	81.9	154.0	102.4	139.0	88.0	194.7	150.4	180.0	176.2	183.9	91.2
Leather and hides	6.7	7.0	19.0	25.5	16.0	16.5	20.4	30.0	33.8	37.7	32.0	39.7	47.4	30.2
Chemicals and pharmaceuticals	7.6	11.4	16.9	32.2	70.7	53.0	44.5	45.9	12.2	60.7	84.5	78.2	76.5	89.7
Basic metals and products	4.9	6.9	10.9	20.9	28.0	21.5	23.6	32.7	36.4	65.9	47.8	62.4	68.0	75.2
Mechanical and electrical equipment	3.7	5.3	7.3	13.1	23.6	23.1	29.4	43.9	41.1	52.1	62.4	63.8	62.7	31.7

(Table continues on the following page.)

Table SA-8 (continued)

Item	1970	1971	1972	1973	1974	1975	1976	1977	1978	1979	1980	1981	1982	1983
Minor exports (cont.)														
Timber and wood products	5.4	5.6	8.7	22.0	30.6	8.0	13.6	14.7	7.5	15.1	11.3	11.7	16.9	7.5
Paper, cartons, and books	3.6	4.4	10.0	11.0	14.2	16.4	25.1	28.3	72.2	53.0	71.0	90.9	74.0	57.0
Cement	3.3	3.2	5.7	6.9	9.8	11.9	23.3	14.9	21.9	30.7	35.7	31.3	34.3	19.9
Glass	4.2	3.9	4.2	4.8	6.6	7.3	10.0	10.0	9.7	14.3	18.0	14.9	11.3	8.2
Plastics	1.3	2.3	3.5	4.7	5.9	7.6	9.8	10.7	14.4	17.3	25.8	25.4	26.9	26.8
Transport equipment	0.7	9.5	2.3	2.8	5.4	7.1	9.2	15.6	21.1	17.9	25.7	30.2	16.2	10.2
Fuel oil	12.1	20.5	21.7	22.5	102.6	119.9	84.0	104.5	124.2	146.3	240.9	265.9	283.8	352.0
Other products	83.9	66.4	112.5	156.4	86.1	51.7	62.5	121.8	63.9	218.9	51.6	42.2	34.6	202.8
Total goods	735.6	690.0	866.0	1,177.3	1,413.3	1,465.2	1,745.2	2,443.2	3,002.7	3,300.4	3,945.0	3,039.8	3,072.7	3,080.9
Balance of payments adjustment	52.4	62.0	113.0	85.7	77.1	281.8	509.8	283.8	267.3	280.6	351.0	440.6	187.0	96.1
Total goods adjusted	788.0	752.0	979.0	1,263.0	1,494.0	1,747.0	2,255.0	2,727.0	3,270.0	3,581.0	4,296.0	3,397.0	3,282.0	3,147.0
Freight and insurance	43.0	49.0	49.0	65.0	98.0	93.0	120.0	144.0	140.0	153.0	142.4	114.1	115.7	103.3
Other transportation	52.0	58.0	55.0	69.0	80.0	82.0	142.0	146.0	165.0	182.0	290.0	366.3	319.6	287.4
Travel	54.0	61.0	59.0	72.0	105.0	141.0	175.0	231.0	260.0	357.0	478.0	437.0	484.4	235.0
Other	63.0	54.0	65.0	79.0	81.0	102.0	113.0	195.0	204.0	385.0	541.0	364.0	583.0	278.0
Total goods and nonfactor services	1,000.0	974.0	1,207.0	1,548.0	1,858.0	2,165.0	2,805.0	3,443.0	4,039.0	4,658.0	5,747.4	4,678.4	4,784.5	4,050.3

... Zero or negligible.

a. Excluding sugar.

b. Excluding cotton fiber.

Source: Customs data.

Table SA-9. *Balance of Payments, 1971–84*

(million U.S. dollars)

Item	1971	1972	1973	1974	1975	1976	1977	1978	1979	1980	1981	1982	1983	1984[a]
Merchandise exports f.o.b.[b]	752	979	1,263	1,494	1,747	2,255	2,728	3,270	3,581	4,296	3,397	3,282	3,147	3,658
Merchandise imports f.o.b.	900	848	982	1,510	1,425	1,666	1,980	2,564	2,996	4,283	4,730	5,358	4,464	3,980
Trade balance	-148	131	281	-16	322	589	748	706	585	13	-1,333	-2,076	-1,317	-322
Nonfactor service receipts	222	228	286	365	418	550	716	769	1,077	1,451	1,281	1,503	903	884
Nonfactor service payments	385	388	442	562	605	656	783	861	943	1,210	1,340	1,381	1,350	1,133
Goods and services balance	-311	-29	124	-213	135	483	681	614	719	854	-1,400	-1,954	-1,764	-571
Net factor income	-176	-196	-215	-193	-263	-313	-272	-301	-255	-315	-564	-1,100	-1,226	-1,504
Receipts	(11)	(10)	(26)	(67)	(61)	(71)	(72)	(132)	(267)	(494)	(647)	(510)	(280)	(124)
Payments	(187)	(206)	(241)	(260)	(324)	(384)	(344)	(433)	(522)	(809)	(1,211)	(1,610)	(1,506)	(1,628)
Net private transfers	3	11	12	23	30	39	40	44	98	165	242	169	164	205
Current account balance	-484	-214	-79	-383	-98	209	449	357	562	104	-1,722	-2,885	-2,826	-1,870
Official grant aid	31	24	23	33	18	12	6	29	3	—	—	—	—	—
Private capital	59	24	8	27	24	-25	37	35	208	108	631	667	587	n.a.
Direct investment	40	17	23	36	32	14	43	67	104	51	228	337	514	411
Loans (net)	19	7	-15	-9	-8	-30	-6	-32	104	57	403	330	73	n.a.
Disbursements	(109)	(104)	(81)	(88)	(58)	(44)	(55)	(65)	(152)	(70)	(690)	(428)	(307)	n.a.
Amortization	(90)	(97)	(96)	(97)	(66)	(83)	(61)	(97)	(48)	(13)	(287)	(98)	(235)	n.a.
Public and publicly guaranteed capital	45	61	310	216	9	141	202	79	505	750	981	960	943	1,116

(Table continues on the following page.)

227

Table SA-9 (*continued*)

Item	1971	1972	1973	1974	1975	1976	1977	1978	1979	1980	1981	1982	1983	1984[a]
Disbursements	(237)	(257)	(441)	(424)	(411)	(295)	(382)	(325)	(950)	(999)	(1,249)	(1,285)	(1,342)	(1,743)
Amortization	(92)	(96)	(131)	(208)	(142)	(154)	(180)	(246)	(445)	(249)	(266)	(325)	(399)	(627)
Special drawing rights allocation	17	18	...	...	...	...	...	...	24	24	24	...	...	...
Short-term capital	n.a.	n.a.	n.a.	n.a.	n.a.	n.a.	n.a.	...	n.a.	107	336	370	−395	−390
Public, net[c]	n.a.	n.a.	n.a.	n.a.	n.a.	n.a.	n.a.	n.a.	n.a.	(−83)	(38)	(41)	(−90)	(4)
Private, net	n.a.	n.a.	n.a.	n.a.	n.a.	n.a.	n.a.	n.a.	n.a.	(190)	(298)	(329)	(−305)	(−394)
Other capital, net	157	79	−37	−257	−74	225	158	110	−65	75	−138	17	−163	n.a.
Capital account balance	409	406	304	19	237	353	403	253	675	1,064	1,834	2,014	972	n.a.
Net change in reserves (minus means increase)	75	−192	−225	364	−139	−562	−852	−618	−1,237	−1,168	−112	871	1,854	n.a.
Central Bank	−19	−178	−180	95	−117	−619	−667	−652	−1,624	−1,310	−214	739	1,812	1,284
Rest of banking system	94	−14	−42	269	−22	57	−185	42	387	142	102	132	42	n.a.

n.a. Not available.

... Zero or negligible.

a. Preliminary estimate.

b. Includes sales of nonmonetary gold.

c. Includes liabilities that represent reserves of foreign authorities.

Source: Banco de la Republica.

228

Table SA-10. *Imports, by Economic Category, 1970–83*
(million U.S. dollars)

Item	1970	1971	1972	1973	1974	1975	1976	1977	1978	1979	1980	1981	1982	1983
Consumer goods	86.9	101.1	105.4	161.6	190.3	168.5	204.5	287.6	503.5	451.1	619.6	667.6	690.6	538.9
Durables	43.9	45.1	48.4	57.5	87.9	78.5	93.7	130.3	187.4	196.8	312.2	336.2	366.7	236.8
Nondurables	43.0	56.0	57.0	104.1	102.4	90.0	110.8	157.3	316.1	254.3	307.4	331.4	323.9	302.1
Raw materials and intermediate goods	366.1	410.7	405.7	490.1	936.4	780.8	843.0	1,076.5	1,434.8	1,705.3	2,458.8	2,701.1	2,771.2	2,542.8
Fuels	1.2	8.1	5.4	2.1	3.0	14.5	39.9	136.2	204.5	322.2	562.8	724.1	656.7	639.1
Agricultural inputs	8.3	10.1	21.2	34.8	99.4	54.8	22.9	69.7	104.5	95.8	162.2	147.0	189.7	158.3
Industrial inputs	356.6	392.5	379.1	453.2	834.0	711.5	780.2	870.6	1,125.8	1,287.3	1,734.0	1,830.0	1,924.8	1,745.4
Capital goods	368.2	397.6	330.8	386.7	464.9	539.3	660.6	664.2	898.0	1,076.8	1,584.2	1,830.5	2,015.9	1,886.4
Construction	20.3	15.8	10.1	18.9	32.4	35.4	42.6	26.1	44.7	63.1	98.3	159.6	213.6	129.3
Agricultural	13.0	8.1	10.6	18.3	24.3	29.0	30.7	44.1	54.2	39.3	63.1	66.1	68.3	66.0
Industrial	194.7	246.3	216.7	225.1	260.5	269.1	330.5	387.8	517.0	603.1	955.0	1,113.2	1,148.9	1,112.9
Transport	140.2	127.4	93.4	124.4	147.7	205.8	156.7	206.2	282.1	371.2	467.8	491.6	585.1	578.2
Unclassified	15.0	20.0	17.1	23.1	5.6	6.2	...	...	...	...	...	...	...	...
Total goods	836.2	929.4	859.0	1,061.5	1,597.2	1,494.8	1,708.1	2,028.3	2,836.3	3,233.2	4,662.6	5,199.2	5,477.7	4,968.1
Balance of payments adjustment	−34.2	−29.4	−11.0	−79.5	−87.2	−69.8	−42.1	−48.3	−272.3	−237.3	−379.6	−469.2	−119.7	−504.1
Total goods adjusted	802.0	900.0	848.0	982.0	1,510.0	1,425.0	1,666.0	1,980.0	2,564.0	2,996.0	4,283.0	4,730.0	5,358.0	4,464.0

. . . Zero or negligible.

Note: Subcategories were calculated on the basis of import registrations as shares of totals for the years 1970–83. Figures for total imports of merchandise have been adjusted by the Banco de la Republica.

Sources: Customs data and DANE.

229

Table SA-11. *Imports, by Principal Product Group, 1970–83*
(million U.S. dollars)

Year	Machinery and electrical equipment	Vehicles and transportation equipment	Fuels, mineral oils, and products	Chemicals and pharma- ceuticals	Iron and steel	Plastics	Paper materials and products	Rubber products	Foodstuffs	Other	Total[a]
1970	231.2	136.8	8.7	76.6	78.6	22.5	35.9	14.0	31.0	200.9	836.2
1971	275.5	127.7	10.8	87.6	81.6	25.4	35.1	16.9	62.7	206.1	929.4
1972	256.0	117.3	5.4	92.4	64.6	21.0	37.8	17.0	46.7	200.8	859.0
1973	359.3	128.0	3.9	127.0	72.2	21.8	48.4	21.3	80.1	199.5	1,061.5
1974	306.7	191.6	3.7	210.8	139.6	45.1	67.9	35.1	143.5	453.2	1,597.2
1975	329.7	238.4	18.4	199.1	135.3	41.1	68.3	28.7	94.8	341.0	1,494.8
1976	406.4	251.4	41.7	200.6	122.9	48.8	66.6	40.5	146.2	383.0	1,708.1
1977	475.5	273.7	136.3	236.8	123.6	61.0	72.2	45.3	156.6	447.3	2,028.3
1978	618.4	380.7	205.1	300.6	180.9	84.0	96.3	55.3	180.6	734.4	2,836.3
1979	719.4	455.4	324.3	291.4	251.6	101.2	103.4	69.4	213.6	703.5	3,233.2
1980	1,099.1	626.0	566.5	409.9	316.1	145.3	169.8	85.8	232.6	1,011.5	4,662.6
1981	1,244.9	661.4	729.1	436.3	382.5	135.6	199.7	95.8	294.9	1,019.0	5,199.2
1982	1,310.0	776.9	661.4	457.2	442.5	139.6	213.1	98.2	297.0	1,081.8	5,477.7
1983	1,227.1	647.9	646.9	446.6	315.2	130.6	187.1	84.2	208.5	1,074.0	4,968.1

a. Before balance of payments adjustment.
Sources: Customs data and DANE.

Table SA-12. *Weighted Average CAT Subsidies, 1978–83*
(percent)

Section	Chapters	1978	1981	1983
1	1–5	3.77	5.58	10.94
2	6–14	2.39	1.61	11.29
3	15	2.00	0.30	0.50
4	16–24	10.05	8.87	13.79
5	25–27	0.63	0.54	1.00
6	28–38	5.11	4.76	10.53
7	39–40	4.93	6.55	14.92
8	41–43	9.97	9.80	12.40
9	44–46	9.77	6.61	9.71
10	47–49	2.63	9.48	14.96
11	50–63	8.81	10.21	14.95
12	64–67	11.97	11.97	14.96
13	68–70	10.52	10.74	14.78
14	71–72	1.00	0.40	0.40
15	73–83	8.72	8.64	11.79
16	84–85	11.93	11.70	14.86
17	86–89	6.69	11.70	14.86
18	90–92	9.96	11.82	15.00
19	93	9.00	9.00	15.00
20	94–98	10.60	11.51	15.00
21	99	0.90	0.00	0.00

Source: Constructed from DNP data.

Table SA-13. *Index of Real Support Prices Established by IDEMA, 1970–82*
(1975 = 100)

Year	Sesame	Paddy rice	Barley	Beans	Corn	Sorghum	Soybeans	Wheat
1970	81.3	138.9	102.8	89.5	89.1	83.6	73.4	90.4
1971	79.1	125.0	99.5	80.6	95.0	77.1	85.9	81.4
1972	79.2	106.5	84.8	79.0	89.1	69.0	73.2	86.3
1973	65.3	86.9	73.8	82.4	84.2	77.9	61.6	77.3
1974	78.4	123.1	91.0	87.3	100.3	88.4	103.6	96.1
1975	100.0	100.0	100.0	100.0	100.0	100.0	100.0	100.0
1976	n.a.	86.9	93.4	99.3	80.9	80.0	86.7	90.3
1977	n.a.	71.4	74.2	81.9	77.0	70.1	73.5	90.3
1978	88.0	86.2	87.1	85.3	91.0	81.1	87.9	68.0
1979	87.7	89.1	78.3	80.6	85.6	77.4	81.9	70.7
1980	91.1	103.0	73.7	75.7	98.5	90.6	80.2	81.2
1981	76.9	104.1	86.5	81.6	111.1	101.1	94.7	85.4
1982	74.7	100.9	92.3	82.5	120.5	114.8	107.9	86.5

n.a. Not available.
Sources: DNP; *Diagnostico del Sector Agrario*, vol. 2, table 76; and IDEMA.

Table SA-14. *Ratio of Support Prices to Producer Prices, 1970–84*

Year	Paddy rice	Corn	Beans	Sorghum	Soybeans	Wheat	Barley	Sesame
1970	1.22	0.91	1.13	0.88	0.68	1.09	1.26	0.77
1971	1.17	0.94	0.65	0.87	0.85	1.09	1.14	0.82
1972	1.20	0.81	0.75	0.61	0.81	1.04	1.05	0.90
1973	0.96	0.66	0.92	0.67	0.66	1.10	0.81	0.83
1974	1.14	0.96	0.82	0.83	0.99	1.05	1.03	0.73
1975	1.06	0.95	0.84	1.00	1.01	0.92	0.92	1.01
1976	1.13	0.84	0.97	0.90	0.97	1.08	0.96	n.a.
1977	0.85	0.68	0.92	0.79	0.76	1.01	0.96	n.a.
1978	0.99	0.98	0.98	0.95	0.95	1.05	1.10	1.06
1979	1.02	0.76	0.70	0.74	0.86	1.02	0.99	0.99
1980	1.14	0.77	0.68	0.85	0.85	1.11	1.00	1.01
1981	1.14	0.92	0.89	0.94	0.96	1.06	1.04	1.01
1982	1.07	n.a.	0.82	0.98	0.77	1.08	1.07	0.88
1983	1.05	n.a.	0.92	1.00	0.95	1.11	1.05	0.94
1984	0.86	1.28[a]	0.51	0.99	0.79	1.20[a]	1.01	0.78

n.a. Not available.

a. Support price/producer price of first semester 1984.

Source: IDEMA.

Table SA-15. *Ratio of Domestic Prices to International Prices of Selected Agricultural Commodities, 1970–82*

Year	Producer price/f.o.b. international price							Wholesale price/ f.o.b. international price	
	Wheat	Corn	Sorghum	Soybeans	Rice	Barley	Cotton	Sugar	Beef
1970	1.84	1.38	1.78	1.37	0.82	1.03	0.93	1.4	0.9
1971	1.53	1.46	1.17	1.21	0.78	1.21	0.84	1.1	0.8
1972	1.66	1.77	1.49	1.05	0.62	0.69	0.74	1.3	0.7
1973	0.86	1.44	1.07	0.63	0.42	0.74	0.76	0.6	0.7
1974	0.97	0.98	0.87	0.84	0.40	0.86	0.71	0.2	0.7
1975	1.51	1.11	0.94	1.02	0.46	0.90	0.95	0.5	1.4
1976	1.51	1.24	1.02	1.00	0.58	1.08	1.00	0.8	1.5
1977	2.07	2.25	1.59	1.18	0.85	1.12	1.02	2.1	1.6
1978	1.54	1.79	1.43	1.21	0.69	1.38	0.95	2.0	1.8
1979	1.42	2.03	1.54	1.20	0.78	0.93	1.01	0.6	1.2
1980	1.54	2.37	1.39	1.31	0.69	0.96	1.29	0.7	1.2
1981	1.92	2.21	1.49	1.47	0.71	0.86	1.14	1.4	1.4
1982	2.08	1.83	1.93	1.89	1.20	0.98	n.a.	3.0	n.a.

n.a. Not available.

Source: Jorge García-García, "Aspects of Agricultural Development in Colombia" (Bogotá, April 1983, processed).

Table SA-16. *Ratio of Production Costs to f.o.b. International Peso Prices of Some Agricultural Commodities, 1970–82*

Year	Rice	Corn	Sorghum	Soybeans	Wheat	Cotton
1970	1.011	2.402	1.090	0.825	2.663	0.446
1971	0.755	2.551	1.004	0.847	2.534	0.362
1972	0.722	2.459	1.024	0.776	1.977	0.270
1973	0.473	1.479	0.767	0.378	0.914	0.185
1974	0.313	0.780	0.674	0.585	0.866	0.232
1975	0.459	0.872	0.758	0.814	1.273	0.342
1976	0.615	1.013	0.963	0.863	1.495	0.257
1977	0.605	1.376	1.243	1.014	1.886	0.389
1978	0.594	1.568	1.240	1.012	1.732	0.700
1979	0.699	1.336	1.000	0.940	1.227	0.393
1980	0.745	1.608	1.084	1.038	1.463	0.310
1981	0.692	1.853	1.388	1.226	1.954	0.390
1982	1.124	2.138	1.586	1.460	1.767	n.a.

na. Not available.
Source: García-García, "Aspects of Agricultural Development."

Table SA-17. *Ratio of Support Prices to f.o.b. International Prices of Selected Agricultural Commodities, 1970–83*

Year	Rice	Corn	Sorghum	Soybeans	Wheat	Barley
1970	0.99	1.25	1.03	0.93	2.00	1.29
1971	0.91	1.37	1.02	1.04	1.66	1.38
1972	0.73	1.44	0.92	0.85	1.73	0.72
1973	0.39	0.94	0.72	0.42	0.95	0.60
1974	0.43	0.94	0.72	0.83	1.02	0.88
1975	0.49	1.05	0.94	1.03	1.40	0.83
1976	0.67	1.04	0.92	0.97	1.63	1.03
1977	0.67	1.54	1.26	0.90	2.09	1.07
1978	0.69	1.76	1.37	1.15	1.62	1.52
1979	0.79	1.54	1.14	1.03	1.44	0.93
1980	0.79	1.81	1.18	1.12	1.71	0.96
1981	0.74	2.04	1.40	1.42	2.03	0.89
1982	1.17	3.93	1.82	1.84	1.96	1.00
1983	1.16	1.86	1.62	2.21	1.68	1.74

Sources: 1970–82, García-García, "Aspects of Agricultural Development"; the 1983 estimate is based on DNP figures.

Table SA-18. Index of Real Peso Value of f.o.b. International Prices of Selected Agricultural Commodities, 1970–83 (1975 = 100)

Year	Butter	Beef	Barley	Corn	Rice	Wheat	Sugar	Palm oil	Coffee	Sorghum	Soybeans	Bananas	Tobacco	Cotton	Sisal
1970	64.1	117.6	59.8	67.4	62.5	56.7	25.3	83.6	95.7	68.4	73.4	93.7	106.3	75.3	36.1
1971	88.1	139.3	54.2	65.8	61.7	61.7	30.0	82.0	80.9	64.1	77.2	77.4	95.4	86.1	39.5
1972	98.4	174.5	91.8	61.3	67.5	65.4	47.3	66.3	89.3	66.3	83.3	86.3	101.0	89.5	54.0
1973	72.3	215.5	104.4	96.5	111.6	116.5	55.4	103.6	104.8	104.2	155.8	79.5	94.8	137.9	106.9
1974	76.2	223.5	87.0	114.2	137.3	133.1	151.3	161.4	98.6	117.0	127.4	77.7	95.2	127.1	188.3
1975	100.0	100.0	100.0	100.0	100.0	100.0	100.0	100.0	100.0	100.0	100.0	100.0	100.0	100.0	100.0
1976	94.9	106.5	77.4	84.1	65.9	79.7	50.0	84.5	172.6	84.0	93.2	94.0	91.1	130.0	72.2
1977	85.7	83.3	64.0	58.4	58.3	50.8	28.9	92.6	215.7	58.0	92.8	81.5	81.4	98.6	64.9
1978	101.2	107.4	49.1	56.1	63.5	157.1	25.4	95.2	151.0	57.3	80.7	77.7	79.7	90.3	56.2
1979	105.9	127.0	67.8	56.5	53.2	62.8	27.5	90.9	131.2	61.5	78.5	77.5	75.9	84.9	71.1
1980	106.9	105.9	59.6	53.4	60.3	58.9	71.0	70.6	111.4	67.3	68.0	77.7	69.9	89.9	67.1
1981	93.4	89.0	73.1	52.2	64.5	56.0	39.3	64.9	74.9	61.6	62.2	78.0	73.9	75.6	54.3
1982	81.5	81.0	65.4	40.7	39.4	48.4	18.4	47.7	77.0	49.5	49.7	68.6	79.3	61.5	46.3
1983[a]	71.1	84.6	n.a.	52.2	41.6	48.5	18.9	54.9	74.2	n.a.	58.5	80.35	82.3	72.9	44.7

a. Preliminary estimate.
Sources: García-García, "Aspects of Agricultural Development"; and DANE.

Table SA-19. *Index of the Ratio of f.o.b. International Prices in Pesos to Production Costs of Some Agricultural Commodities, 1970–82*

(1975 = 100)

Year	Rice	Corn	Sorghum	Soybeans	Wheat	Cotton
1970	45.4	36.3	69.5	98.6	47.8	76.7
1971	60.8	34.2	75.5	96.1	50.2	94.5
1972	63.6	35.5	74.0	104.9	64.4	126.5
1973	97.0	59.0	98.8	215.5	139.3	184.5
1974	146.6	111.9	112.5	139.1	147.1	147.2
1975	100.0	100.0	100.0	100.0	100.0	100.0
1976	74.6	86.1	78.7	94.3	85.2	132.9
1977	75.9	63.4	61.0	80.3	67.5	88.0
1978	77.3	55.6	61.1	80.5	73.5	48.9
1979	65.7	65.3	75.8	86.6	103.7	87.0
1980	61.6	54.2	69.9	78.4	87.0	110.1
1981	66.3	47.1	54.6	66.4	65.1	87.6
1982	40.8	40.8	47.8	55.7	74.7	n.a.

n.a. Not available.

Source: García-García, "Aspects of Agricultural Development."

Table SA-20. *Ratio of Basic Prices to Market Producer Prices of Selected Agricultural Commodities, 1970–81*

Product	1970	1971	1972	1973	1974	1975	1976	1977	1978	1979	1980	1981
Barley	135.1	114.1	104.5	80.3	89.7	92.4	79.8	86.1	77.8	67.1	86.1	123.3
Beans	113.1	65.4	65.4	50.8	39.7	74.8	67.8	59.7	60.3	39.0	45.8	n.a.
Cocoa	92.5	94.1	90.9	74.5	65.0	106.2	98.8	67.0	64.0	54.1	77.9	95.9
Corn	87.2	76.7	66.8	73.6	93.6	94.1	82.0	55.7	70.1	49.3	51.2	91.8
Cotton fiber	126.8	106.2	94.1	89.9	82.9	106.8	68.6	83.9	94.8	68.3	102.3	102.0
Cottonseed	131.3	95.0	93.4	105.9	80.2	97.5	80.9	72.1	63.2	50.6	73.6	100.7
Palm oil	97.1	93.9	90.2	61.8	41.1	38.4	34.9	27.0	23.5	18.6	36.6	103.9
Rice (paddy)	109.2	104.6	107.3	80.4	67.7	101.1	101.4	66.7	67.9	58.2	73.5	88.9
Sesame	95.0	93.0	87.4	74.6	44.2	101.0	87.5	74.6	61.5	49.4	94.5	94.8
Sorghum	n.a.	84.9	57.1	42.1	85.0	100.0	87.6	67.0	76.1	58.3	60.3	86.7
Soybeans	88.3	85.2	81.2	64.4	82.4	100.9	86.9	57.8	58.7	47.7	60.5	111.9
Wheat	108.6	108.6	89.5	85.9	53.4	89.7	90.4	82.5	87.6	69.9	73.3	92.4

n.a. Not available.

Source: Calculations by the DNP.

Table SA-21. *Effective Rate of Interest for Banks on Bonos de Prenda, 1970–81*

Year	Market interest rate[a]	Effective rate bonos de prenda[b]
1970	13.3	22.0
1971	16.4	22.0
1972	15.6	22.0
1973	20.3	22.0⁻
1974	30.4	22.4
1975	23.8	22.6
1976	22.4	22.6
1977	22.9	22.6
1978	25.9	22.6
1979	36.5	22.6
1980	41.5	29.8
1981	52.5	32.1

a. CAT, 120-day maturity, average annual rate.

b. $R_e = [R_m - (R_t)(M_r)]/(1 - M_r)$, where R_e = effective rate of interest, R_m = market rate of interest, R_r = rediscount interest rate, M_r = margin of rediscount.

Sources: Calculations by the DNP, based on Banco de la Republica, *Resoluciones de la Junta Monetaria*; Asobancaria.

Table SA-22. *Value of Discounts and Rediscounts under the Bonos de Prenda System and the Distribution of the Cost of the Implied Subsidy, 1981*
(thousand pesos)

Product	Value discounted	Value rediscounted	Total cost[a]	Paid by government[b]	Paid by banks[c]
Beans	6,759	1,660	1,602	476	1,126
Corn	225,875	80,421	53,532	23,081	30,451
Cotton fiber	1,995,175	758,997	472,856	217,832	255,024
Cottonseed	568,298	215,353	134,687	61,806	72,881
Rice (paddy)	1,419,137	475,056	336,335	136,341	199,994
Sesame	45,561	22,382	10,798	6,424	4,374
Sorghum	897,613	325,966	212,734	93,552	119,182
Soybeans	681,131	264,781	161,428	75,992	85,436
Tobacco	1,066,679	238,222	252,803	68,370	184,433
Other agricultural products[d]	483,461	168,969	114,580	48,494	66,086
Other products[e]	2,329,949	115,373	552,198	33,112	519,086
Total	9,719,638	2,667,180	2,303,553	765,480	1,538,073

a. Total cost = value rediscounted · $(r_m - r_s)$, where r_m = market interest rate and r_s = subsidized interest rate for bonos de prenda.

b. Amount paid by government = value rediscounted · $(r_m - r_r)$, where r_r = rediscount interest rate.

c. Amount paid by banks = total subsidy less amount paid by government.

d. Barley, cocoa, malt, and wheat.

e. Manufactured products and products for export.

Source: World Bank estimates.

Table SA-23. *Supply and Distribution of Export-Grade Green Coffee,*
1958/59 through 1983/84

(thousand sixty-kilogram bags)

| Coffee year[a] | Stocks carry-in | Production[b] | Domestic consumption | Exports | | | Stocks carry-out[c] |
				ICA quota markets	Non-ICA quota markets	Total	
1958/59	11	7,442	908	6,372	59	6,431	114
1959/60	114	7,648	1,197	5,597	74	5,671	894
1960/61	894	7,500	1,270	5,990	53	6,043	1,081
1961/62	1,081	8,035	1,526	5,536	58	5,594	1,996
1962/63	1,996	7,500	1,416	5,952	104	6,056	2,024
1963/64	2,024	7,800	1,375	6,228	82	6,310	2,139
1964/65	2,139	8,547	1,354	5,612	131	5,743	3,589
1965/66	3,589	8,224	1,202	5,670	195	5,865	4,746
1966/67	4,746	7,507	1,250	5,421	213	5,634	5,369
1967/68	5,369	7,995	1,270	6,344	251	6,595	5,499
1968/69	5,499	7,375	1,290	6,204	330	6,534	5,050
1969/70	5,050	8,266	859	6,467	407	6,874	5,583
1970/71	5,583	6,872	989	6,008	322	6,331	5,135
1971/72	5,135	5,958	1,035	6,198	289	6,487	3,571
1972/73	3,571	8,564	1,046	6,046	209	6,255	4,834
1973/74	4,834	7,066	1,252	6,873	535	7,408	3,240
1974/75	3,240	7,981	1,279	7,102	440	7,542	2,400
1975/76	2,400	7,804	1,369	6,554	469	7,023	1,812
1976/77	1,812	8,939	1,305	4,891	401	5,292	4,154
1977/78	4,154	10,463	1,420	7,144	414	7,558	5,639
1978/79	5,639	12,300	1,638	10,714	717	11,431	4,870
1979/80	4,870	11,848	1,728	10,692	848	11,540	3,450
1980/81	3,450	13,037	1,478	8,310	721	9,031	5,978
1981/82	5,978	12,893	1,592	8,052	938	8,990	8,289
1982/83	8,289	12,810	1,695	8,465	709	9,174	10,230
1983/84	10,230	13,464	1,553	9,130	836	9,966	12,175

a. October through September.
b. Series deduced from data on stocks, consumption, and exports.
c. Stocks include private holdings.
Source: FEDERACAFE.

Table SA-24. *The Direct Share of Main Agricultural Entities in National Budget Allocations, 1970–83*
(million pesos and percent)

Year	Total budget Current pesos (1)	Total budget Constant 1970 pesos[c] (2)	Agriculture sector[a] Current pesos (3)	Agriculture sector[a] Constant 1970 pesos[c] (4)	Agriculture sector[a] Participation in total budget (percent) (3 ÷ 1)	Public agencies in agriculture sector only[b] Current pesos[d] (5)	Public agencies in agriculture sector only[b] Constant 1970 pesos[c] (6)	Participation of public agencies in total agriculture sector budget (percent) (5 ÷ 3)
1970	20,644.2	20,644.2	5,186.9	5,186.9	25.1	1,518.7	1,518.7	29
1971	25,522.1	22,446.9	5,413.9	4,761.6	21.2	1,287.3	1,132.2	24
1972	31,279.5	24,191.4	6,388.0	4,940.4	20.4	1,550.3	1,199.0	24
1973	38,492.0	24,753.7	8,103.2	5,211.1	21.1	1,764.3	1,134.6	22
1974	50,726.5	26,255.9	8,688.6	4,497.2	17.1	2,071.8	1,072.4	24
1975	60,719.5	25,384.4	7,124.4	2,978.4	11.7	2,696.0	1,127.1	38
1976	86,185.9	30,050.9	12,852.4	4,481.3	14.9	2,715.6	947.2	21
1977	112,805.7	32,763.8	16,738.9	4,861.7	14.8	3,348.3	972.5	20
1978	174,875.7	40.830.2	16,972.0	3,962.6	9.7	3,993.0	932.3	24
1979	234,160.1	42,404.9	20,693.7	3,747.5	8.8	5,448.0	986.6	26
1980	332,382.3	47,496.8	28,277.4	4,040.7	8.5	7,054.7	1,008.1	25
1981	438,678.7	50,020.4	33,218.3	3,787.7	7.6	8,990.1	1,025.1	27
1982	574,404.5	55,912.4	40,834.2	3,974.8	7.1	10,679.0	919.8	26

Note: Tables SA-24 through SA-31 were prepared by Aichin Wee and Kei Kawabata.

a. The agriculture sector includes the Ministry of Agriculture (Dirección Superior); its ascribed agencies (Entidades Adscritas), the ICA, INCORA, INDERENA, and HIMAT; agriculture-related investments of the autonomous regional corporations, essentially the CVC, Corpouraba, CAR, and Codechoco; and other public enterprises or entities (Entidades Vinculades), mainly IDEMA, COFIAGRO, and EMCOPER, that at various times receive investment funds from budget allocations. The figures include investment funds (Inversion) from both budget allocations (Presupuesto Nacional) and own resources (Recursos Proprios) and recurrent funds (Funcionamiento) from both the budget and own resources.

b. Includes only the Entidades Ascritas—ICA, INCORA, INDERENA, and HIMAT—which account for about 23 percent of total public allocations in the agriculture sector (see table SA-4).

c. Deflated, using the implicit price deflator for current government purchases of goods and services, with assumed annual rates of inflation for 1982–86.

d. Figures for 1970–81 are derived from the actual figures for 1982 and 1983 in column 6 and from projected allocations for investment and recurrent expenditures for 1984–86 supplied by OPSA.

Sources: Based on calculations of the Ministry of Agriculture and OPSA.

Table SA-25. *Public Allocations to Agriculture, by Entity, 1970–81*
(million constant 1970 pesos and percent)

Year	Total agriculture		Ascribed agencies (ICA, INCORA, HIMAT, INDERENA)		Regional corporations		Other entities	
	Million pesos	Percent	Million pesos	Percent	Million pesos	Percent	Million pesos	Percent
1970	5,186.9	100.00	1,518.7	29.28	219.9	4.24	3,448.3	66.48
1971	4,814.0	100.00	1,132.2	23.52	477.2	9.91	3,204.6	66.57
1972	4,977.0	100.00	1,199.0	24.09	634.7	12.75	3,143.3	63.16
1973	5,211.1	100.00	1,134.6	21.77	839.1	16.10	3,237.4	62.13
1974	4,497.2	100.00	1,072.4	23.85	759.5	16.89	2,665.3	59.26
1975	2,988.4	100.00	1,127.1	37.72	532.9	17.83	1,328.4	44.45
1976	4,481.3	100.00	947.2	21.14	628.7	14.03	2,905.4	64.83
1977	4,315.4	100.00	972.5	22.53	623.0	14.44	2,719.9	63.03
1978	4,081.0	100.00	932.3	22.84	666.7	16.34	2,482.0	60.82
1979	3,856.1	100.00	986.6	25.59	793.6	19.91	2,101.7	54.50
1980	4,214.2	100.00	1,008.1	23.92	1,064.5	25.26	2,141.6	50.82
1981	3,787.7	100.00	1,025.1	27.06	1,179.7	31.15	1,582.9	41.79

Source: Ministry of Agriculture, Oficina de Planeamiento del Sector Agropecuario, on the basis of data from the Contraloria General de la Republica.

Table SA-26. *Area under Cultivation, by Principal Crop, 1971–84*
(thousand hectares)

Crop	1971	1972	1973	1974	1975	1976	1977	1978	1979	1980	1981	1982	1983[a]	1984[a]
Cereals														
Rice (paddy)	241.8	258.2	291.0	354.5	372.5	365.6	324.4	406.1	442.0	415.8	420.7	446.0	396.5	364.1
Barley	55.6	63.5	52.4	59.1	75.6	68.0	46.6	68.4	73.9	62.8	36.0	34.9	17.6	17.4
Wheat	46.9	60.7	56.5	45.1	30.1	32.8	33.0	29.7	30.7	37.6	44.0	45.3	46.3	42.9
Corn	666.5	624.5	580.3	570.1	572.7	647.5	580.5	670.9	615.6	614.4	629.0	636.0	582.3	593.0
Sorghum	92.1	84.0	135.4	151.2	134.0	173.6	189.5	224.8	221.2	206.0	231.3	291.1	271.9	237.6
Other food crops														
Yuca	248.8	251.3	249.8	250.8	256.7	223.3	218.3	216.9	221.7	207.7	207.0	170.0	172.7	183.0
Potatoes	88.3	89.5	98.6	92.0	110.0	125.0	130.0	141.6	148.0	142.0	159.5	165.2	160.5	160.7
Plantain	324.9	324.8	326.7	327.9	341.0	340.1	386.3	400.1	412.1	432.6	433.0	358.2	356.8	366.9
Panela	183.0	188.0	194.0	196.9	173.5	171.5	178.9	197.8	200.0	209.0	187.0	170.7	176.5	186.2
Beans (common)	68.0	84.6	87.0	90.7	120.7	101.0	115.8	110.9	112.4	115.4	117.3	112.2	112.5	109.6
Cocoa	49.0	52.6	54.9	57.9	52.6	54.5	57.5	60.5	62.7	64.1	68.0	77.3	84.6	89.3
Cotton and oilseeds														
Seed cotton	219.0	242.3	250.8	258.4	280.7	285.6	377.2	327.9	186.5	216.9	221.1	99.2	76.7	140.8
Soybeans	55.1	54.0	54.0	57.0	87.8	37.6	56.7	69.0	71.3	78.1	43.9	49.4	59.5	50.6
Sesame	47.0	43.2	37.0	32.2	41.6	36.1	23.7	24.9	27.7	24.2	19.4	12.3	9.0	8.3
African palm oil	13.8	15.0	16.5	18.2	15.7	16.0	17.4	19.0	21.8	24.6	25.2	31.6	35.4	38.3
Other export crops														
Sugarcane[b]	64.0	72.9	78.6	75.1	75.7	83.0	76.5	86.5	91.1	93.2	92.1	92.9	94.8	93.4
Bananas[b]	14.0	15.7	13.3	14.9	14.2	16.3	19.5	20.8	22.0	20.9	21.0	21.8	22.5	23.1
Tobacco[b,c]	23.0	26.3	26.2	25.5	34.1	29.7	33.3	28.8	30.6	28.5	30.1	29.0	29.8	27.3

a. Preliminary estimate.
b. Refers to calendar year.
c. Combination of white and dark tobacco.

Source: Ministry of Agriculture, Oficina de Planeamiento del Sector Agropecuario, and the DNP.

Table SA-27. *Production of Principal Crops, 1971–84*

(thousand metric tons)

Crop	1971	1972	1973	1974	1975	1976	1977	1978	1979	1980	1981	1982	1983[a]	1984[a]
Cereals														
Rice (paddy)	851.9	997.5	1,151.1	1,540.4	1,614.0	1,560.0	1,307.0	1,714.7	1,932.5	1,797.9	1,798.7	2,018.2	1,779.8	1,695.8
Barley	107.2	98.0	81.5	96.9	121.8	71.4	81.3	118.9	136.6	109.5	56.4	55.6	27.8	28.2
Wheat	53.2	69.2	72.4	58.8	38.9	45.3	38.5	37.7	42.0	45.7	62.3	70.7	77.8	59.3
Corn	818.5	806.2	739.1	791.5	722.6	883.7	752.8	862.2	870.2	853.6	880.0	898.5	863.8	864.3
Sorghum	239.6	210.0	280.2	336.6	335.0	427.7	406.2	516.7	501.3	430.5	532.0	568.4	595.2	589.6
Other food crops														
Yuca	1,990.4	2,010.4	1,998.4	2,125.9	2,021.1	1,845.7	1,972.6	2,044.1	1,908.9	2,150.4	2,150.1	1,552.3	1,554.8	1,674.5
Potatoes	868.9	823.4	1,030.5	1,012.0	1,320.0	1,515.8	1,608.5	1,995.6	1,966.1	1,726.7	2,006.1	2,149.0	2,186.7	2,462.9
Plantain	1,517.3	1,562.3	1,653.1	1,678.9	1,791.7	1,852.0	1,844.0	2,192.0	2,235.8	2,348.0	2,400.0	1,993.0	2,247.9	2,277.4
Panela	457.0	508.0	524.0	557.2	805.6	833.6	837.6	965.4	984.7	987.8	802.6	734.8	779.6	824.6
Beans (common)	35.6	61.1	56.9	67.1	89.9	67.6	74.9	74.8	74.7	83.6	79.3	72.8	81.8	80.1
Cocoa	19.0	20.0	22.0	23.0	21.2	29.2	27.0	31.0	32.3	35.7	38.3	39.4	38.6	41.6
Cotton and oilseeds														
Cotton	322.4	412.1	344.8	420.3	400.9	408.6	480.4	330.3	281.6	353.2	366.2	153.6	130.4	243.3
Soybeans	100.7	104.6	97.2	114.0	168.9	75.1	102.9	130.8	143.6	154.5	89.0	98.8	122.4	94.1
Sesame	31.4	28.3	18.1	17.2	20.7	20.7	13.0	13.7	15.6	12.9	11.6	7.2	4.9	4.9
African palm oil	36.2	41.4	44.0	50.8	39.2	38.6	48.1	52.6	59.6	70.0	79.9	85.2	101.9	118.2
Other export crops														
Sugarcane[b]	744.0	823.7	809.9	894.8	969.7	934.6	853.3	1,025.9	1,096.0	1,188.6	1,148.1	1,302.9	1,330.0	1,177.6
Bananas[b]	351.0	282.0	301.0	469.7	559.0	521.5	593.1	719.0	800.5	944.3	1,109.6	1,146.6	1,043.4	1,106.1
Tobacco[b,c]	39.3	36.1	39.7	41.1	57.6	38.6	58.3	46.6	51.4	46.3	49.4	48.7	47.9	43.8

a. Preliminary estimate.
b. Refers to calendar year.
c. White and dark tobacco.

Sources: Ministry of Agriculture, Oficina de Planeamiento del Sector Agropecuario and the DNP.

Table SA-28. *Yields of Principal Crops, 1971–84*
(metric tons per hectare)

Crop	1971	1972	1973	1974	1975	1976	1977	1978	1979	1980	1981	1982	1983[a]	1984[a]
Cereals														
Rice (paddy)	3.5	3.9	4.0	4.3	4.3	4.3	4.0	4.2	4.4	4.3	4.2	4.5	4.5	4.6
Barley	1.9	1.5	1.6	1.6	1.6	1.1	1.7	1.7	1.8	1.8	1.6	1.6	1.6	1.6
Wheat	1.1	1.1	1.3	1.3	1.3	1.4	1.2	1.3	1.4	1.2	1.4	1.6	1.7	1.4
Corn	1.2	1.3	1.3	1.4	1.3	1.4	1.3	1.3	1.4	1.4	1.4	1.4	1.5	1.5
Sorghum	2.6	2.5	2.1	2.2	2.5	2.5	2.1	2.3	2.3	2.1	2.3	2.0	2.2	2.5
Other food crops														
Yuca	8.0	8.0	8.0	8.5	7.9	8.3	9.0	9.4	8.6	10.4	5.5	9.1	9.0	9.1
Potatoes	9.8	9.2	10.5	11.0	12.0	12.1	12.4	14.1	13.3	12.2	13.2	13.0	13.6	15.3
Plantain	4.7	4.8	5.1	5.1	5.3	5.4	4.8	5.5	5.4	5.4	5.5	5.6	6.3	6.2
Panela	2.5	2.7	2.7	2.8	4.6	4.9	4.7	4.9	4.9	5.0	4.3	4.3	4.4	4.4
Beans (common)	0.59	0.62	0.61	0.64	0.7	0.7	0.6	0.6	0.7	0.7	0.6	0.6	0.7	0.7
Cocoa	0.39	0.38	0.40	0.40	0.35	0.54	0.47	0.51	0.5	0.5	0.6	0.5	0.5	0.5
Cotton and oilseeds														
Seed cotton	1.5	1.7	1.3	1.6	1.4	1.4	1.3	1.0	1.5	1.6	1.7	1.5	1.7	1.7
Soybeans	1.8	1.9	1.8	2.0	1.9	1.0	1.8	1.9	2.0	2.0	2.0	2.0	2.1	1.9
Sesame	0.67	0.66	0.49	0.53	0.5	0.6	0.5	0.6	0.6	0.5	0.6	0.6	0.5	0.6
African palm oil	2.6	2.8	2.7	2.8	2.6	2.4	2.5	2.5	2.7	2.8	3.2	2.7	2.9	3.1
Other export crops														
Sugarcane	11.6	11.3	10.3	11.9	12.8	11.3	11.2	11.9	12.0	12.8	12.5	13.5	14.0	12.6
Bananas	25.1	18.0	22.6	31.5	39.4	32.0	30.4	34.6	35.6	45.0	52.8	52.7	46.4	47.9
Tobacco[b]	1.7	1.4	1.5	1.6	1.7	1.3	1.8	1.6	1.9	1.6	1.6	1.6	1.6	1.6

a. Preliminary estimate.
b. Dark tobacco.
Source: Ministry of Agriculture, Oficina de Planeamiento del Sector Agropecuario.

Table SA-29. *Gross Domestic Product and Gross Output, by Main Economic Activity, 1970–83*
(million current pesos)

	Gross domestic product						Gross output				
Year	*Agriculture*[a]	*Pergamino coffee (01)*	*Processed coffee (08)*	*Sugar (12)*	*Rest of the economy*	*Total*	*Agriculture*[a]	*Processed coffee (08)*	*Sugar (12)*	*Rest of the economy*	*Total*
1970	32,052	4,417	3,561	581	96,574	132,768	37,321	10,116	1,358	171,694	220,489
1971	35,396	3,919	3,584	615	116,291	155,886	41,677	9,850	1,594	208,863	261,984
1972	44,034	5,192	4,555	850	140,175	189,614	51,908	12,404	2,142	248,388	314,842
1973	56,460	6,690	7,761	982	177,957	243,160	67,638	17,354	2,532	313,716	401,240
1974	75,441	7,841	6,960	1,985	237,998	322,384	92,345	19,281	4,573	432,722	548,921
1975	93,164	8,971	12,816	2,510	296,618	405,103	113,991	26,629	5,949	537,773	684,342
1976	120,908	17,017	23,839	2,553	384,970	532,270	145,451	45,723	6,078	693,691	890,943
1977	172,900	30,898	33,831	4,485	504,813	716,029	202,674	64,530	8,803	900,252	1,176,259
1978	201,111	35,426	33,906	5,116	669,354	909,487	239,178	84,955	10,706	1,176,242	1,511,081
1979	244,477	41,098	33,399	7,647	903,294	1,188,817	294,841	96,222	14,599	1,570,314	1,975,976
1980	292,524	47,269	53,060	16,491	1,217,055	1,579,130	361,411	125,627	26,815	2,107,969	2,621,822
1981	364,760	57,489	26,264	16,625	1,560,120	1,982,773	452,292	112,216	28,875	2,707,970	3,301,353
1982	445,387	63,256	39,218	19,292	1,923,401	2,497,298	553,008	121,790	35,585	3,407,525	4,117,908
1983[b]	539,379	n.a.	47,233	25,627	2,424,422	3,036,661	666,824	146,565	46,972	4,104,222	4,964,583

n.a. Not available.

a. Consists of pergamino coffee (01), other agricultural products (02), and animal products (03).

b. Preliminary estimate.

Sources: DANE, *Cuentas nacionales de Colombia: 1970–1982* (Bogotá, August 1984), and unpublished information for 1982 and 1983.

Table SA-30. *Gross Domestic Product and Gross Output, by Main Economic Activity, 1970–83*
(million 1975 pesos)

	Gross domestic product						Gross output				
Year	Agriculture[a]	Pergamino coffee (01)	Processed coffee (08)	Sugar (12)	Rest of the economy	Total	Agriculture[a]	Processed coffee (08)	Sugar (12)	Rest of the economy	Total
1970	75,338	8,370	10,062	1,088	221,008	307,496	91,119	20,850	3,824	400,178	515,971
1971	76,195	7,784	10,344	1,520	237,766	325,825	92,155	21,434	4,070	437,141	554,800
1972	81,565	8,595	10,468	1,739	257,041	350,813	98,650	21,691	4,566	464,142	589,049
1973	83,354	8,636	10,787	1,881	278,376	374,398	100,814	22,190	4,546	498,935	626,485
1974	87,918	8,793	11,020	2,006	294,966	395,910	108,250	22,911	5,009	536,693	672,863
1975	93,164	8,971	12,816	2,510	296,618	405,108	113,991	26,629	5,949	537,773	684,342
1976	95,839	9,386	10,830	2,136	315,458	424,263	116,801	23,552	5,074	567,940	713,367
1977	98,946	10,853	8,909	2,049	332,002	441,906	120,587	19,288	4,842	595,366	740,083
1978	107,088	11,852	14,193	2,343	355,711	479,335	130,157	30,728	5,583	639,547	806,015
1979	112,379	13,482	17,189	2,738	372,813	505,119	136,736	37,335	6,547	671,800	852,418
1980	114,849	13,945	17,565	3,085	390,266	525,765	140,256	38,140	7,458	703,254	889,108
1981	118,667	15,391	14,799	2,819	401,536	537,821	144,316	31,943	6,767	724,446	907,472
1982	116,149	16,081	15,045	3,397	408,245	542,836	142,401	32,188	7,951	728,095	910,635
1983[b]	118,153	n.a.	15,801	3,491	410,610	548,055	144,603	33,508	8,086	727,175	915,372

n.a. Not available.

a. See note a, table SA-29.

b. Preliminary estimate.

Sources: DANE, *Cuentas nacionales de Colombia: 1970–1982* (Bogotá, August 1984), and unpublished information for 1982 and 1983 and extraction of pergamino coffee (01).

Index

Adjustment, economic. *See* Macroeconomic policy (adjustment and)

Ad valorem export tax, 101, 110, 111, 112, 113

AGD. *See* Almacenes Generales de Depósito

Agricultural commodities: domestic consumption of, 9, 62, 63; domestic demand for, 7, 22, 62, 81, 83; domestic prices of, 12, 46, 54, 66, 67, 69, 73, 74, 76, 77, 82, 83, 87, 97, 98; domestic supply of, 22; employment share of, 5; export earnings share of, 5; export prices of, 5, 12, 34, 67, 69, 84, 123; export quotas of, 62; exports of, 3, 4, 5–6, 7, 9–10, 22, 23n8, 28, 30, 33–35, 38, 41, 43, 62, 67, 72, 77, 162; export subsidies for, 62; foreign demand and, 5, 9, 22; foreign exchange and, 3, 5, 10, 86; growth rate and, 3, 5, 6, 7, 10, 144, 156, 158, 161; import-competing commodity price of, 67; import prices of, 63, 68–69, 70, 71; imports of, 9–10, 14, 46, 47, 54, 61, 62, 70, 72, 137, 160; import trade restrictions on, 62; incentives and, 4, 61, 77, 156, 161; inputs to, 46, 47, 61, 63, 69, 136–40, 151, 152, 154; processing costs of, 69; producer prices of, 14, 62, 70–71, 74, 82, 149; production of, 4–5, 9, 10, 14, 21, 22, 28, 43, 46, 47, 61, 66, 68, 70, 72, 73, 76, 81, 136–37, 141–42, 161; production costs of, 14, 15, 22, 47, 62, 63, 72, 83, 136, 145, 147, 154; production incentives and, 71–73, 77, 84, 157, 158, 161; relative prices of, 13, 61, 73–76; as share of GDP, 5, 6, 9, 10; stocks of, 151; surplus of, 41, 62, 77; value added in, 46, 137; yields of, 14, 15, 52, 137, 141, 152. *See also* Marketing; Research and extension; Storage (agricultural); Technology; *specific commodities*

Agricultural Development Bank. *See* Caja Agraria

Agricultural equipment, 47, 136, 137, 153; rental of, 147, 154

Agricultural fund. *See* Fondo Financiero Agropecuario

Agricultural income, 61, 63, 66, 69–70, 81, 82, 83, 108, 143–44, 147, 152

Agricultural investment, 14, 61, 81, 82, 123–34, 136, 141, 159, 161–62. *See also* Infrastructure (agricultural)

Agricultural loans, 132–33, 145–49, 161

Agricultural Marketing Institute. *See* Instituto de Mercadeo Agropecuario

Agricultural practices, 140. *See also* Coffee production technology

Agricultural trade policies. *See* Decree; Plan Vallejo; Resolution

Almacenes Generales de Depósito (AGD), 88, 93

Almagrario (agricultural storage), 93, 99n8

Almapopular (agricultural storage), 93, 99n8

Andean Group, trade with, 28, 48

Andean Pact, 44, 48

Asociación Colombiana de Productores de Flores (ASOCOLFLORES), 131

Asociación Colombiana de Productores de Semillas (ACOSEMILLA), 131

Asociación de Cultivadores de Caña de Azúcar de Colombia (ASOCAÑA), 62, 134

Asociación Latino Americana de Desarrollo y Integración (ALADI), 48–49

Auctioning. *See* Licenses (auctioning of)

Balance of payments, 20, 43, 44; current account of, 3, 19, 26, 157; factors affecting, 9, 10, 16,

Oficina de Planeación del Sector Agropecuario (OPSA), 80, 150

Output. *See* Gross domestic product; *specific crops (production of)*

⅄ Palm oil, 72, 88, 133

PAN. *See* Plan Nacional de Alimentación y Nutrición

Pasilla (grade of coffee), 110, 111

Pergamino (processed coffee), 110, 111, 113, 116

Peso (Colombian), 10, 159; appreciation of, 11, 18, 21, 26, 30, 36, 43, 53, 67; depreciation of, 13, 17, 21, 26, 29, 32, 33, 37, 40, 55, 107; possible devaluation of, 36, 37, 38, 40; real value of, 72

Peso-dollar rate, 30, 31, 32, 35, 39

Pesticides, price controls on, 62, 151

Petroleum, 20, 26, 39, 44, 46, 50, 158

Plan Nacional de Alimentación y Nutrición (PAN), 127, 149, 151, 153

Plan Nacional de Investigación Forestal (PLANIF), 47, 143

Plan Vallejo (import-export regime), 27, 28, 39, 41

Policies, government. *See* Agricultural trade policies; Development plan; Import policy; Macroeconomic policy; Monetary policy; Stabilization policy; Trade reform

Port-handling costs, 47, 67, 68, 69, 71, 145, 153, 154, 160

Ports, 68, 153

⅄ Potatoes, 82, 88, 131, 137

PPP. *See* Purchasing power parity

Price controls, 62

Price distortions, 78

Price fixing, 62

Price interventions, 61, 63, 66–71, 76–78, 107, 110, 145, 160

Prices: basic, 92–93, 94, 97; border, 47; clearing, 56; constant, 19, 30; factor, 36; import parity, 71; input, 4, 136, 137–40, 145, 151, 160; internal, 49, 73, 107, 118; market, 66, 93, 94, 100*n*17, 132; output, 4, 62, 137, 140; relative, 12–13, 15, 18, 53; retail, 69; wholesale, 69; World Bank' projections of commodity, 34. *See also* Consumer prices; Domestic prices; Farmgate price; International prices; Producer prices; *price entries under specific commodities*

Price stabilization, 4, 11, 77, 80, 81–82, 97–99, 156; annual and seasonal aspects of, 80–81, 83–97

Price supports, 4, 14, 46, 47, 61, 62, 63–66, 70, 71, 76, 77, 81, 85, 150, 151, 156, 159, 160

Prior deposit requirements for imports, 44, 52–53

Private sector, 14, 29, 39, 50–51, 116, 151, 157; agricultural investment and, 123, 130–33, 134, 142, 161; agricultural research and, 140; storage and, 95, 97, 98

PROCAÑA. *See* Productores de Caña

Processing: of agricultural products, 131, 132, 149, 150, 153, 161; and exports, 35, 39, 69

PRODESARROLLO. *See* Programa de Diversificación y Desarrollo de Zonas Cafeteras

Producer prices, 6, 11, 14, 47, 62, 67, 80, 98, 152, 153, 159–60; relative, 21, 22

Producers' associations, 91, 93, 106, 123, 127, 131–32, 150

Productores de Caña (PROCAÑA), 62

PROEXPO. *See* Export Promotion Fund

Profitability in agriculture, 61, 82, 96, 140

Programa de Desarrollo Rural Integrado (DRI), 127, 149, 151, 153

Programa de Diversificación y Desarrollo de Zonas Cafeteras (PRODESARROLLO), 114, 149, 153

Protectionism, 35, 41, 44, 48, 50, 53, 56, 61, 62, 67–71, 77, 78, 159, 160

Public Investment Fund, 128, 161

Public sector: accounts, 16, 20, 22; agricultural investment and, 123–30, 133, 134, 136, 154, 159, 161; expenditures, 16, 29, 40, 127, 128, 158; imports and, 50–51

Pulp and paper, imports of, 47

Purchasing power parity (PPP), 25–26

Quantitative restrictions. *See* Quota system

Quota system: for exports, 77, 83; for imports, 54, 56, 62, 63, 76. *See also* Coffee (export quotas on)

Recession, international, 10, 22. *See also* Colombia, recession in

Reforestation, 47, 142, 143

Refrigeration of agricultural products, 150, 151

Regional corporations for development, 126–27

Reintegro mínimo (minimum surrender price for coffee), 111

Relative prices, 12–13, 15, 18, 53. *See also* Agricultural commodities (relative prices of)

RER. *See* Exchange rate (real)

Research and extension: agricultural, 14, 61, 123, 127, 131, 134, 140, 142, 144, 152, 159, 161; in forestry, 143; stations, 124

The most recent World Bank publications are described in the annual spring and fall lists. The latest edition is available free of charge from Publications Sales Unit, Department B, The World Bank, Washington, D.C. 20433, U.S.A.

Vinod Thomas is a senior economist in the Country Programs Department of the Latin America and the Caribbean Regional Office of the World Bank.